Successful Trucking After Deregulation

by
Thomas J. Hays

Pacific Standard Publishing Co.

First Printing March 1995

95

Library of Congress Cataloging-in-Publication Data

Hays, Thomas J. (Thomas James), 1932-
    Successful trucking after deregulation/Thomas J. Hays.
      p.   cm.
    Includes index.
    ISBN 0-9645222-0-9
      1. Trucking–United States. 2. Trucking–Deregulation–United States. I. Title.
HE5623.H39   1995
388.3'24'0973–dc20
                                        95-8015
                                          CIP

Acknowledgments

The author thanks the following individuals for their contributions to this book:

Barbara Braasch, for her excellent work developing and editing this book, including original concepts and chapter organization. It could not have been written without her help.

Artwerks, for the layout of pages, the design of the book format, and the extra hours of labor. Cupertino, California

Chris Chope, for the cover and graphics design and assistance with promotional materials. Cupertino, California

Proof reading department: John Pietrowicz and Dorothy Freeman

Babylon Printing, Milpitas CA. for the quality work and quick turnaround.

Special thanks to my wife Dotte for her support and encouragement. Her advice and criticism kept the project in focus.

The book is dedicated to my children, Mark, Nancy, Judy, and Brian.

Contents

 # Preface

This book comes at a time when the trucking industry is experiencing the most significant change in its short history. The industry has been regulated by federal and/or state governments since about 1935. This regulation has taken many forms, depending upon the governmental entity involved and the segment of the industry regulated. For example, household goods transportation has been the most heavily regulated segment, ostensibly because it is the only portion of the industry that serves the consuming public directly. Geographically, California is the only jurisdiction that was regulated under a system of *minimum* rates for most of the industry. Most other jurisdictions were regulated with a system of *minimum* and *maximum*, or fixed, rates.

In 1975, various regulatory agencies began to consider whether continued regulation of truck prices was in the public interest. At the onset, most industry policy-makers resisted the philosophy of relaxed regulation. By the late 1970s, however, it became apparent that the forces of deregulation, or reregulation, would succeed in changing the pricing patterns for trucking industry services. Finally, in 1980, passage of the Motor Carrier Act forever changed the face of the industry. While it did not "deregulate," it certainly began the process that culminated in the passage of Public Law 103-305, the Federal Aviation Administration Authorization Act of 1994, and final economic deregulation within the various states.

Since 1975, I have participated in a myriad of events designed to implement farther industry deregulation. In most of these cases, an erosion of the regulatory system occurred, and resulting changes produced a half-hearted system with little, if any, positive effects on the marketplace. For example, the federal system allowed for the retention of bureau tariffs with the right of the individual carriers to discount indiscriminately from the published rate. In the

1980s, tariff bureaus increased some of their published rates in excess of 100%. During the time base rates were being increased, individual carriers were also increasing the percentage of discount. In the writer's opinion, this system produced no meaningful result for either the industry or its customers.

As a participant in several of the regulatory change proceedings, I was only one of those who became aware that it was only a matter of time until the industry would be competing in an open, price-competitive market. I also learned that issues of regulatory change were being discussed in sessions where few trucking company owners and executives had an opportunity to participate. Their only exposure to the issues was through industry trade journals that, while highlighting various matters, rarely attempted to offer information or advice to constituents on the consequences of regulatory change.

From this history, I determined that the industry needed material to ease its entrance into these new competitive circumstances. My intent is to frame a complete analysis in language that can be readily understood without further reference material. One objective is to create a book that can be used by trucking company executives to construct competitive strategies best suited to their individual needs.

The other objective is to fill the void left by cancellation of anti-trust immunity. Under such immunity, carriers have relied upon tariff publishing bureaus to provide rates. In the new environment, carriers are left to determine rates without bureau guidelines. This book is intended to provide the industry with methods to independently construct operating cost and rates in a fashion that will be responsive to competitive markets.

T.J.H.

 Introduction

The trucking industry is on the threshold of the greatest change in structure since its origin. After nearly 20 years of regulatory analysis and discussion, the industry is free to set individual prices in an open and competitive environment. Although many states had previously deregulated trucking rates, it was not until the end of 1994 that the entire intrastate industry was thrust into an open market.

Left to its own devices, the industry will likely pass through a period of adjustment where it will search for answers to a myriad of questions relative to price competition. No longer will it cling to old tariffs and rates that have little, if any, relation to reality. No longer will a competitor know the exact prices assessed by its competition. No longer will customers pay each carrier essentially the same price. No longer will state agencies approve or establish rates. No longer will price guidelines be published. No longer can trucking companies continue to do business in the old ways.

Successful survivors of the transition period will have to search for new ways to compete. Many have already begun to ask questions. What are the competitive forces that drive the trucking industry? What actions should I expect from my competitors? How should I respond to those actions? In what market should I concentrate? Will prices plunge because most of us do not know how to compete in an open market? How do I determine my rate structure? How can I best position myself to compete over the long term and enable my company to prosper in the future?

This book provides some answers to these questions. It is designed to stimulate trucking company executives into action. Organized into three parts, the book's first section presents an analysis of the industry from the viewpoint of the economist. It is intentionally written in language that obviates the need for additional reference material. Included in this section are discussions of the framework of competition, structure of the industry, and competitive strategies.

Readers can view the industry from a vantage point they may not have previously considered. Under a price-regulated environment, it has not been necessary to focus upon the need for competitive pricing, or to learn how competitive forces can be changed to benefit the individual. The first part of the book provides some definitions and terms for motor carriers to consider in determining how to pursue their new-found freedom. Most importantly, this book is not a doomsday prophecy. It is intended to provide the reader with a new look at an industry that really does need rejuvenation. It also delivers the message that competition does not necessarily mean price wars or price gouging.

It also discusses various forms of competition. In connection with price competition, in particular, it concludes that the lifeline of that form of competition is the level of product cost. Before a company can compete in an open market, it must know the cost to produce its product.

The second part presents an in-depth analysis of methods proven to be effective in establishing cost-based pricing. Its organization allows carriers to develop cost-based prices for all services. In the future, customer needs may dictate that prices be set in terms of rate per trip, per ton, per hour, per hundredweight, per mile, or per carton. The methodology to accomplish these objectives has several advantages over the traditional method of allocating cost from the income and expense statement. Whereas financial statements describe financial history and operating results from a previous period, these new methods use present and future cost. Methods and procedures described in this book provide the operator with systems to determine what the expected operating cost will be, and what the resulting cost-based price should be.

The other difficulty that arises when using the historical financial statement as the basis for cost-based pricing is the nature of the trucking service itself.

Transportation service involves unlimited lengths of haul and an almost unlimited number of shipment sizes, ranging from 50 pounds and one carton to in excess of 200,000 pounds in a multiple-lot shipment. The cost system must be capable of determining costs for all of these circumstances. Allocations from a financial statement are simply not reliable because too many of them are subjective.

The methods described in this book determine, as nearly as possible, the precise costs of providing virtually all types of truck transportation service, from LTL (less-than-truckload) general commodities to household goods. Though actual operations differ, principles of cost analysis are the same for each type of service. In addition to the illustrated discussion of actual cost determination, the book also describes how the methodology can be used to measure all types of truck transportation service.

The book's second part is arranged so the reader can follow, through illustration and example, the logic of the cost-finding methodology. It describes, in detail, each element of cost, and points out the pitfalls that will be encountered if consistency is not maintained. The labor cost section provides a method for calculating all of the elements necessary to prepare total labor cost for each employee classification required to provide a given service. The section also portrays several rate-making concepts, using labor cost as a basis. One concept deals with pricing based upon a single straight time hourly rate versus a combination of straight time and overtime.

The section also shows how to determine vehicle fixed cost, which is the cost of procuring a vehicle and preparing it for service. Typically, this cost includes purchase or lease outlay, licensing fees, and vehicle insurance. By illustration and example, the reader learns exactly how the final total cost is obtained. In addition to discussing the mechanics of cost development, the section also describes related circumstances, such as the effect of inflation on the methods used to determine vehicle fixed cost. It also addresses the problems encountered if this cost element is not properly considered and calculated.

The final component of what the book describes as "direct cost" is vehicle running cost, a category that includes fuel, oil, tires, and maintenance. When this cost element has been calculated and added to labor cost and vehicle fixed cost, the result is referred to as 'total direct cost.' Direct cost in this book is much the same as production cost for the manufacturing firm. Both terms include labor and capital as the productivity elements. All of these terms really describe cost that varies as a result of the particular transportation service or manufacturing cost incurred. In truck transportation, driver labor cost, vehicle fixed cost, and vehicle running cost all respond to, and change with, the service provided. These costs are opposed to what is commonly referred to as overhead, or 'indirect cost.' The latter cost does not necessarily change with a particular volume of business, but must be at least partially retained to maintain the flow of business.

The third section discusses particular pricing problems peculiar to specific segments of the industry. These range from the transportation of LTL general freight to household goods, cement, liquid products, and dump-truck commodities. A portion of this section also discusses vehicle rental concepts and price applications as well as independent owner-operator or subhauler situations. A chapter is devoted to each of these issues.

The book is written for the mainstream trucking company owner or executive who is looking for a new in-depth discussion of trucking business practice. It is presented in a fashion that will make it easy for any reader to prepare an operational cost analysis upon which competitive prices can be structured. Though the reader should keep in mind that the pricing of services such as trucking is more closely akin to an art than to science, cost-based pricing is the lifeline upon which that art is perfected. Without knowledge of the production cost, the effort to price at a profit will be futile. Every motor carrier interested in cost-based pricing should read Chapters 4 through 8 before continuing to the chapters describing specific types of service.

Readers are urged to use the book for more than mere cost calculation. Each of the cost centers discussed includes the opportunity to reduce the level of cost incurred. Not only is the method valuable for determining operating costs and rates, but it also shows areas where costs can be reduced to produce an improved competitive position.

Methods for cost construction and rate design in this book are long-standing. Shortly after World War II, the California Public Utilities Commission issued the first LTL general freight studies using methods described here. These studies have been continuously refined and expanded to include nearly all types of trucking operations. It was common for cost studies and rate proposals to be subjected to many days of cross-examination in formal proceedings. The systems described in this book have stood the tests of time and intense scrutiny, and upgrades and improvements over the years have produced results of unequaled accuracy and reliability. Expansion of the system to other states and to individual carrier applications attest to its success.

Economic Structure of the Industry

Economists describe the trucking industry as fragmented, with a large number of vendors selling to a smaller number of buyers with more economic clout than the sellers. There are a wide variety of reasons why the industry is fragmented. The following summary highlights the major ones.

Low Overall Entry Barriers

Entry into the trucking business is now easier and cheaper than ever before because no regulatory requirements exist, and equipment can be easily obtained. In recent years, the Interstate Commerce Commission has eliminated most of the regulatory requirements for entry into the trucking business. Evidence of insurance and some minor safety requirements are all that have been needed. At state regulatory levels the same conditions have existed with only a few variations. Some states had no regulatory requirements for entry, some had minor requirements, and a relatively few had maintained strict entry requirements until the recent federal preemption.

Financially, the cost to acquire trucks, tractors, and/or trailers has been low in comparison to most industries, and financing is readily available at competitive money market rates. These conditions have introduced a relatively new type of competition to many segments of the trucking industry: former customers have entered the field. During the 1970's and 1980's, when inflation increased for-hire transportation prices, a number of shippers purchased rolling stock in the belief that they could distribute their products more efficiently and at a lower cost than could be achieved through for-hire trucking. Though many of these arrangements proved to be profitable and constructive, some failed. However, once a shipper acquires trucking equipment, it tends to continue the operation even though it may be an economic failure.

Not only does this trend infringe upon for-hire industry revenue and profitability, it also creates conditions for the loss of related business. As private fleet operators discover their operations are not economically viable, and regulatory agencies relax entry requirements, many companies elect to enter for-hire trucking. The reasons for their decisions is two-fold.

First, shippers transport products from manufacturing facilities to distribution points or customer warehouses. Because vehicles are loaded only one way, this activity is not viable economically. To obtain return shipments, therefore, many shippers solicit other shippers through their for-hire operation. The second, and more obvious, reason for the phenomenon is that shippers tend to increase their fleets in the mistaken belief that larger size will produce productivity gains.

Absence of Economies of Scale

Economies of scale may be defined as the reduction of long-term cost by addition to the unit of production. In trucking, the unit of production is the truck (in combination with trailing equipment), which is limited by size, weight, and speed laws. The unit of production can only be so large, and it can only travel so fast, depending upon the legal jurisdiction. Therefore, the unit of production (truck) cannot be increased by the industry except to produce a vehicle from lighter materials, which would increase carrying capacity and reduce fuel consumption. The addition of more trucks to a fleet does little to lower long-term transportation costs as all trucks are essentially the same, and all use the same highway network. Accordingly, there are a large number of small truck operators operating relatively few vehicles; hence, a fragmented industry.

This is not to say, however, that no economies of scale exist in the industry. Productivity gains are obviously available through improved load factors, reduced fuel consumption, better employee morale, fewer empty miles, and so on. Productivity adjustments are discussed in all chapters that illustrate pricing concepts for specific sub-industries.

No Size Advantage

The trucking industry, in general, is structured so that no one firm is large enough to dictate terms to its suppliers. For example, IBM, Apple Computer, and General Motors are so large that the trucking companies who solicit their business are at an economic disadvantage. This imbalance is particularly apparent where the carrier transports specialized commodities, such as bulk cement, petroleum products, or construction materials, in dump trucks. It is common for shippers of such commodities to dictate transportation rates in the absence of economic regulation. These shippers arbitrarily set rates with little, or no, consideration for the carrier's cost.

The imbalance of economic strength also exists when the carrier is the buyer of vehicles and other major assets. Few trucking companies are in position to dictate purchase terms for acquisition of rolling stock. Certainly, those who can buy 100 to 150 units in a single purchase can realize more favorable terms than can smaller carriers, but, in general, even the largest trucking firms do not exert substantial pressure upon the overall fleet market.

The industry is also fragmented in size because of the wide-ranging types of transportation service required. The public perceives the industry as consisting of large LTL general commodities carriers, but, in fact, they make up only a small portion of the entire industry. It also includes tank truck, dump truck, household goods, automobiles, and truckload general commodities carriers, among others. Each of these specialized carriers exist to fill the needs of specific shippers with specific equipment requests. Because the specialized sub-industries operate unique equipment, meet differing market characteristics, and serve specialized shippers, it is uncommon for a carrier to serve more than two of the specialties. Consequently, the industry is fragmented by both shipper-carrier relationship limitations and diverse market needs for its services.

Erratic Sales Fluctuations

Most of the subgroups in the trucking industry suffer from seasonal volume fluctuations. In the transportation of cement, petroleum products, household goods, construction materials, and even general commodities, it is not uncommon for volume during the year to fluctuate by 50%, or more. Most carriers do not, and many cannot, acquire sufficient rolling stock to handle the high peak season, and to support that equipment during the off-season. Thus, the specialized carrier uses underlying carriers to assist in the peak season, maintaining only a base fleet. This circumstance keeps both the overlying and underlying carriers rather small in comparison to their customers. Consequently, this condition contributes to continued industry fragmentation.

Exit Barriers

Exit barrier refers to the ease with which an entity can leave the industry. If the industry involves large capital investment, such as railroads, automobile manufacturing, or computer systems, there is little turnover. Even marginal companies stay in an industry if the exit cost is too high for investors to incur. On the other hand, in trucking, exit barriers are almost nonexistent. If a company elects to leave the industry, it is not too difficult to place equipment for sale, and there are no regulatory penalties associated with leaving.

There are other types of exit barriers, as well. In fragmented industries, managerial exit barriers are often present. For some, the trucking operation has been a family-owned business for as long as three generations. It is not unusual for the present ownership to feel a loyalty to both the family tradition and its employees. This loyalty is an exit barrier because ownership continues the business even though results are marginal, at best. Retention of these businesses contributes to industry fragmentation.

Economic Effects of Fragmentation

What has fragmentation to do with the current competitive environment of the trucking industry? The answer is everything! Most economists agree that fragmented industries, such as trucking, create a more competitive environment. If any of the conditions mentioned above are present, an economist will say the industry is blocked from consolidation. Without consolidation, the industry remains fragmented, and, therefore, highly competitive. Competition, by definition, drives profits to marginal levels.

Without consolidation, competition is more acute because there is an imbalance between the numbers of buyers and sellers. A large number of trucking companies are vying for business from a smaller number of shippers or customers.

In summary, the trucking industry is highly competitive because it is relatively easy to enter and relatively easy to exit. There is no reason to believe this condition will change in the post-regulation era. In fact, it is more likely that turnovers will increase. From a practical viewpoint, it is not likely the industry will consolidate in the near future. The industry does not have the financial resources do to so, and is presently in a transition mode that precludes daring management decisions.

Trucking industry fragmentation is the result of underlying economics that cannot be overcome in the short term, if ever. Marginal profitability is the likely outcome from continued fragmentation, making strategic positioning an absolute necessity for survival. The challenge is to become one of the successful players, even though only a moderate market share is obtainable. However, just because fragmentation causes stringent competitive conditions, it does not necessarily follow that competition creates uncontrolled downward pricing spirals.

For-hire trucking had its genesis in the railroads, and, early on, most observers analyzed trucking as if it were an extension of that industry. Prior to the 1930s, railroads monopolized the transportation system. As the country grew, communities developed away from rail spurs, and relied upon trucking as the intermediate transportation mode. Economists of that era also viewed trucks as an extension of the railroads. They tried to apply the same economic theory to trucking as that applied to railroads, but, over time, it has become clear that trucking has its own economic structure, one that is quite different from railroads. This is particularly true in terms of cost and distribution structure. Railroads have a high fixed, or overhead, cost in track and track beds, terminals, and power equipment as opposed to trucking, which has a very low fixed cost. For this reason, it has been common for railroads to price services below out-of-pocket cost on occasion and still generate profits.

When a high fixed cost exists, a portion of that cost must be recovered on each segment of business. The railroads can, and do, assess rates below out-of-pocket cost to move traffic in order to cover fixed cost. Examples of this pricing include back-haul traffic that would not be moved without severely reduced rates or an imbalance of freight cars that would require movement back to the mainstream flow of business. Under these conditions, it is not necessary to cover costs above fixed cost.

The concept of pricing below fully allocated, or total, cost is explained by economists and others in terms of levels of fixed and variable costs. The railroad industry is a good example because it provides transportation service under a different cost structure from trucking. Though railroads incur a very high level of fixed cost in relation to total cost, they incur a very low level of variable cost. Economists assert that entities of this type can, and do, generate profit even when prices are pegged at the level of fixed cost plus one unit of variable cost. Using this yardstick, railroads generate a wide range of cost-based pricing strategies.

Trucking, on the other hand, is a low fixed cost, high variable cost industry. In excess of 90% of all trucking cost varies as traffic flow changes. Because trucks do not own the highways over which they travel, they have no investment in what is probably the industry's greatest asset, the network of pickup and delivery roadways. The trucking industry, however, pays its fair share for highways through fees, but even these fees vary with volume and highway use.

It has been estimated that, in many segments of the trucking industry, labor cost accounts for as much as 70% of total cost. Labor is a variable cost in the sense that it changes with both business volume and type of service. Trucks, which account for about 15% of total cost, are also variable with volume and service because fleet size is relatively inexpensive to adjust as volume changes. Some might even advance the notion that real estate cost is variable because it can be adjusted to some extent as major volume changes occur. Real estate cost is nearly 8% of total cost. While terminal and warehouse cost is less variable than labor and vehicles, it is, nonetheless, a variable cost. All these variable costs account for approximately 93% of total cost.

If motor carrier costs are variable, the rate-making considerations in relation to railroads or other high fixed-cost industries are significantly different. Since virtually all trucking costs are variable, there are narrow limits within which a carrier can price its service below fully allocated cost. All costs must be recovered in almost all trucking rates as opposed to the rates quoted by high fixed-cost industries. Additionally, there is less emphasis on the value-of-service concept in trucking because value to the buyer must still recover variable cost, which differs with the service provided. Railroads can move some traffic at rates only high enough to cover fixed cost if the traffic would not otherwise be moved. Trucking firms, on the other hand, cannot price below fully allocated cost because that cost is variable and must be paid from each service provided.

Another way to view this variable-versus-fixed cost phenomenon is in connection with long-run and short-run costs. It is difficult for the railroad to substitute another service for rail beds; the beds serve only one purpose, and cannot be otherwise used, or disposed of, to ready buyers. Production plants also suffer from the same infirmities; ready buyers for large facilities are limited both in number and financial ability. (This may explain why the government has entered the railroad industry.) Accordingly, fixed cost tends to be long term in nature and cannot be substituted or disposed of easily. Truck cost is a short-term cost and more variable because it is inexpensive to adjust fleet size to meet fluctuating demand.

Finally, this fixed-versus-variable cost issue can be better understood by reviewing the overall regulatory concept employed by the Interstate Commerce Commission during the past 60, or so, years. In determining whether rate increase applications by railroads were justified, the commission applied the fair-return-on-fair-value measure. Simply, this concept attempted to measure the value of service against the railroad's return on investment, or equity, a typical measure used in public utility regulation where high fixed cost is the norm.

IMPORTANT!

On the other hand, the trucking industry has been required to meet the operating ratio test, where rates are designed to cover all operating expenses. The commission recognized that truck cost is predominately variable, and that measurements such as return on investment or return on equity have little meaning as they are so minimal that their measurement produces no usable information for rate setting.

The trucking industry is fragmented for reasons set forth above, and this fragmentation contributes to increased competition. However, because the cost structure of the industry is predominately variable, competition should not create a downward price spiral if participants understand operating cost, and create prices accordingly.

Most fragmented industries contain disparate entities that make it difficult to propound specific strategic moves that will work in all cases. The trucking industry is no exception. Many alternatives must be examined to evaluate the individual strategic position.

Decentralization

Fragmented industries, such as trucking, commonly require precise coordination, a hands-on management style, and high personal service. Rather than increasing the size of the central operation, it may be preferable to keep individual operations small and tightly controlled by central management, which, in turn, places responsibility upon local managers who are compensated on a performance basis. Generally, a promote-from-within program augments the decentralization strategy to build employee loyalty and responsibility. Such a decentralization strategy requires strong central management and a willingness by the ownership to delegate authority and responsibility. In many cases, this strategy can be highly profitable.

Decentralization also requires that management recognize the causes of industry fragmentation and address these causes by selecting highly qualified and motivated local managers. The decentralization strategy also establishes a "boiler plate" approach to management, with each decentralized location operating in an identical fashion. Under a tightly controlled management philosophy that includes standard procedures, each local operation should be operated to achieve lower cost and higher productivity.

Keep It Simple

Because competition is intense in fragmented industries, a simple yet powerful strategy is to develop a no-frills approach to business. Vehicles acquired for a specific function should include no chrome or strings of lights and should be standardized by manufacturer and model. Acquisition of all vehicles from the same manufacturer reduces the complexities of maintenance and the number of replacement parts.

The "keep it simple" strategy requires low-skilled and low-paid employees, low overhead, tight cost control, and constant attention to detail. The term "attention to detail" means that management should always be aware of its operating cost for servicing each book of business and should be in a position to immediately respond to cost changes. If this strategy is strictly followed, the firm is in the best position to compete on price and still realize a reasonable return. Alternatively, if the "keep it simple" approach is not maintained, chances of success are limited.

Value-added Methods

Some segments of the trucking industry have the ability to participate in product manufacturing cost. For example, many dump truck operators also own or lease sand pits. Sand is sold to existing customers, and the transportation cost is added for a delivered product price. Not only does the carrier realize a profit on the sand, the transaction also produces increased productivity for the truck fleet.

Other examples of this type of increased productivity include tank truck operators transporting their own fuel or operating automobile service stations and bulk distribution plants, household goods carriers storing customer products in existing warehouses, or general commodities carriers fabricating products from raw materials. All of these value-added methods contribute to profitability by increasing sales and productivity. Moreover, many of these activities can be enlarged to include wholesaling or retailing of the product.

Specialization by Order

Carriers can choose to specialize only in those shipments that contain some urgency. In this situation, the customer is less price sensitive and more service sensitive. Many customers need immediate handling of a portion of their shipments because of production failures, inadequate warehouse facilities, or human error. The carrier who specializes in solving these distribution problems will be rewarded with higher prices and repeat business. The down-side to this kind of specialization is limited volume and a greater need for attention to detail.

As an offshoot of this strategy, carriers can choose to service only custom orders where special handling is required to cope with intense competition. Examples of this practice include servicing only small orders, orders requiring immediate service, or orders of special commodities, such as convention displays and exhibits. Such specialized quality service can command higher than normal pricing.

Specialization by Geographic Area

Nationwide truck service is out of reach for most trucking companies. Even interstate service may be out of reach or undesirable from an economics perspective. However, there may be significant gains to be realized by blanketing a specified geographic area with concentrated facilities, sales effort, and marketing attention. Such a program reduces the size of the sales force, allows for more efficient advertising, increases equipment utilization, and improves management efficiency. A focus on servicing a specific geographic area often enables a firm to tally additional profits.

Fragmented Industry Traps

The trucking industry holds some disastrous traps for those who do not recognize its fragmented condition. Fragmentation necessarily means it is extremely difficult, if not impossible, to dominate the industry. Seeking domination in such a fragmented industry is doomed to failure because the underlying causes of fragmentation ensure that the firm will be exposed to inefficiency, loss of control over its product, and loss of contact with customers and suppliers as growth occurs. If the firm tries to be all things to all people, it will experience a vulnerability difficult to overcome.

Another trap is the tendency of the unaware to stray from the strategy of discipline. Members of fragmented industries can operate only with hands-on management because the underlying causes of the fragmentation we have discussed are always present. Firms in such an industry must be constantly alert to changes in the firm's position in relation to its competitors. Once a strategy has been formulated, the firm must maintain a tight focus, never wavering or changing that strategy unless it is not working. Strategy focus may mean rejecting some business or going against the conventional wisdom of how things should be done.

Competition in fragmented industries requires personal service, many local contacts, close managerial control, ability to adjust to changing circumstances, commitment to cost measurement and analysis, and so on. If the management style becomes too centralized and too rigid, it will slow the firm's reaction time to changing circumstances, remove incentives at lower management levels, and, perhaps, cause the loss of its most skilled employee-managers. Too much centralization will weaken, not strengthen, a firm.

By definition, a fragmented industry consists of many small privately owned companies. As we have seen, there are a myriad of reasons why these firms exist, and not all of them are economic. Accordingly, it is a serious mistake for company management to assume that all competitors sustain the same overhead cost, labor cost, or productivity levels. Some competitors may work out of their homes, use family labor, operate obsolete vehicles, fail to meet safety criteria, pay no fringe benefits, operate facilities closer to the market, and so on. This does not necessarily mean their overall operating costs are relatively higher or lower; it simply means they operate for different motives. It can also mean that the competitor is willing to operate at lower profit margins, maintain volumes alone without regard to profit levels, or only to provide work for employees.

 While it is extremely important to learn as much as possible about competitors, it is a serious error to make any assumptions about their operating cost. It is more important that a firm compete with as much information about its own cost as possible. Without this data, the firm will have no understanding of price levels or price competition. Though not all prices must return full cost, it is utterly essential to know and understand the operating cost to provide specific service. This subject will be discussed throughout this book.

A dialogue on economic structure in the industry would not be complete unless some discussion is devoted to available methods for developing a strategy. In this chapter we emphasized the need for self-evaluation as a basis for action in a non-regulated environment. Because the trucking industry is, in fact, several sub-industries, the first step in formulating a strategy should be a thorough analysis of the immediate sub-industry being addressed. This first step should also include a study of market competitors and their relative position.

The second step is to determine why the sub-industry is fragmented by using the underlying causes discussed in this chapter. If one or more of these causes are present, it is wise to determine the relative importance of each.

Step three should be to determine whether fragmentation can be overcome by consolidation possibilities. If it is concluded that consolidation cannot be attained, or, if attainable, would not be profitable, a determination should be made as to whether fragmentation can be overcome by other methods.

The final step should be to develop the competitive strategies necessary to survive in this fragmented industry.

Competitive Strategies in the Industry

There are three generic types of competition common to all fragmented industries: differentiation, cost leadership, and focus. A competitor should choose the philosophy its firm is best suited to employ. Within these types of competition, there are two types of sellers, price-makers and price-takers. Price-makers are those who set the competitive stage by aggressively establishing price structure at any level they choose. Price-takers are those who take the price stated by the market. Price-takers use the established prices to operate their firms, adjusting prices over time to meet existing competition.

All three generic competitive forms require knowledge of the infrastructure of both the firm and its competitors. The company must first develop a data base from which it can readily determine its operating cost to provide service. This operating cost system should provide enough information for top management to make cost adjustments without jeopardizing their generic competitive strategy. The management and organizational structures must then be evaluated to determine if the structure is compatible with the competitive direction to be taken. Finally, employees must be trained to understand the new competitive direction.

Decisions made during this evaluation are not easy as they may directly involve employee compensation or performance evaluation. It is human nature to resist change, but adjustments may be the only formulas for success. Any of the generic headings will prove successful if the competitive strategy results in outperforming rivals.

Focus

The focus concept involves selecting a particular buyer, product, or geographic area as a target. Once the target is selected, the strategy is to focus all of the firm's energy upon servicing that target better than rivals can do at prices that are both competitive and reflective of the company's operating cost. By focusing on a particular market, the company will develop skills not available to buyers from its rivals. This strategy can lead to higher profits and net returns along with the reduced possibility of service substitutions. The customer who receives above average service at competitive prices is less likely to substitute its own fleet, and potential competitors entering the field will not seek to attract the targeted customer.

This focus strategy may be seen in many industries. One example would be a trucking company formed for the purpose of focusing upon the fast-food industry. This particular company is not the low-cost leader, nor is it differentiated from other companies. It simply focuses upon another industry's need, and provides the required service.

Differentiating

Another competitive strategy, one we call "differentiating," involves creating a unique image recognized in the industry by both competitors and customers. It means setting the firm apart from its rivals by perception or in fact. Examples of this strategy include Mercedes, IBM, JennAir, and Mitsubishi's big screen television division.

How this strategy is implemented varies according to individual images. IBM is still recognized as the first computer company, as a company that has developed exceptional employee programs, and as a company with impeccable service. Despite competition from BMW and Lexus, Mercedes Benz is another company recognized as the ultimate status symbol.

The differential strategy does not permit the firm to ignore its operating cost, but that cost is not the company's primary concern. In most cases, the differentiated firm is free to set prices above those of competition as long as service commitments are consistently met. The differentiated firm must know its cost in advance, as well as the approximate cost and strategy of its competitors. With that information, it is relatively simple to adjust prices upward.

One benefit of this differentiated strategy is the ease in justifying higher prices. Where the customer perceives it is receiving added benefits, it will usually reward the supplier. The differentiated firm also understands this customer loyalty and realizes that there is little threat of new competition.

Competitive strategy recognizes that all shippers cannot pay higher prices to the differentiated firm because of philosophical differences or ability to pay. Accordingly, market share may suffer. The fortunate firm is the one that selects a differential strategy that does not involve heavy cost.

An example of such low-cost differentiation would be the firm that maintains exceptional equipment through color combinations, cleanliness, or quality maintenance. Another would be a company that uses employee morale to advertise the quality of the firm. In trucking, the driver employee is in constant contact with the customer. Training the driver to advertise the company by emphasizing quality in-house programs is a relatively inexpensive method of differentiation. Well trained sales personnel with a personal stake in company success will meet the customer with confident and positive attitudes.

Low-cost Leader

The third generic competitive strategy is the low-cost leader. This strategy requires the most aggressive behavior and efficient management. The low-cost leader develops and maintains accurate and functional accounting and cost-finding systems, and operates a more efficient and productive firm than any competitor. It usually has achieved the lowest cost in a major cost center, such as in overhead, labor, or vehicle operating efficiency. An unlimited energy in cost determination and control is required of the low-cost competitor. Low cost is the goal that guides every action of this competitor.

This type of competition has several advantages. Having the lowest cost can return increased yields because it is possible to construct prices just under those of the competition and still obtain significant profits. This method also creates a formidable defense against new rivals as they must incur entry costs not incurred by the low-cost firm.

The low-cost competitor can even stand off most established competitors that struggle to compete and ultimately suffer from diminished profits. Moreover, the low-cost firm is also able to ward off pressure exerted by strong buyers that can only drive down prices to the level of the next lowest competitor. Accordingly, the low-cost company is protected from all of the competitive forces existing in a fragmented industry. The overall low-cost position may require a high market share, however, in order to generate enough return to maintain its position.

Generally, the low-cost competitor needs sufficient yield to reinvest in state-of-the-art equipment to maintain its position. It may even require special equipment to take advantage of productivity or service gains. A high market share and modern vehicles also create additional cost cutting, which will further enhance the low-cost position.

There are significant drawbacks to this generic competitive stance. Low-cost positioning requires the establishment of, and commitment to, cost-finding and accounting systems that provide decision-makers with accurate and timely data. Operating cost is not static, and changes in individual items without reflection on the price structure can either take the firm out of its position or critically reduce its profit. Management must be forever vigilant. While continual attention to detail and cost structure is a necessity for the low-cost leader, rewards can be exceptional.

The universal competitive strategies discussed in this chapter differ from each other in terms of management style, organizational structure, control procedures, and market approach. The motor carrier's objective should be to analyze the firm from within, and choose a strategy that best fits its needs. Once the strategy is selected, it must receive unwavering commitment. Upon selection of the strategy, management must put into place a system of cost information that is both accurate and timely. The cost data must be arranged so that a price structure can be built to sustain the firm over time. Secondly, the cost system must provide sufficient information for management to determine ways to reduce cost and/or increase productivity.

There are two fundamental risks if the firm does not pursue one of the competitive strategies. The most obvious is a failure to reach its objective and/or the inability to nourish it properly, once achieved. The second risk involves changing strategy without a proven cause. It is important to note that all three of these approaches require different management and operational methods. If the firm waivers or changes competitive direction periodically, it will lose momentum and fail.

What happens if a firm fails to choose one of the strategies? First of all, that company is put into a very poor competitive position because it will lack market share, cost data upon which to make intelligent decisions, equipment investment, and buyer confidence. Most importantly, it will have demonstrated that the firm lacks the expertise or incentive to play the game.

Once the strategy is selected, the next task is to set up appropriate competitive moves for given situations. This part of the competitive environment relies, to a large extent, upon the competitor's knowledge of the industry and its intuition in decision-making. If the firm has a history of quality client service, it should use this strength to increase market share. If its goal is to maintain reasonable return on investment, it should keep constant, relatively high rates as long as possible, and make competitors and buyers aware that its objective is to maintain a sufficient return to continue quality service.

At the first sign of price competition, this competitor should have a predetermined strategy. This might involve reducing its price below an initial reduction to send a signal that price conflict will be met with force.

Another, more drastic, strategy in response to a price reduction where the firm provides a needed service is to withdraw the service. This strategy requires real commitment, but generally produces results. It puts the buyer on notice that the firm knows it is needed, knows its cost, is not willing to succumb to price wars, and will be available to provide quality service when prices produce the desired result.

A third method is to solicit business from the most important buyer of the price-reducing rival. This sends a clear message that the company is willing to join in reducing prices, if necessary, and that the firm will not sit by while business is lost.

All companies must be prepared to deal with competitors' actions. A competitor may test the firm's resolve through a selected price reduction, for example. The best way to address this activity is with a swift, well-designed retaliation on a preselected course. This swift and calculated response will cause a competitor to take the action as a certainty, and it may try to avoid future price wars. If a competitor understands that the firm is committed to fair prices, but has the ability and willingness to retaliate, the competitor realizes it would be well advised to find a new strategy. This is particularly true where the competitor is aware that the firm is on sound footings in terms of cost structure and management resolve. The trick is to select the best strategy to enhance the firm's market position.

On the other hand, it is equally important that the firm makes both buyers and competitors aware that it will take no action to start price wars. The idea is to project the firm as being in control of a destiny from which it will not waiver. This competitive move requires the building of trust and reliability. If the firm makes a statement or takes an action that projects a particular image, it must have the courage and resolve to stand by it.

The commitments made by a firm must be conveyed to all of the players. There are several ways to accomplish this. One way is through consistency. The firm that has built a reputation of standing by its commitments should have this history extolled repeatedly by its sales force.

A second method of communicating a firm's commitment is through well-placed leaks from employees. If you want something known outside the firm, tell drivers and other people. These leaks will reach the desired targets in short order, and can be used to convey future strategy and place competitors on notice. Care should be taken that only leaks of true conditions are made. To do otherwise reduces the target's reliance on such leaks.

Another communication device is the signing of long-term contracts. Not only does this ensure long-term business, but it also conveys to competitors the fact that the firm is in the game for the long term, and has agreed with buyers to perform under written conditions. Other methods include large equipment acquisitions, preferably purchases not leases. Adding to the sales force also demonstrates aggressive behavior. Written commitments to buyers that price reductions by competitors will be met is another strategy. Once competitors realize they face strong, committed, capable, and aggressive competition, price wars will be less likely.

We have tried to emphasize, so far in this book, that the ability to develop, understand, and adjust the firm's operating cost is a primary criteria for success in the fragmented industry. Each of the strategies discussed begin with an accurate and responsive cost development. This is important because the purpose of the strategies is to establish and maintain a pricing philosophy that will retain the desired business and still yield desired returns. The best pricing structure is one that attracts business and generates profits. The term cost development has a number of connotations. To a tax accountant, it may mean expense development for income tax purposes; to a financial manager, it may represent the cost to run the business; and, to an economist, it may denote the cost of lost opportunity. A financial manager analyzes accounts to determine how much money was spent on a given cost center, while an economist determines lost opportunity cost because of trucking company ownership.

This book is only concerned with cost preparation for the purpose of setting prices. Such an analysis cannot be prepared solely from the balance sheet or income statement because normal financial statements, while crucial to business management, do not contain the necessary data to isolate specific functions. Operating cost for pricing purposes requires analysis of the individual operation by observation and compilation of data.

Thus far we have shown that for-hire trucking is fragmented, and we have provided the various reasons for it. One might conclude that such fragmentation would drive prices to rock bottom. However, this should not be the case if the participants understand the effect of cost on the pricing structure. The concept that virtually all motor carrier costs are variable is the most important element in the future of the industry. It's vital that a firm recognize that variable cost must be consistently recovered in the price structure if the firm is to survive. While variable cost will vary among rivals, the range of variance will be narrow because the basic cost to provide service is constant. Firms must acquire vehicles, employ drivers, and pay for fuel, maintenance, and tires. For the motor carrier who understands this concept, and prepares appropriate analyses of operating cost, the future should be anticipated with confidence.

Shipper Deregulated Environment Strategies

The Motor Carrier Act of 1980, and its related studies, provide a number of lessons about shipper behavior when major disruptions occur in motor carrier economics. The impact on the motor carrier industry is well-documented. Thousands of carriers found themselves in financial difficulty; many failed, and hundreds of new carriers entered the field.

It is interesting to note that shippers also responded to the act with changes in buying attitudes and new purchasing procedures. These trends were being studied and reported as early as 1985. A study presented at the 1987 annual meeting of the Council of Logistics Management found that immediately following passage of the act, 54 percent of reporting shippers said that cost reduction was the most important element in the purchasing decision. Five years later, that percentage was reduced to 42 percent, with 58 percent of shippers saying service and reliability were most important in carrier selection.

Whether history will repeat itself in 1995 is not clear. It must be remembered that the national economy was in a recessionary period in the early 1980s. At least some of the industry turmoil in that period was created by external economics not related to the Motor Carrier Act. In 1995, however, the economy is improving, and it is expected to continue to do so. A sound economy should minimize stress on the trucking industry resulting from the current legislation.

A paper written by Alfred Marcus of the University of Minnesota, and published in the Transportation Journal in 1987, described the evolution of the purchasing practice as moving from a theory of "market dominance" to "credible commitments." According to the Marcus theory, shippers that practice market dominance try to obtain carriers who are particularly competitive with each other. They may set their own low-rate schedule, shift volumes among carriers to make them more dependent, threaten proprietary carriage, and search for alternate modes of transportation.

Using these techniques, market-dominating shippers drove carriers to financial instability by requiring rates below reasonable levels. The pushy purchaser can switch carriers with ease; it does not develop longstanding relationships with carriers. They also study their own transportation cost as well as that of competing carriers, and continuously monitor changes in distribution patterns of the organization. In short, the dominating shipper continually updates its data base to be aware of changing transportation conditions.

All of these activities are geared to obtaining the lowest cost for service. Skill in negotiating and preparing information are the hallmarks of the market dominator. It is also common for this buyer to continually obtain bids to build its data base. Even though it actually uses a small number of carriers, it maintains the domineering role.

Initial shipper reaction to deregulation was an attempt to develop market dominance through the use of these techniques. It is interesting that during the escalation of such attempts for market dominance the industry suffered its greatest turbulence. From the studies reported, it is clear that the strategy failed, creating carrier instability. Without financial stability in the carrier industry, market-dominating shippers found it difficult to sustain their roles.

Transition to the alternative shipper strategy that Mr. Marcus described as "credible commitments" began to replace market dominance. Shippers and carriers started to realize that common ground existed where mutual respect could be developed. Shippers searched for more long-lasting relationships with carriers, developed computer systems to be shared with carriers for distribution efficiency, and integrated portions of their business with carrier operations. Both sides found that improved communications resulted in a greater efficiency through common language and better trust.

The transition also included greater commitment through establishment of service contracts. Shippers initially selected financially sound carriers as partners for long-lasting relationships. Strong communication prior to contractual commitment prevented disputes and established incentives for additional efficiency. In short, shippers in the newly deregulated environment have come to realize that reliability and performance of service produce the best long-term results.

A study by Edward Bardi of the University of Toledo, also reported in the Transportation Journal, made similar determinations. This study sampled 1,000 shippers, with 296 responding. From this core group, Bardi determined that reliability and service are the most important criteria for shippers selecting carriers. Price considerations were second in importance. The group also reported that price considerations changed more than any criteria in the period after passage of the Motor Carrier Act: shippers considered price far more after deregulation. This is a rather obvious result because carrier rates were generally static prior to deregulation.

The Bardi study also found that the average time a carrier stays with a shipper increased for half of the reporting shippers. Fifty-five percent of the shippers used the same carriers longer than five years. Accordingly, after the initial shakeout period in the early 1980's, both shipper and carrier operating practices have tended to stabilize.

The final interesting Bardi statistic is that 82 percent of the reporting shippers use carriers who perform to expectations 81 percent of the time. This means that carriers who are not reliable will find the new environment extremely difficult.

An improved economy during the early 1990's, shipper awareness of the importance of long-term commitments, and carrier realization that virtually all operating cost is variable and must be recovered in its rates all contribute to a smoother transition in this second round of regulatory relaxation.

Cost accounting for pricing purposes will be indispensable as a competitive tool in the 1990s and on into the 21st century. If variable cost characteristics preclude pricing fluctuations below fully allocated cost, and competition precludes pricing above fully allocated cost plus marginal profit, how can a successful pricing strategy be developed and maintained unless cost is known? Cost determinations will be the yardstick and standard by which prices and services are structured in the industry. Both shippers and carriers must become better informed on the economics of truck transportation. The examination and analysis provided in this book will prove invaluable to the firm that chooses to compete intelligently through the coming transition period.

The Cost/Price Formula

Methods described in this book show how trucking companies can establish prices for specific products and services based upon known cost levels. Because of competition, it is not possible to set all prices at cost, or at cost plus an increment of profit. However, it is essential that management be aware of the cost/price relationship on all traffic handled. This allows the firm to set cost-based pricing, compare cost levels with competitor pricing, avoid setting prices below cost, and, if prices must be set below cost, to understand why that is to be the case. Without cost analysis, the firm could price below cost and never realize it until it was too late.

The discussion and examples presented are designed to provide management with a method for allocating operating costs so that the firm can construct transportation bids, formulate contracts with buyers, negotiate terms with sub-haulers, distribute costs over various weights of shipment and lengths of haul, establish and maintain cost-based pricing, provide price guidelines to sales staff, prepare employee compensation packages, and control cost through detailed analysis.

In this book, trucking cost studies for pricing purposes are constructed in accordance with four general principles: that the direct cost of providing service includes labor, vehicle fixed cost, and vehicle running cost; that costs are measured in terms of individual asset productivity; that individual costs must relate to the operational processes under study; and that overhead, or indirect, cost must be recovered in each established rate. The analyst must design the study within this framework before actual data is collected.

The study plan should be based on the following:

- Understanding of the specific transportation service.

- Price structure to be obtained, including units of measurement.

- Segments of operations to be studied.

- Selection of weight brackets and mileage points to serve as study focal points.

- Productivity measurements necessary.

- Source information required.

- Acquisition of data from existing records.

- Methods for collecting unavailable data.

- Company staff required to complete data collection and perform analytical work.

- Time schedule for completion.

Data required to produce cost studies and rate designs described in this book is available from several sources. Direct labor cost data comes from payroll records, payroll tax returns, and purchase invoices supporting payments for employee fringe benefits. Underlying vehicle fixed cost records include equipment lists, depreciation schedules, vehicle registration documents, and insurance policies or supporting schedules. Vehicle running cost is determined from accounting records, maintenance agreements, and/or purchase invoices. Indirect cost is determined by analysis of expense accounts listed in the income statement.

Unless carriers have performed similar studies, productivity measurements are determined from field investigations that measure time and distance to perform the operating processes. Appendix A provides forms for collecting and compiling field data. The time and the amount of data required depend upon the carrier's size, rate design, and volume of shipments and traffic available for study. Care must be exercised to assure that the field results reflect the entire makeup of the transportation under study. Statistical sampling formulas are also available to assist in establishing correct procedures. Ensuing chapters take a detailed look at all of these study elements as they relate to particular types of truck transportation.

Cost studies for price determination address either specific rates for a specific purpose or a broad scale of rates, such as those found in an LTL class rate structure. If the study will result in specific commodity rates for specific shippers, such as those ordinarily found in contract transportation, the analyst must be aware of all transportation conditions at the time the study plan is prepared. These conditions include daily loading and unloading availability, origin and destination points, shipment frequency, type and quantity of equipment, number of employees required in addition to the driver, product to be transported, and special buyer needs. From this broad definition, the analyst can begin to formulate the study parameters.

The more broadly based cost/price studies found in both truckload and less-than-truckload transportation of general commodities dictate a more comprehensive plan because tariff or price schedule construction involves a series of rates. That is, LTL rates are normally applied to a wide range of customers shipping a broad range of commodities, and are constructed to reflect relative prices based upon weight, distance, and susceptibility to damage. Typical of this rate structure are the LTL tariffs with which most carriers are familiar.

An understanding of rate applications is central to developing a study plan. To construct a rate structure, the analyst must determine selected shipment weights and mileage increments that will provide the required result. These elements make up the study format. Cost is determined at the specific mileage points and average weights within each weight bracket. These rates are then "flowed" through the weights and distances in a smooth progression that evenly distributes cost. The weight brackets are used to allocate cost according to average shipment weight. From the cost points, graphic illustrations determine cost and rate at any specific weight or distance. Accordingly, an understanding of rate applications is central to developing the study plan.

Once the overall transportation rate system is determined, the analyst can select the appropriate productivity measurement. For example, in a study designed for truckload service for one shipper, a limited number of productivity measurements are required. There would be no need to determine loading and unloading pounds per man hour, for instance, as the number of pounds loaded or unloaded in an hour has no significance when the vehicle is loaded to capacity in a given period, and that time period is the measure of cost. Only the loading and unloading time for the entire shipment would be the essential ingredient in the cost determination. If the objective is to determine the cost for loading and unloading multiple shipments of varying weights, however, the measurement of pounds per man hour to load or unload each shipment is extremely important.

IMPORTANT!

Study design relies heavily on the units of productivity to be related to the determined cost increments. These productivity measurements are determined by the end result to be achieved. In truckload transportation for specific commodities or specific shippers, the required productivity measurements are average weight per shipment, vehicle capacity, running speed, and loading and unloading times.

The final ingredient for a successful study plan is deciding on what source documents to use and how to collect the data. What information is necessary and what is already available from current records? The analyst must also ascertain staff requirements for data collection, methods for collecting the data, and the time frames to be used.

Cost Increments

We stated previously that one of the four principles of cost-based pricing is that a trucking company employs direct costs for labor, vehicle fixed cost, and vehicle running cost. Direct labor normally consists of the driver in truckload operations; drivers, helpers, and packers for household goods transportation;

and several categories of employees in the LTL general freight transportation industry, including local pickup and delivery drivers, line drivers, and platform workers. Specialized carriers may elect to include other types of employee in direct cost.

The second increment of direct cost is vehicle fixed cost. Simply stated, it is the cost to acquire and prepare vehicles for service, including purchase or lease cost, licensing fees, and insurance expense. When designing this cost, the term "economic value" is used to describe the level of cost to be imputed into the formula to recover the vehicle acquisition cost for all vehicles employed in the process being measured. The economic value concept is different from depreciable value accounting provisions, and will be discussed in detail in following chapters.

The third component of direct cost is vehicle running cost. Typically, vehicle running cost includes fuel, oil, tires, and maintenance, and is expressed in terms of cost per mile for the vehicles employed in the service under analysis. These vehicle operating costs can be difficult to measure because many firms do not maintain detailed maintenance cost-per-vehicle records. However, as more manufacturers offer extended warranties that require carriers to maintain detailed records on the breakdown and replacement of parts, companies have started to develop new maintenance control systems.

Collectively, the three cost increments outlined above are referred to as direct cost, a cost that will vary according to the service provided. Though economists would refer to these costs as labor and capital, this cost-based pricing differs from their pricing theory in that it does not include all labor and capital in determining direct production cost. While the manufacturing cost of goods produced normally includes all labor and capital costs, the distribution cost includes only the vehicle driver, other vehicle workers, and the vehicle itself.

The final cost increment in the formula is referred to as indirect cost. Though accountants and economists may refer to this cost category as overhead or burden, there is a distinct difference between the accounting and economics terms and the concept discussed here. In this formula, indirect cost is not the same as fixed cost.

Indirect costs in the trucking industry are simply those costs that are not readily expressed in terms of productivity, and are not always necessary to produce service. We refer to these costs as "indirect" only because this portion of the total cost cannot be allocated to specific traffic flows. Though we do not argue with those who take the position that these costs are overhead or burden, we prefer to add the indirect cost to the direct cost so that the proposed cost-based prices will return full cost.

Indirect cost is determined by analyzing individual expense accounts in the income statement and isolating those accounts that may consist of indirect cost, either in total or in part. This analysis will produce an indirect ratio to be applied to direct cost. In the process described in this book, the total of direct and indirect cost produces a break-even cost, or cost at a 100 operating ratio.

Productivity Measurement

The second principle of trucking cost analysis for pricing purposes is the measurement of productivity used to express the cost and the rate in terms acceptable to a firm and its buyer. For example, the calculation of cost/rate per trip requires determination of vehicle configuration, running speed (MPH), and loading and unloading times. These components convert raw direct cost to a figure that can be used for pricing purposes. For example, if the transportation is by truckload, the loading and unloading time is 1.5 hours and the labor cost is $15 per hour, the loading and unloading driver cost per trip is $22.50 (1.5 x $15.00 = $22.50). Obviously, the productivity factor that must be determined is loading and unloading time.

In another example, the trip loaded is 100 miles in length. To determine driver labor cost per trip, running speed must be determined. If that speed is 35 miles per hour, the running time (round-trip) is 5.71 hours (200 miles ÷ 35 MPH = 5.71). When the driver labor cost per hour is $15, the driver cost per trip is $85.65 ($15.00 x 5.71 = $85.65). The total trip cost for the driver for loading, travel, and unloading would be $108.15.

Once the direct cost per unit of measure (per hour, per mile, etc.) is determined, it must be related to production in order to measure cost in the same terms as the rates expressed. In addition to load and unload time and running speed, production is stated in terms of pounds per man hour, average weight per shipment, average weight per truckload, annual hours worked, ratio of loaded to total miles, vehicle annual hours, and so on. The three elements of direct cost are measured in terms of one or all of the production categories detailed in this book, depending upon the motor carrier operation under study.

A brief look at other productivity measurements will contribute to a better understanding of the cost formula. Pounds per man hour measures loading or unloading performance at the point of pickup or point of delivery when rates are expressed in terms of weight (per 100 pounds or per ton) and multiple shipments are involved. Later discussion of LTL general freight cost construction will provide significant details on the importance of this measurement.

Pounds per man hour is employed in measuring cross-dock handling on the carrier's platform. It is a measurement of the time necessary to transfer a shipment from one point to another. In the loading process, measurement of time expressed as pounds per man hour is necessary to move a shipment from its point of rest to the carrier vehicle; in the unloading process, the time measurement is from the carrier vehicle to the point of rest.

Average weight per shipment is the measurement used to convert a known cost to the basis in which the rate will be expressed. For example, if the cost to unload a 5,000 pound shipment is $50, the cost per 100 pounds for those shipments is $1. Average weight per shipment is a conversion factor when rates will be expressed in terms of 100 pounds or tons. Average weight per truckload is a similar measurement except that it is used to convert a cost per line-haul trip to either a cost per 100 pounds or cost per ton. For example, if a trip costs $250, and the truckload weight of all shipments transported in a single unit of the carrier's equipment is determined to be 50,000 pounds, the cost per 100 pounds would be $.50.

Annual hours worked is a productivity measurement used to convert some of the driver labor cost from a cost-per-month or cost-per-year to a cost-per-hour basis. Typical of this type of cost is the monthly company contribution to medical insurance programs. It is also the measurement used to convert annual vehicle fixed cost to a cost per hour. Simply, if the annual or monthly cost is known, the annual hours worked will be the productivity measurement to convert that cost to a cost per hour (annual cost ÷ annual hours = hourly cost).

In many specialized product transportation systems, the carrier can load only one way because of trailer design limitations or other external conditions. Bulk cement carriers, for example, normally use pneumatic hopper trailers which are limited in terms of product compatibility because the unloading point is distant from typical loading points, a quick turnaround to point of origin for reloading is necessary, or a compatible product is not available. Accordingly, the ratio of loaded to total miles is 50% as the vehicle is only loaded half of the total trip time. This ratio becomes an important productivity measurement to reduce price.

IMPORTANT!

Costs and prices in this example must be constructed on a round-trip basis because the carrier must be compensated for all time and miles from a single buyer. If the haul is 100 miles, for example, costs are constructed for 200 miles to recover the return miles in the rate. Accordingly, when this imbalance occurs, the rate is higher than when back-haul or cross-haul loads are achieved. On the other hand, when the carrier can obtain other loads to go with the outbound shipment, all buyers share in the cost distribution through application of a concept we refer to as "ratio of loaded to total miles." All buyers in the loop benefit when the carrier efficiently dispatches its equipment, a principle that will be demonstrated in the chapters that discuss specific cost development.

Operating Processes

We have noted that the operating processes for truckload transportation are not complex. They are limited to loading, unloading, and running time. Cost preparation for the LTL operation requires considerably more productivity measurement and process analysis because of the distinct operations required to provide the service. The LTL operation requires measurement of local pick-up and delivery, platform handling, and line haul as separate cost centers or operating processes. Before any analysis is begun, there must be a predeter-mination of the study design in terms of these processes. The type of rate to be assessed must be established. If the rate will be expressed in terms of hun-dredweight, all costs must use that standard of measurement. If another unit of measurement is to be used, such as per ton or per piece, the cost study should be so designed. As most LTL rates have been expressed in terms of hundredweight, that method will be used in our examples.

LTL rates are affected by both distance and weight; therefore, initial planning must include selection of study shipment weights as well as particular dis-tances. Careful selection of these criteria is necessary in order for the cost study and rate design final result to flow through the weight brackets and mileage scales.

The pickup and delivery operation in LTL service is considered separately from platform handling or the line-haul portion of the study. Appendix A, Form 1, is a typical form that can be used to gather productivity measurements for the pickup and delivery operation; Form 2 may be used for platform han-dling.

The pickup and delivery operation is divided into two parts, "stop" time and "en route" time. Stop time is the time the vehicle and driver are at each stop to pick up and/or deliver shipments. The stop time is expected to differ at each stop because of the sizes of shipments being handled. The higher the weight, the longer the stop time. Additionally, stop time includes all of the time at the stop, including waiting time, time to complete paperwork, and time for obtaining signatures on documents. En route time is all other time incurred in performing the pickup and delivery, including the time from the carrier's terminal to the first stop, and the time from the last stop to the carrier's terminal, referenced as "stem time" in this book.

The objective of the platform study is to determine the pounds per man hour for handling shipments of various sizes across the carrier platform. Pounds per man hour increase as shipment weight increases, primarily because the use of mechanical aids increases as weight increases. In preparing a platform study, the analyst uses the same shipment weight groups as those selected for the pickup and delivery analysis. Observers are used to time shipments from the local vehicles to the line-haul vehicles as well as from the line vehicles to the pickup and delivery vehicles. Separate analysis is necessary for shipments that come to rest on the dock so that both handlings (vehicle to rest and rest to vehicle) are recorded and included for accurate results.

The line-haul portion of the LTL study is similar to the truckload operation. The major difference is that if trip manifests are not routinely prepared, it is necessary that Form 3 be used during the study period. The trip manifest will provide the analyst with the load weight, which is used as the productivity measurement for the line-haul cost center or operating process. Line-haul productivity is not a function of average weight per shipment; it is a function of average weight per trip. Total trip time is determined by the length of the haul, and the cost for that trip is divided by the hundredweight carried to determine the cost per hundred pounds for line-haul service.

Formulas examined in this book will provide the firm with direct, indirect, and total costs to perform the various functions relative to most types of truck transportation. Each of the cost elements are expressed in terms of productivity for each of the processes furnished in the overall transportation system. Table 3.1 shows the format of the data used throughout the book:

TABLE 3.1

BASIC COST FORMULA

Line No.	Item	Cost Per Unit
1.	Labor Cost	$xxxxxxx
2.	Vehicle Fixed Cost	xxxxxxx
3.	Vehicle Running Cost	xxxxxxx
4.	Subtotal - Total Direct Cost	$xxxxxxx
5.	Indirect Cost	xxxxxxx
6.	Total Cost at 100 Operating Ratio	$xxxxxxx
7.	Total Cost Including Net Income	$xxxxxxx

Direct Labor Cost

Direct labor cost is the most significant of all motor carrier costs. It ranges from about 35% to 65% of the total cost, depending upon the carrier operation. Specialized carriers transporting truckload quantities are at the lower end of the spectrum, and household goods carriers and LTL general freight carriers are at the other end. Controlling direct labor cost is a major objective of the industry.

Components

The industry uses several methods to pay employees directly involved in transportation operations, and rates utilized to recover labor cost are assessed on several bases. Major payment methods as well as labor rate issues are discussed in this chapter. The methods and illustrations used in the following chapters to describe cost-finding procedures use a fully allocated labor cost. This direct labor cost, regardless of employee classification (driver, helper, platform, or packer), includes the following components:

TABLE 4.1

DIRECT LABOR COST COMPONENTS

Base Wage Rate	Federal Unemployment Fund
Overtime Increment	State Payroll Taxes (if any)
Vacation, Holidays, and/or Sick Leave	City Payroll Taxes (if any)
Medical Insurance (Health and Welfare)	Other Payroll Taxes (if any)
Retirement Funds	Workers Compensation
Social Security (FICA)	Non-revenue Time

Direct labor cost per hour, including all applicable taxes and fringe benefits, must be developed for each category of employee directly involved in the service under study. Most LTL carriers and household goods carriers hire a variety of employees, including platform workers, warehousemen, pickup and delivery drivers, line-haul drivers, packers, and helpers. Each of these wage classifications include employees who earn different rates of pay. Accordingly, the Base Wage Rate is determined by weighting the pay rates for all employees in the same classification.

Wage Rates

Table 4.2 sets forth a method to determine wage classification pay rates.

TABLE 4.2

EMPLOYEE PAY RATES — LINE DRIVERS

Number of Employees	Hourly Pay Rate	Percent of Total	Weighted Average
6	$9.00	25.0	$2.25
9	10.25	37.5	3.84
5	11.00	20.8	2.29
4	12.00	16.7	2.00
24		100.0	$10.38

Weighting by the number of drivers in each work classification, such as line driver, produces a Base Hourly Wage Rate of $10.38. The same calculation must be made for each employee classification in the direct cost development. This becomes the wage rate carried forward in the process to determine the total cost for the service under analysis.

The number of employees in each classification paid the same wage is determined first. By weighting all the rates by the number of employees in each pay rate, the final weighted rate is then determined. In Table 4.2, for example, 6 employees earn $9 per hour. These 6 employees represent 25% of the work force in the classification of line driver. Accordingly, $9 is weighted by 25% to obtain a weighted average pay rate of $2.25.

After each of the pay rates is weighted in the same fashion, the resulting rates are added to obtain a line driver weighted wage of $10.38. Using this procedure, the analyst can utilize one pay rate to represent the cost of line drivers in subsequent total cost calculations.

Overtime Cost.

The next item in the preparation of the total hourly direct cost for labor is overtime, if the firm pays overtime to employees. The analyst needs to decide how the freight rates will be assessed in the overall study plan. There are two methods commonly used to assess hourly freight rates in connection with overtime. The first method designs rates so that all hours worked and charged in the freight rates recover the cost of overtime; the second method designs separate freight rates for straight time and overtime.

In the first method, costs are calculated so that each hour worked recovers an increment of overtime cost. Over an annual period, the carrier will be compensated for all overtime. In the second method, the rates are expressed separately for both straight time and overtime.

These procedures apply only if the objective is to construct hourly rates. If the study is for the purpose of designing rates on a hundredweight basis, the underlying labor cost calculations should include overtime in the hourly cost so that each hundredweight transported recovers an increment of overtime cost. If the study is designed to produce both hundredweight rates and hourly rates with overtime stated separately, the analyst must determine hourly cost by using both methods. In other words, the hourly labor cost to establish a hundredweight rate must include overtime in the basic hourly labor cost calculation. The alternative hourly cost study must state the overtime cost separately or combine it with straight time, depending upon the desired method of rate assessment.

In the first example, overtime is included in the hourly labor cost because the rate assessment will be on a hundredweight basis that requires recovery of the cost in a single rate. It is not practical, nor useful, to develop a hundredweight rate for service provided during straight time hours and another hundredweight rate for overtime hours.

The overtime increment is calculated from the annual employee payroll record. These records show both straight time and overtime hours worked in addition to the dollar amounts accumulated for annual payroll tax purposes.

The relationship of overtime to total time must be determined for each employee classification in a manner similar to the summary in Table 4.3. Determining the exact annual hours worked is critical to accurate pricing. The study should not be constructed by using 2,080 hours or 2,088 hours per year. These figures are inaccurate, and will produce faulty results.

IMPORTANT!

Cost per hour for components such as employer contributions to employee welfare programs is determined on the basis of annual hours worked. This hourly cost is understated if too many annual hours worked are used as a denominator, or overstated if too few annual hours worked are used. Using the figure of 2,088 hours will not produce the desired results for several reasons: employees receive holiday and vacation pay for periods when they are not working; overtime hours are not included in that figure; and seasonal layoffs tend to reduce annual hours worked. Hourly rated employees simply do not work 8 hours per day, 5 days per week, 52 weeks per year.

TABLE 4.3

ANNUAL HOURS WORKED — LINE DRIVERS

Line No.	Item	Hours	Percent
1.	Straight Time	1,550	87.3
2.	Overtime	225	12.7
3.	Total Annual Hours Worked	1,775	100.0

TABLE 4.4

GROSS ANNUAL EARNINGS — LINE DRIVERS

Line No.	Item	Amount
1.	Straight Time ($10.38)	$16,089.00
2.	Overtime (one and one-half)	3,503.25
3.	Gross Annual Earnings	$19,592.25

In the example in Table 4.3, the line driver classification works 1,775 hours annually at a straight time hourly pay rate of $10.38 and 1.5 times the hourly rate of $15.57 during overtime hours. These hourly rates and annual hours produce annual earnings of $19,592.25. The annual earnings consist of $16,089.00 in straight time and $3,503.25 in overtime, as shown in Table 4.4. From this data, analysts must determine the amount to be added to each straight time hourly rate assessed to recover the overtime cost. Using this method, one rate will recover straight time and overtime cost on an annualized basis.

STOP

IMPORTANT!

When overtime pay is 1.5 times the straight time pay rate, the penalty for having the employee work on an overtime rate is one-third of the overtime rate. Using the overtime rate of $15.57 per hour, the overtime penalty is $5.19 ($15.57 - $10.38 = $5.19). The employee worked 225 hours annually at a penalty rate of $5.19, which produced an annual penalty that must be recovered in the rates assessed to the buyer. The annual penalty cost is $1,167.75, or 5.96% of annual earnings ($1,167.75 ÷ $19,592.25 = 5.96%). Accordingly, if 5.96% is added to the hourly base wage rate of $10.38, the ultimate rate assessed to the buyer will recover the overtime penalty annual cost.

This calculation is accomplished by dividing the complement of the overtime penalty percentage into the straight time rate to obtain the whole amount. If the overtime penalty percentage is 5.96%, the complement of that number is 94.04% (5.96% + 94.04% = 100%). When the straight time Base Hourly Wage Rate is $10.38 and the overtime penalty is 5.96%, $10.38 is divided by 94.04% for a result of $11.038.

When the cost study in the example includes $11.038 as the Base Hourly Wage Rate, the firm will recover the cost of overtime on an annualized basis. This can be tested by multiplying the cost of $11.038 times the annual hours worked of 1,775. This produces $19,592.45, the same figure (except for rounding) as the annual earnings shown in our example above. Thus, the new Base Hourly Wage Rate is correct, and the final total cost will recover the correct labor cost insofar as overtime is concerned.

As mentioned above, this is only one method to establish labor cost for pricing purposes. If the study objective is to determine straight time and overtime rates separately, a different analysis is required. Rates of this type are normally found in contract transportation where the buyer is assessed rates on an hourly basis. In this calculation, overtime during off-hours on weekdays and all hours on weekends become an issue. This issue will be discussed later in the chapter.

TABLE 4.5
PROGRESSIVE TOTAL LABOR COST CALCULATION — LINE DRIVERS

Line No.	Item	Amount
1.	Base Hourly Wage Rate	$10.380
2.	Overtime	.658
3.	Subtotal	$11.038

Fringe Benefits

The next labor cost component to be determined is vacation, holidays, and sick leave as a unit of cost measurement. These fringe benefits may be calculated as a single unit because their measurement uses annual hours worked as a common denominator. Vacation pay is based upon what is termed "tenure of employment"; the longer employees are with the firm, the greater the vacation benefits. Tenure of employment for each employee classification might appear as shown in Table 4.6.

TABLE 4.6
TENURE OF EMPLOYMENT — LINE DRIVERS

Line No.	Number of Employees	Number of Years	Weeks Vacation	Percent
1.	6	0-1	0	18.8
2.	19	1-5	1	59.4
3.	5	5-10	2	15.6
4.	2	Over 10	3	6.2
	32			100.0

The number of vacation hours for the wage classification of line drivers can be determined by the method shown in Table 4.7. Using the tenure of employment in Table 4.6, and the vacation policy of the firm, the over-all vacation hours paid each line driver, on the average, are obtained.

TABLE 4.7

WEIGHTING OF VACATION HOURS — LINE DRIVERS

Line No	Percent	Vacation Hours	Weighted Hours
1.	18.8	0	0
2.	59.4	40	23.76
3.	15.6	80	12.48
4.	6.2	120	7.44
5.	100.0		43.68

Hence, all employees in this classification would earn a weighted average vacation pay of 43.68 hours per year.

Holiday pay is the simplest of the fringe benefits to calculate because all employees receive the same number of holidays in the employment package. If there are 8 annual holidays, the number of hours is 64, 8 hours per day for 8 days.

Sick leave and funeral leave (if any) are determined from an analysis of payroll records. For example, if the employer has a policy that pays for up to 5 sick days per year and 2 funeral days at the death of family members, the obvious result is that the employee may be paid for as much as 7 days per year while not working. However, this calculation overstates the cost because not all employees take 7 days per year. The use of payroll records will determine the number of days that each employee within a work classification is paid while not on duty. Our illustration uses 3.6 days for both of these fringe benefits, or 28.8 hours.

Using this process, the total annual hours for vacation, holidays, sick leave, and funeral leave are 136.48. These total fringe benefit hours are then divided by the annual hours worked (1,775) to obtain a percentage to apply to the Base Hourly Wage Rate. In the examples shown above, that percentage is 7.69%. Applying that percentage to the Base Hourly Wage Rate results in the hourly cost for these fringe benefits ($10.38 x .0769 = $.798). Table 4.8 shows the completed determination.

TABLE 4.8
PROGRESSIVE TOTAL LABOR COST CALCULATION — LINE DRIVERS

Line No.	Item	Amount
1.	Base Hourly Wage Rate	$10.380
2.	Overtime	.658
3.	Subtotal	$11.038
4.	Vacation, Holidays, and Sick Leave	.798
5.	Subtotal	$11.836

Line 1 is multiplied by the percentage for vacation, holidays, and sick leave because these fringe benefits are paid at the straight time rate.

The next labor cost components to be determined are weekly or monthly company contributions to employee health and retirement programs. Only the employer contributions should be considered in this calculation. In our example in Table 4.9, the employer pays $250 per month for each employee's health insurance and puts $30 per week into a retirement fund. The annual costs for these employee benefits are $3,000 for health and welfare and $1,560 for retirement. The total of $4,560 is divided by the annual hours worked (1,775) to produce a cost per hour of $2.569.

TABLE 4.9

PROGRESSIVE TOTAL LABOR COST CALCULATION — LINE DRIVERS

Line No.	Item	Amount
1.	Base Hourly Wage Rate	$10.380
2.	Overtime	.658
3.	Subtotal	$11.038
4.	Vacation, Holidays, Sick Leave	.798
5.	Subtotal	$11.836
6.	Health, Welfare, and Pension	$ 2.569

Payroll Taxes

Payroll taxes may be calculated as a single figure, or considered separately. Our example calculates them separately.

Social Security taxes paid by the employer are expressed as a percentage of earnings to a maximum amount of earnings. If annual earnings exceed the taxable wage, the analyst would use the statutory taxable wage limit as the basis for the calculation. Because earnings are subject to tax but fringe benefits are not, the percentage is applied to the subtotal in line 5 in Table 4.9. That result is $.905 ($11.836 x .0765). This calculation may be tested by multiplying the hourly cost in line 5 by the annual hours worked (1,775), which produces a figure of $21,008.90. The rate of 7.65% would produce an annual cost of $1,607.18. Dividing the annual hours worked into that figure proves the result of $.905. The maximum earnings subject to FICA changes periodically. When an employee's annual earnings exceed the maximum, the percentage is applied to the statutory maximum annual wage. That figure is divided by the annual hours worked to obtain the hourly cost. The tax for Federal

Unemployment Insurance is shown as .8% of the first $7,000 of wages, or an annual cost per employee of $56. Dividing that figure by the annual hours worked (1,775) produces a cost per hour of $.032. State payroll taxes and some city and/or county taxes are expressed as a percentage of maximum annual earnings ($7,000). Our example uses a rate of 3.5% on $7,000 of annual earnings, resulting in an annual cost of $245. Again, dividing the annual cost by the annual hours produces the cost per hour; the figure in this case would be $.138. Table 4.10 illustrates the calculation of the total direct labor cost per hour, excluding workers compensation.

TABLE 4.10

PROGRESSIVE TOTAL LABOR COST CALCULATION — LINE DRIVERS

Line No.	Item	Amount
1.	Base Hourly Wage Rate	$10.380
2.	Overtime	.658
3.	Subtotal	$11.038
4.	Vacation, Holidays and Sick Leave	.798
5.	Subtotal	$11.836
6.	Health, Welfare and Pension	2.569
7.	FICA	.905
8.	Federal Unemployment Fund	.032
9.	State Payroll Taxes	.138

Workers Compensation

The final component of the labor cost is workers compensation insurance. As not all jurisdictions employ the same method of premium assessment, the illustration in Table 4.11 may not apply. However, studying the illustrations of cost measurement should enable an analyst to discover a method of cost allocation for workers compensation insurance.

IMPORTANT!

The example below bases premiums on a standard rate within precise work descriptions, and assumes that rates are modified by the firm's experience rating. Drivers, helpers, packers, and platform workers are rated differently from outside sales people or clerical staff, but the modification rating of the individual firm applies to all job classifications. The example in Table 4.11 uses $15 per $100 of earnings for all employees in the direct cost development. It also assumes an individual firm modification rate of 90%. In other words, the firm in the example has an improved loss ratio in worker injury over the industry work classification as a whole. Accordingly, the effective rate is $13.50 per $100 of earnings.

Workers compensation premiums in most states are paid on all earnings except the penalty portion of overtime. When this is the case, the hourly premium cost is determined by using the cost of Base Hourly Wages of $10.38 plus the cost of Vacation, Holidays, and Sick Leave of $.798, which results in a numerator of $11.178. The illustration produces an hourly cost of $1.509 for workers compensation insurance ($11.178 x .135 = $1.509).

TABLE 4.11

TOTAL LABOR COST DEVELOPMENT — LINE DRIVERS

Line No.	Item	Amount
1.	Base Hourly Wage Rate	$10.380
2.	Overtime	.658
3.	Subtotal	$11.038
4.	Vacation, Holidays and Sick Leave	.798
5.	Subtotal	$11.836
6.	Health, Welfare and Pension	2.569
7.	FICA	.905
8.	Federal Unemployment Fund	.032
9.	State Payroll Tax	.138
10.	Workers Compensation	1.509
11.	Total Hourly Labor Cost	$16.989

Non-revenue Time

The total Hourly Labor Cost of $16.989 represents the cost per hour the firm must recover in its rate structure to break even on that portion of the total cost. This figure is predicated upon the firm assessing rates to buyers for each hour the employee is on the payroll. In the example above that assessment is not possible because the employee is paid for time that cannot be charged to individual work assignments. Examples of this non-chargeable time are employee "start time," the time until the driver and vehicle leave the point of domicile, and the time from the entry to the point of domicile to the time-out recording. At the beginning of the day, drivers are required to complete vehicle safety inspections before operation; at the end of the day, the driver completes shipping-related forms and performs duties related to vehicle operation. The driver is paid for this time, which must be recovered in the rate structure.

The analyst should perform some field observations to obtain time measurements for these activities. In addition to determining costs, these observations may reveal activities that can impair driver productivity. For example, if the driver punches in and then drinks coffee for 15 minutes, the time must be included as non-revenue time, or the company must absorb the cost. In either circumstance, the firm will not be competitive if these conditions persist. If the firm passes the cost along to its buyers, the added cost may lose potential business. If the firm tries to absorb the cost, its expenses become a burden.

STOP
IMPORTANT!

In the example below, the driver spends 15 minutes in the morning visually inspecting the vehicle for obvious safety failures and 15 minutes at the end of the shift completing vehicle inspection reports, turning in paperwork to clerical staff, and obtaining instructions for the following day. Clearly, the daily 30 minutes the employee is on the payroll must be recovered in the rate structure. If the employee is on duty an average of 8 hours per day, the 30 minutes is 6.25% of the time. To recover this cost, the total figure in Table 4.11 should be increased by 6.25%, producing a figure of $18.051 to be imputed into the total cost for purposes of pricing.

Reference was made earlier in this chapter to determining rates where straight time and overtime prices are to be assessed separately. Clearly, the illustrations above will not accomplish that objective. If a separate rate for overtime is the objective, the cost of overtime must be separately stated, and some modifications must be made to our examples.

TABLE 4.12

OVERTIME LABOR COST PER HOUR — LINE DRIVERS

Line No.	Item	Amount
1.	Overtime Base Hourly Wage	$15.570
2.	Vacation, Holidays, and Sick Leave	.798
3.	Subtotal	$16.368
4.	Health, Welfare, and Pension	2.569
5.	FICA	1.252
6.	Federal Unemployment Fund	.032
7.	State Payroll Tax	.138
8.	Workers Compensation	1.509
9.	Total Overtime Labor Cost Per Hour	$21.868
10.	Non-revenue Time (6.25%)	$23.235

When the objective is to determine labor cost for overtime hours, the Base Wage Rate is changed to the rate that is paid for such work, or 1.5 times the straight time rate. The increment for overtime in Table 4.11 is removed since it will no longer be included in an overall labor cost per hour. Vacation, Holidays, and Sick Leave are not changed because the method of calculation uses annual hours worked as the divisor. Annual hours worked do not change because two rates will be employed. The same explanation also applies to Health, Welfare, and Pension; the cost per hour was determined in Table 4.11 using annual hours worked. FICA is increased in Table 4.12 because that tax is based on earnings, and the earnings on overtime are higher than straight time. State payroll taxes and the Federal Unemployment contributions are fixed because of the low level of wages subject to the taxes; therefore, these costs are not changed from Table 4.11. Table 4.11 must be changed when rates are to be assessed separately for straight time and overtime. Such changes are indicated below.

TABLE 4.13

STRAIGHT TIME HOURLY LABOR COST — LINE DRIVERS

Line No.	Item	Amount
1.	Straight Time Base Hourly Wage	$10.380
2.	Vacation, Holidays and Sick Leave	.798
3.	Subtotal	$11.178
4.	Health, Welfare and Pension	2.569
5.	FICA	.855
6.	Federal Unemployment Fund	.032
7.	State Payroll Taxes	.138
8.	Workers Compensation	1.509
9.	Straight Time Hourly Labor Cost	$16.281
10.	Hourly Cost Including Non-revenue Time (6.25%)	$17.209
11.	Annual Hours Worked	1,775

In Table 4.13, the cost of overtime has been removed because that cost is recovered in the cost shown in Table 4.12. This adjustment also reduces the cost of FICA because a portion of that tax is recovered in overtime cost.

Other Labor Cost Issues

Other issues arise in connection with the measurement and payment of labor cost, including payment on a mileage basis or payment as a percentage of revenue. Because labor cost is a major component of motor carrier operating cost, an understanding of this cost is necessary. Payment on a mileage basis generally applies to the general freight long-haul carrier who routinely performs trips exceeding 1,000 miles. As the length of haul increases, the impact of loading and unloading time, which is labor-intensive, is less relevant, and vehicle operating cost becomes a greater portion of the total cost. Virtually all of the cost and revenue is generated by miles traveled. Short-haul operations involve more loading and unloading, which are not a function of distance. Cost per mile becomes erratic as the number of loadings and unloadings increase. For these reasons, expression of labor cost in longer haul operations on a mileage basis is consistent with related operating cost.

An example will illustrate the concept. If the loaded vehicle travels 1,500 miles at an overall speed of 45 miles per hour, the trip takes 33.3 hours of actual driving time. For the driver to earn the equivalent of the Base Hourly Wage Rate used in earlier examples, he or she would need to be paid $345.65 for the trip ($10.38 x 33.3 = $345.65). The trip labor cost divided by 1,500 miles produces a pay rate per mile of $.23 ($.23 x 1,500 = $345.00).

One of the difficulties in this payment method is that the driver must be paid for empty return miles if loads to the originating point cannot be achieved on a timely basis. If the firm has exceptionally good loading balance in both directions, this may be an appropriate payment method. The advantage is that the firm controls driver labor cost by fixing the labor cost per trip and by forcing the efficient driver to run the miles quickly. Safety considerations are, of course, inherent in this operational method.

When union contract applications of the 1970's dissipated, trucking firms began to search for ways to compensate employees on the basis of revenue generated by the employee. Many firms settled on a percentage of revenue as a way of controlling cost. In many cases, this proved advantageous to both the firm and the employee. In other cases, firms found that the percentage payment method created shoddy service, with employees rushing the work and sacrificing quality. However, efficient employees usually discover that wages paid on a percentage basis produce greater annual earnings than other payment methods. Percentage payment hovers near 25% of revenue for the base wages of drivers in truckload transportation such as tank truck, cement, dump truck, and agricultural hauling. Once the base wage is determined, the study follows the same procedures for calculation of payroll taxes, insurance, and fringe benefits as those discussed in connection with hourly wages. Accordingly, even though wages are paid as a percentage of revenue, the number of annual hours worked must be recorded in payroll records so fringe benefit cost per hour can be determined.

When the percentage method is used, the base wage is determined in two ways. If the revenue and the percentage are known in advance, the base wage is determined by simple calculation. The other method for figuring base wage is to determine the total cost other than direct wages for the service, and impute the wage cost. For example, if the other costs, excluding driver pay and the labor cost fringe and tax loading, are 75% of the total cost, a single calculation determines the total. If the cost to perform a specific service, excluding driver labor cost, is $150, dividing that figure by 75% results in a total cost of $200, with driver earnings of $50.

Once the analyst has completed the other costs in this book, the total cost will be known, and the overall wage on a percentage basis may be easily determined. The methods for this determination will be discussed in connection with the final analysis of the total cost.

When a mileage-pay basis is used, the method of determining the cost is similar to the hourly cost preparation. The primary difference is that the annual-miles-driven figure must be determined so that it can be used as the common denominator for figuring out the fringe benefit cost on a mileage basis. The major difficulty is that annual mileage driven by individual drivers is not normally a statistic maintained in payroll records. When mileage records are not a part of driver payroll records, other sources such as driver vehicle inspection reports or logs are reliable sources for this data.

The demonstration in Table 4.14 employs a figure of 80,000 annual miles driven. If a driver does 80,000 miles annually, and the average trip is 1,500 miles, he or she will make 53.3 trips per year. If the trips require 33.3 hours, that driver will work 1,775 hours. (It will be noted that this figure corresponds to the number of hours used in earlier demonstrations.)

TABLE 4.14

LABOR COST PER MILE — LINE DRIVERS

Line No.	Item	Amount
1.	Base Wage Per Mile	$.230
2.	Vacation, Holiday, and Sick Leave	.018
3.	Subtotal	$.248
4.	Health, Welfare, and Pension	.057
5.	FICA	.019
6.	Federal Unemployment Fund	.001
7.	State Unemployment Insurance	.003
8.	Workers Compensation	.033
9.	Total Labor Cost Per Mile	$.361

Since the driver is paid only for miles operated, there are no non-revenue costs to be imputed into the labor cost. Further, the firm pays no overtime to the driver under this formula. For comparison purposes, multiplying the cost per mile by 80,000 annual miles produces an annual cost per driver of $28,880. Using the Total Hourly Labor Cost from Table 4.11, the driver's annual cost to the firm is $30,155.48 ($16.989 x 1,775 hours = $30,155.48). The difference is the overtime cost and the related reduction in FICA cost due to the nonpayment of overtime on a mileage basis.

In Table 4.14, fringe benefits are determined by dividing the annual cost of each benefit by the annual miles (80,000 in our example). FICA is the subtotal of Table 4.14 multiplied by the applicable rate. Federal and State Unemployment costs are determined by dividing the annual cost by the annual miles, and the Workers Compensation cost per mile is determined by application of the effective rate of 13.5% times the subtotal in Table 4.14.

In truck transportation, labor cost is a major portion of the direct cost. This chapter has touched upon several components of cost and productivity that must be controlled if the firm expects to be price competitive. The firm that intends to be cost and price competitive will analyze each of the components to determine if reductions in cost or increases in productivity are achievable.

The tables in this chapter have developed the cost for one wage classification - line drivers. To prepare a final labor cost schedule, the company will have to analyze costs for all direct cost classifications employed by the motor carrier. A typical final labor schedule is shown below.

TABLE 4.15

HOURLY LABOR COST — DIRECT WAGE CLASSIFICATIONS

Line No.	Item	Local Driver	Line Driver	Helper	Platform Worker
1.	Base Hourly Wage Rate	$10.080	$10.380	$ 9.560	$10.280
2.	Overtime	.720	.658	.410	.585
3.	Subtotal	$10.800	$11.038	$ 9.970	$10.865
4.	Vacation, Holidays, Sick, and Fnl Leave	.655	.798	.746	.637
5.	Subtotal	$11.455	$11.836	$10.716	$11.502
6.	Health, Welfare, and Pension	2.171	2.569	2.606	2.073
7.	FICA	.876	.905	.820	.880
8.	Federal Unemployment Fund	.034	.032	.032	.025
9.	State Payroll Tax	.148	.138	.140	.111
10.	Workers Compensation	1.449	1.509	1.391	1.474
11.	Hourly Labor Cost	$16.133	$16.989	$15.705	$16.065
12.	Non-revenue Time	1.006	1.062	.982	1.004
13.	Total Hourly Labor Cost	$17.141	$18.051	$16.687	$17.069
14.	Annual Hours Worked	1,650	1,775	1,750	2,200
15.	Annual Overtime Hours	300	225	150	250

Although tenure of employment for each employee classification would be different in actual practice, this demonstration uses the same figures for all classifications. It also uses a figure of 6.25% for non-revenue time for all wage classifications. Cost studies to establish prices should use actual tenure of employment and nonproductive time for each wage classification.

 # Vehicle Fixed Cost

The term "Vehicle Fixed Cost" should not be confused with an economist's definition of fixed versus variable cost. Vehicle fixed cost is that portion of the vehicle cost that remains constant over the life of the vehicle, as opposed to vehicle running cost, which is the cost incurred as the vehicle is operated. The fixed portion of vehicle cost is the cost of the acquisition plus the cost of licenses and insurance. These costs continue over the life of a vehicle, and do not vary with use. Once the vehicle life is established, the vehicle fixed cost is stationary.

Vehicle fixed cost is determined only for revenue-producing vehicles, including trucks, tractors, trailers, and dollies. It does not include shop pickup trucks, sales cars, or other types of vehicles.

The purpose of this portion of the cost study is to determine the cost per hour or mile to acquire vehicles, and to record the cost of making those vehicles ready for service. Acquisition cost is incurred either through purchase or lease. If acquired by purchase, the firm incurs the investment cost of vehicles and the added costs of licensing and insurance. Leases take many forms, with licensing costs shared by the lessee and lessor varying from lease to lease. Leases are simply a series of monthly payments designed to recover the original costs. These costs include the cost of the lease, the cost of money, and a profit for the lessor.

Financing the cost of vehicles is not included in the vehicle fixed cost in either instance because the methods described include such cost as non-operating expense. Though our discussion will be devoted mainly to acquisition by purchase, lease cost can be substituted for purchase cost, and monthly or annual cost can be converted to an hourly or mileage cost in a similar fashion. The annual hours or miles operated determine the cost per unit of measure.

The formula presented for the determination of acquisition cost includes sales tax but excludes tire cost. Sales or use taxes are included because these taxes must be recovered in the direct cost since they vary according to the type of vehicle used in the particular trucking activity under study. Tire cost is excluded because that cost is recovered in the vehicle running cost discussed in the next chapter.

Acquisition Cost

The initial determination of acquisition cost is made from the firm's depreciation schedule or equipment list, if those schedules record the original cost of individual vehicles. If not, the analyst must review invoices to determine the original acquisition cost. When depreciation schedules are used as the source, the analyst must be assured that the figures include sales tax and exclude tires. Invoices, when selected as the source document, will provide that information. At the time of acquisition, each vehicle cost is recorded by year and vehicle category. An equipment list such as that shown in Appendix A, Form 4, will provide the information for vehicle historical cost.

Before actual cost calculations are begun, analysts must determine the vehicle categories that will fit the transportation rates under study. If the study is for general freight LTL operations, the analyst might record the vehicle acquisition cost for bobtails, two-axle tractors, three-axle tractors, long semitrailers (over 28 feet), short semitrailers (under 28 feet), and converter gears or dollies. A similar selection for truckload operations might include two-axle tractors, three-axle tractors, flatbed trailers, and van trailers. The worksheet or software spreadsheet will appear as follows for an LTL operation:

TABLE 5.1

ECONOMIC VALUE OF SELECTED VEHICLES

Line No.	Item	Local Truck	2-Axle Tractor	3-Axle Tractor	Semi (S)	Semi (L)	Conv. Gear
1.	Economic Value	$20,000	$30,000	$45,000	$18,000	$28,000	$3,000

Truckload vehicle fixed cost categories will also reflect the types of specialized equipment employed in providing the service under analysis. If the service is bulk cement, the categories would be two- and three-axle tractors as well as two-axle pneumatic trailers and sets of pneumatic double trailers.

Salvage Value

Examples indicated above are taken from depreciation schedules or invoices accompanying the purchase. When recorded in the cost study, the worksheet or software spreadsheet would also include the value received for vehicles retired from the fleet during the period of time covered by the analysis of acquisitions. An analysis of this information will indicate, in summary, the trade-in or salvage value of vehicles retired in the categories selected for acquisition cost. The purpose of this determination is to find the net economic value that must be recovered in the rate structure during the fleet life.

IMPORTANT!

TABLE 5.2

ECONOMIC VALUE AND SALVAGE VALUE

Line No.	Item	Local Truck	2-Axle Tractor	3-Axle Tractor	Semi (S)	Semi (L)	Conv. Gear
1.	Economic Value	$20,000	$30,000	$45,000	$18,000	$28,000	$3,000
2.	Salvage Value	10%	10%	12%	12%	12%	10%

Though the value of retired vehicles over the life of the existing fleet can be determined from historical data, that information is merely a reference point for additional analysis. External economic forces influence the market for used motor carrier vehicles. As the cost of new vehicles increases, the value of good used equipment also escalates, although usually not in the same increments. The analyst must first determine the reference point from historical data, and then project the possible future value of the present fleet. For example, it may be determined from firm records that bobtails retired from the fleet returned only 10% of original cost. However, current and projected market conditions could indicate strong bobtail resale values. In that event, the salvage value imputed into the study might be increased to 15%. While external forces are important, the condition of the vehicle at disposal is also paramount. When Salvage Value is deducted from Economic Value on Line 1 in the illustration below, Net Value is the amount that must be recovered in the price structure.

TABLE 5.3

DETERMINATION OF NET VALUE

Line No.	Item	Local Truck	2-Axle Tractor	3-Axle Tractor	Semi (S)	Semi (L)	Conv. Gear
1.	Economic Value	$20,000	$30,000	$45,000	$18,000	$28,000	$ 3,000
2.	Salvage Value	10%	10%	12%	12%	12%	10%
3.	Net Value	$18,000	$27,000	$39,600	$15,840	$24,640	$ 2,700

Vehicle Life And Fees

Net values indicated must be recovered in the price structure over the life of each vehicle category. For example, if the vehicle fixed cost study of the current fleet of bobtails indicates an average age of 12 years, the value of $18,000 must be recovered over a 12-year period to replace the bobtail on the same life basis as the current fleet, if company fleet acquisition programs remain unchanged. The analyst should recognize that because the present fleet of bob-tail vehicles averages 12 years of age, it does not mean that the firm is satisfied with the replacement policy. The analyst must be well aware of management philosophy in connection with vehicle utilization, configurations, and replacement.

Management philosophy in connection with vehicle replacement varies widely in the industry. Carriers who choose the differential competitive strategy replace vehicles on a planned rotation system. When a 3-axle tractor reaches the age of 6 years or 700,000 miles, it might be replaced by the firm that uses its fleet as a differential tool for marketing purposes.

The low-cost carrier, on the other hand, might plan to retain the current fleet as long as possible. This carrier avoids financing cost, high vehicle acquisition cost, and higher license fees when a part of such fees are predicated upon value. However, this competitor incurs greater maintenance cost as opposed to the carrier that employs the differentiation strategy; as age increases, so does maintenance cost.

Intelligent vehicle replacement decisions involve detailed cost and economic analysis. Aside from income tax considerations, a laundry list of financial considerations may be used in the decision-making process. A table similar to that set forth in Table 5.4 will provide data to assist in the process.

TABLE 5.4

VEHICLE REPLACEMENT ANALYSIS

INCURRED COST:	
New Vehicle	$ 75,000
Less Trade-in At Replacement Time	20,000
Net Cost	$55,000
Life	8 Yrs.
Annual Cost	$ 6,875
Finance Charge	2,800
Additional License Fee	400
Additional Insurance	700
Total Annual Incurred Cost	$ 10,775
AVOIDED COST:	
Maintenance Per Mile	$ .050
Annual Miles	100,000
Annual Cost	$ 5,000
Fuel:	
Savings Per Mile	$ .034
Annual Miles	100,000
Annual Cost	3,400
Annual Avoided Cost	$ 8,400
Net Acquisition Cost	$ 2,375

The illustration above makes several assumptions to demonstrate a procedure. The new tractor cost is assumed to be $75,000, and the trade-in value of the retired vehicle is expected to be $20,000 at retirement. These assumptions leave a cost of $55,000 to be recovered in the rate structure over the life of the new vehicle.

The new vehicle is expected to operate over a useful life of 8 years and 100,000 miles annually. Under these conditions, the carrier's annual vehicle investment cost recovery is $6,875. Finance charges in the illustration are calculated at $2,800 per year over the 8-year period. The vehicle is financed for 5 years at a total charge of $22,500. Assuming part of the license fees are based upon the value, the new vehicle requires an additional license fee of $400. Finally, insurance cost is increased by $700. These assumptions bring the total annual incurred cost for the acquired vehicle to $10,775.

Avoided costs are those that can be reduced by retiring a unit ready for major maintenance. By eliminating that cost, and acquiring a vehicle with techno-logical improvements and a drive train warranty for 3 years, it is anticipated that maintenance cost per mile will be reduced by 5 cents over the 8-year life of the new unit.

In our example, the carrier believed that 3.4 cents per mile could be saved on fuel cost because the retired vehicle was using an excessive amount of fuel as it neared time for a major overhaul. Additionally, the carrier realized that newer vehicles experience much improved fuel consumption. All of these assumptions resulted in an increase in annual cost of $2,375. When increased productivity and potentially reduced income taxes are factored into the equa-tion, it was possible that the new vehicle would result in the same cost as that incurred with the retired vehicle.

Table 5.5 depicts a process to determine annualized vehicle fixed cost for the more common types of trucking vehicles. This procedure uses the average value of the existing fleet, the expected Salvage Value at retirement, and the Economic Life over which Net Value will be recovered in the rate structure. Annual fees and insurance are added to the vehicle annualized cost to obtain the vehicle fixed cost. Annual figures may be combined into vehicle sets, and the cost per hour or per mile obtained by employing annual hours or miles as the divisor.

TABLE 5.5

ANNUAL VEHICLE AND LICENSE COST

Line No.	Item	Local Truck	2-Axle Tractor	3-Axle Tractor	Semi (S)	Semi (L)	Conv. Gear
1.	Economic Value	$ 20,000	$30,000	$ 45,000	$18,000	$28,000	$ 3,000
2.	Salvage Value	10%	10%	12%	12%	12%	10%
3.	Net Value	$ 18,000	$ 27,000	$ 39,600	$15,840	$24,640	$ 2,700
4.	Economic Life (Years)	12	10	10	15	15	15
5.	Annual Cost	$ 1,500	$ 2,700	$ 3,960	$ 1,056	$ 1,643	$ 180
6.	License Fees:						
7.	Registration	25	25	25	25	25	25
8.	Weight Fee	500	700	900	800	950	-
9.	Value	450	675	875	400	550	35
10.	Subtotal	$ 975	$ 1,400	$ 1,800	$ 1,225	$ 1,525	$ 60
11.	Federal Hwy. Use Tax	550	550	550	-	-	-
12.	Total Annual Fees	$ 1,525	$ 1,950	$ 2,350	$ 1,225	$ 1,525	$ 60

The fees shown in Table 5.5 are simply examples and are not related to actual costs that should be recovered in the price structure. They are typical costs assessed by some states for the licensing of commercial vehicles. The actual cost may be determined from current registration payments or from formulas available in effective statutes. Many states base registrations upon a fixed fee, with another increment predicated upon vehicle weight, and a final portion based upon a table of present values. Federal Highway Use Tax is common in the various commercial fleet industries, and should be included as applicable.

Insurance

The final segment of vehicle fixed cost is insurance. Insurance premiums are predicated upon either a set amount per vehicle or a percentage of revenue. If premiums are quoted on a per-unit basis, the cost should be included as a segment of vehicle fixed cost. If premiums are assessed as a percentage of revenue, the cost should be included in Indirect Cost, which will be discussed in a later chapter. It is preferable to include insurance in the vehicle fixed cost preparation because such handling provides an accurate accounting of total vehicle cost.

Insurance premium levels fluctuate widely, depending on exposure. The premiums in our examples have no relation to a particular case. The actual figures to be used should include bodily injury and property damage liability as well as any vehicle damage coverage. Liability insurance covering other aspects of the business, such as buildings, should not be included in the vehicle fixed cost.

TABLE 5.6

ANNUAL VEHICLE FIXED COST — HISTORICAL

Line No.	Item	Local Truck	2-Axle Tractor	3-Axle Tractor	Semi (S)	Semi (L)	Conv. Gear
1.	Economic Value	$ 20,000	$30,000	$45,000	$18,000	$28,000	$ 3,000
2.	Salvage Value	10%	10%	12%	12%	12%	10%
3.	Net Value	$ 18,000	$27,000	$39,600	$15,840	$ 24,640	$ 2,700
4.	Economic Life (Years)	12	10	10	15	15	15
5.	Annual Cost	$ 1,500	$ 2,700	$ 3,960	$ 1,056	$ 1,643	$ 180
6.	License Fees:						
7.	Registration	$ 25	$ 25	$ 25	$ 25	$ 25	$ 25
8.	Weight	500	700	900	800	950	-
9.	Value	450	675	875	400	550	35
10.	Subtotal	$ 975	$ 1,400	$ 1,800	$ 1,225	$ 1,525	$ 60
11.	Federal Hwy. Use Tax	550	550	550	-	-	-
12.	Total Annual Fees	$ 1,525	$ 1,950	$ 2,350	$ 1,225	$ 1,525	$ 60
13.	Insurance Cost	2,700	3,400	4,400	1,450	1,800	150
14.	Total Annual Vehicle Fixed Cost	$ 5,725	$ 8,050	$10,710	$ 3,731	$ 4,968	$ 390

Total Annual Vehicle Fixed Cost on line 14 is determined by adding lines 5, 12, and 13.

Determination of vehicle fixed cost is the most subjective of all of the cost factors. The annual cost figures for each vehicle category in the example were determined using the assumptions outlined in this chapter. The analysis was based on historical data from depreciation schedules, past invoices, and other empirical information about previous transactions. Unfortunately, past history only describes what has happened; it tells us little about what will be needed in the future. In the context of price setting, the analyst must, therefore, consider other conditions in determining vehicle fixed cost.

IMPORTANT!

Some readers may wonder why our examples do not reflect current real cost, given modern vehicle prices. However, these figures were selected especially to illustrate that circumstance. If the cost study for pricing purposes uses only historical data in determining vehicle fixed cost, the final price structure will probably not return full cost when inflation rates are high. Consequently, the analyst must make subjective adjustments to lines 1, 2, and 4 of the previous table.

Formulas and calculations found in later chapters build on earlier data. Accordingly, in Table 5.7, we updated the cost shown in Table 5.6 for external economic conditions to more nearly reflect present cost circumstances. These figures are carried into the following illustrations so that the final results will appear more realistic given 1995 operating cost.

TABLE 5.7

ANNUAL VEHICLE FIXED COST

Line No.	Item	Local Truck	2-Axle Tractor	3-Axle Tractor	Semi (S)	Semi (L)	Conv. Gear
1.	Economic Value	$ 30,000	$55,000	$65,000	$22,000	$28,000	$ 4,500
2.	Salvage Value	15%	15%	15%	15%	15%	15%
3.	Net Value	$ 25,500	$46,750	$ 55,250	$ 18,700	$23,800	$ 3,825
4.	Economic Life (Years)	8	6	6	10	10	12
5.	Annual Cost	$ 3,190	$ 7,790	$ 9,210	$ 1,870	$ 2,380	$ 320
6.	License Fees:						
7.	Registration	$ 25	$ 25	$ 25	$ 25	$ 25	$ 25
8.	Weight	500	700	900	800	950	-
9.	Value	550	800	950	500	650	40
10.	Subtotal	$ 1,075	$ 1,525	$ 1,875	$ 1,325	$ 1,625	$ 65
11.	Federal Hwy. Use Tax	550	550	550	-	-	-
12.	Total Annual Fees	$ 1,625	$ 2,075	$ 2,425	$ 1,325	$ 1,625	$ 65
13.	Insurance Cost	2,700	3,400	4,400	1,450	1,800	150
14.	Total Annual Vehicle Fixed Cost	$ 7,515	$13,265	$ 16,035	$ 4,645	$ 5,805	$ 535

Using the individual vehicle total cost in Table 5.7, the cost for vehicle combinations on an annualized basis is readily available:

TABLE 5.8

ANNUAL VEHICLE FIXED COST IN COMBINATIONS

Line No.	Item	2-Axle Tractor	3-Axle Tractor	Short Semi	Long Semi	Conv. Gear	Total
1.	Bobtail						$ 7,515
2.	Two-axle Tractor and Short Semi	$13,265		$4,645			$ 17,910
3.	Two-axle Tractor and Doubles	$13,265		$4,645		$ 535	
				4,645			
		$13,265		$9,290		$ 535	$23,090
4.	Three-axle Tractor and Long Semi	$16,035			$ 5,805		$21,840

Using the totals set forth in Table 5.7 for individual units of equipment, Table 5.8 demonstrates that the annual cost for a three-axle tractor and long trailer is $21,840 and a similar combination cost for a two-axle tractor with doubles is $23,090. The totals in Table 5.8 are achieved by adding the column figures horizontally. Numbers used in this analysis are merely estimates and do not reflect precise cost.

Vehicle Miles and Hours

Annual costs set forth in Tables 5.7 and 5.8 are not figures that can be used in the preparation of total cost for specific pricing. Each of the costs shown must be converted to a cost per hour or per mile. Such conversion requires the use of annual vehicle hours or vehicle miles (or both) by vehicle classification as a divisor. This information comes from maintenance records, driver logs, trip reports, or other documents. Driver payroll records will provide the data if the driver is assigned the same vehicle and the driver non-revenue time is deducted. Non-revenue time is the time the driver is on the payroll on the carrier's premises but the vehicle is not operating.

If none of the sources mentioned above produce reliable results, the analyst might conduct a trip report sampling study. This requires drivers to complete forms such as the documents provided in Forms 1 or 3 in the Appendix. If the sampling technique is used, care must be taken to be sure the sample reflects the correct annual results. If, for example, the trip analysis covers all vehicles for a 2-week period, the total hours per vehicle can be multiplied by 26 to obtain annual hours if the 2-week period selected is representative of the annual period.

Analysts may need to use all of the above documents to obtain reliable results. If answers determined from all of the available sources are similar, the analyst can be certain of accuracy. If such records are not maintained by carriers at present, they are encouraged to develop documents reflecting accurate annual miles and hours for future use by each vehicle.

A summary similar to that furnished in Table 5.8 will indicate the final figures to be carried forward to the overall cost summaries.

TABLE 5.9

VEHICLE FIXED COST PER HOUR AND MILE

Line No.	Item	Annual Cost	Annual Hours	Annual Miles	Cost/ Hour	Cost/ Mile
1.	Bobtail	$ 7,515	1,600	44,000	$ 4.697	$ .171
2.	2-Axle Tractor and Short Semi	$ 17,910	2,000	65,000	$ 8.955	$ .275
3.	2-Axle Tractor and Doubles	$ 23,090	1,800	85,000	$ 12.828	$ .272
4.	3-Axle Tractor and Long Semi	$ 21,840	1,800	85,000	$ 12.133	$ .257

The annual hours and miles indicated in Table 5.9 illustrate an easy method for converting annual cost to a cost per hour or cost per mile. To obtain the desired results, the annual cost in Table 5.9 is divided by either annual hours or annual miles.

Vehicle Fixed Cost Summary

As illustrated by the comparative numbers in Tables 5.6 and 5.7, considerations other than historical cost must be applied in determining the proper figure for Economic Value in the vehicle fixed cost table. One of the major considerations is the philosophy of firm ownership toward company objectives. We discussed earlier the competitive strategy of "differentiation" areas in which a firm can set itself apart from its competitors. One of these areas is the condition of its rolling stock.

Differentiating ownership may determine that it must strive to operate only vehicles of up to 5 years of age. The purpose may be to project a successful image that says, "we operate the best equipment because we are successful and our service is second to none." Though new and/or clean vehicles are noticed favorably by buyers, competitors, and the general public, the real reason for the newer fleet may be to reduce maintenance cost. Warranties provided by truck manufacturers cut maintenance cost significantly in the 1990s environment, and new vehicles usually require less maintenance. Other reasons for the decision may be tax considerations and investment incentives. All of these reasons, plus others, will enter into the firm's future pricing direction.

On the other hand, ownership could well determine that its competitive strategy will be that of a price-maker. The management philosophy is to achieve the lowest cost and price, with every component of overall cost being operated at the lowest levels. In this case, the price-maker would be expected to maintain an existing fleet in a way that would extend the fleet life and lower the annual cost. The price-maker engineers acquisitions on a lowest-cost basis, operates more used vehicles, and probably incurs higher maintenance cost, even though some maintenance is deferred. The low-cost firm will operate vehicles with lower vehicle fixed cost than shown in our examples. The price-maker can be expected to exist for a shorter period than other competitive types because any change in industry circumstances would tend to disrupt this type of operation. The low-cost carrier enters the market at reduced rates, finds that circumstances change, has no reserves for adjustment, and quickly exits the market since no margin of adjustment is provided. Even small cost changes may create severe consequences.

In the first example, the differentiating competitor incurs higher Economic Value for vehicles, shorter Economic Life, and higher Salvage Value. In the second example, the price-leader incurs lower Economic Value, longer Economic Life, and lower Salvage Value. In the following table, the items shown previously for a bobtail are compared with those for a differentiating firm and a price-maker.

TABLE 5.10

COMPARATIVE BOBTAIL ANNUAL COST

Line No.	Item	Bobtail T 5.6	Price Leader	Differentiating Carrier
1.	Economic Value	$ 20,000	$ 16,000	$ 28,000
2.	Salvage Value	10%	6%	20%
3.	Net Value	$ 18,000	$ 15,040	$ 22,400
4.	Economic Life (Years)	12	16	5
5.	Annual Cost	$ 1,500	$ 940	$ 4,480

It is apparent that the differentiating firm incurs significantly higher vehicle fixed cost than that of the price-maker or the carrier in our previous example. In our discussion of vehicle running cost we will discuss this phenomenon in terms of maintenance cost, and illustrate its relationship to vehicle fixed cost.

Inflation is another condition to be considered in setting Vehicle Economic Value. If the vehicle fixed cost is established solely on the basis of historical cost, and the inflation rate is high, the ultimate cost and rate would be insufficient to cover the replacement cost. This concept can be illustrated with another example. Assume that the present fleet life for the bobtail fleet is 12 years, as indicated in the illustration in Table 5.5. Assume also that bobtail vehicles were purchased in each of the 12 years and an average purchase cost in each year was established.

CHART 5.1

HISTORICAL BOBTAIL ACQUISITION COST

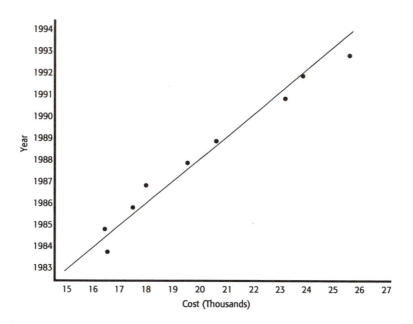

Cost (Thousands)

The objective is to determine the typical cost over the life of the fleet. To determine the Economic Value of $20,000 for the existing fleet, the chart should be read from the midpoint, between 1988 and 1989 in this example. If the inflation rate was high during the term, the selected cost would be understated in terms of current cost. If inflation was held in check during the period, it is conceivable that historical cost could represent current cost, and a line drawn similar to Chart 5.1 would be flat. Accordingly, this technique reflects historical cost, but does not necessarily represent present value.

In addition to the determination of historical cost as indicated, the analyst should review current economic indicators, and impute into the cost formula the appropriate Economic Value predicated upon management and ownership philosophy as well as expected inflation rates.

As we have seen in the illustrations in this chapter, Economic Value, Salvage Value, and Economic Life are closely related. Historical data is the precursor to the final establishment of these cost components. Once the empirical data is accumulated, the subjective considerations set forth in this chapter serve to finalize the annual vehicle fixed cost to be recovered in the price structure. Additionally, the complete analysis will reflect management's approach to price competition.

Cost per hour for vehicle fixed cost can be converted into a unit of measure for pricing purposes by converting the annual cost to cost per mile or cost per hour, as appropriate. Stop time and running time will provide cost per trip, and average weight per load will convert trip cost to cost per 100 pounds. For example, if the trip time is 5 hours, and the vehicle fixed cost per hour is $12.83, the cost per trip is $64.15. If the average load is 52,000 pounds, the cost per 100 pounds is $.123 for vehicle fixed cost.

Vehicle fixed cost may be expressed as a cost per mile, as indicated in Table 5.8. To do this, the analyst must determine annual miles instead of annual hours, and divide these miles into the annual vehicle fixed cost. Fixed cost on a mileage basis is used in a similar fashion to labor cost on a mileage basis. Long-haul, high-mileage operations generally employ cost and rate per mile as the unit of measure while short-haul operation costs and rates are expressed per hour.

In summary, vehicle fixed cost requires a determination of Economic Value by vehicle type, Salvage Value expected at retirement of the vehicle, expected vehicle life in years, annual licensing and insurance costs, and either annual miles, annual hours, or both. With this information, the firm will fully understand both the statistical application and the company philosophy in price-setting as it relates to vehicle fixed cost

 # Vehicle Running Cost

The final element of direct cost to provide motor carrier service is vehicle running cost. Running cost is composed of fuel (including fuel taxes), oil, tires, and maintenance. This chapter focuses upon the methods by which these components are determined, and their relative importance to overall cost and pricing.

Running cost varies in terms of importance according to the type of service provided. As the length of the haul increases, the running cost is increasingly significant. On the other hand, it is an insignificant cost element for the local household goods carrier where the length of the haul is short, and the vehicle is stopped for long periods of time for loading and unloading. For the LTL carrier of general freight, running cost is very important because the operation creates high local pickup and delivery and line-haul miles. As one would expect, the transcontinental carrier must closely monitor running cost as it is a major cost component.

Fuel and Oil Cost

Fuel cost per mile is dependent upon three components: cost per gallon, fuel consumption, and vehicle type. If the fuel cost is $1.20 per gallon, and the rate of consumption is 6 miles per gallon, the cost per mile for fuel is $.20.

IMPORTANT!

Determining fuel consumption is relatively simple. If records on this component are not maintained, consumption rates can be determined from a one-week vehicle sample. To do a sample survey, the vehicle must begin with full fuel tanks. Vehicle odometer readings are taken at the beginning of the survey and at the end, after the tanks are filled. During the test period, additional gallons of fuel loaded are recorded. From this data, the miles traveled and the gallons of fuel added are determined. Obviously, fuel invoices during the period will disclose the cost of the fuel. Results of individual vehicle samples are tabulated using the same vehicle classifications that were used in connection with labor cost and vehicle fixed cost. Table 6.1 illustrates results that will be achieved.

TABLE 6.1

FUEL COST PER MILE

Line No.	Item		Cost Per Gallon	Miles Per Gallon	Cost Per Mile
1.	Bobtail Truck	- Gas	$1.25	8.2	$.152
		- Diesel	$1.20	8.4	$.143
2.	2-Axle Tractor	- Gas	$1.25	6.6	$.189
		- Diesel	$1.20	6.9	$.174
3.	3-Axle Tractor	- Gas	$1.25	5.7	$.219
		- Diesel	$1.20	6.2	$.194

The example in Table 6.1 determines fuel cost per mile for various vehicle types, both gasoline and diesel powered. It may be important for management to know the difference in cost, but the fuel type has no significance in cost studies for pricing purposes. Rates are not established for gasoline and diesel units. To obtain accurate results, however, it is important that the final running cost per mile be expressed for the same vehicle types as those selected in the vehicle fixed cost study.

IMPORTANT!

Once the fuel cost per mile is determined for these vehicles, the figures can be combined for any particular trucking service. If, for example, the cost to be determined is for line-haul distances up to 100 miles, the analyst must determine the mixture of vehicles used in that service. Table 6.2 illustrates this point.

TABLE 6.2

EQUIPMENT WEIGHTING — 100 MILE LINE HAUL

Line No.	Item	% of Trips	Fuel Cost Per Mile	Weighted Cost
1.	Bobtail - Gas	30	$.152	$.046
2.	Bobtail - Diesel	15	.143	.021
3.	2-Axle Tractor - Gas	45	.189	.085
4.	2-Axle Tractor - Diesel	10	.174	.017
5.	3-Axle Tractor - Diesel	-	-	-
		100%		$1.69

In this demonstration the fuel cost per mile for all vehicles performing 100-mile, line-haul service is $.169.

Oil cost per mile is the least significant cost of the running cost components. Its determination can be as simple as $2 per gallon and 2,000 miles per gallon for a cost per mile of $.001. Even if this figure is 100% incorrect, the impact of the error is still only a tenth of a cent per mile.

Tire Cost

STOP

IMPORTANT!

Tire cost per mile is available from several sources. The most obvious is from a record of maintenance cost for the vehicles. Another method is to locate the cost per tire from purchase invoices for various tire sizes. Tire manufacturers supply wear figures for different types of tires, and tire repair shops will provide data on the recap cost and frequency for typical carcasses. If accurate tire cost-per-mile records are not available, an analysis similar to that in Table 6.3 will provide necessary data.

TABLE 6.3

COMPARATIVE TIRE COST PER MILE

Line No.	Item	Local Truck	2-Axle Tractor	3-Axle Tractor	Short Semi	Long Semi	Conv Gear
1.	NEW TIRES:						
2.	Miles Per Tire	50,000	65,000	85,000	95,000	95,000	95,000
3.	Cost Per Tire	$ 260	$ 280	$ 280	$ 280	$ 280	$ 280
4.	Tires Per Unit	6	6	10	4	8	4
5.	Cost Per Unit	$ 1,560	$ 1,680	$ 2,800	$ 1,120	$ 2,240	$ 1,120
6.	New Cost Per Unit Per Mile	$ .031	$ .026	$ .033	$ .012	$ .024	$ .012
7.	RECAP TIRES:						
8.	Recap Miles-Total, All Cap	50,000	65,000	85,000	95,000	95,000	95,000
9.	Cost Per Tire	$ 65	$ 80	$ 80	$ 80	$ 80	$ 80
10.	Recaps Per Tire	1.5	1.5	1.5	1.5	1.5	1.5
11.	Cost Per Recap- Total	$ 98	$ 120	$ 120	$ 120	$ 120	$ 120
12.	Recaps Per Unit	3	3	5	4	4	4
13.	Recap Cost Per Unit	$ 294	$ 360	$ 600	$ 480	$ 480	$ 480
14.	Recap Cost Per Unit Per Mile	$ .005	$ .006	$ .007	$ .005	$ .005	$ .005
15.	Tire Cost Per Mile	$ .036	$ .032	$ .040	$ .017	$ .029	$ .017

TABLE 6.4

TIRE COST IN VEHICLE COMBINATIONS

Line No.	Item	Combination	Per Mile	Cost per mile
1.	Bobtail		$.036	$.036
2.	3-Axle Tractor and Semi Trailer:			
	Tractor	$.040		
	Semi Trailer	.029		
	Total			$.069
3.	2-Axle Tractor and Double Trailers:			
	Tractor	$.032		
	Semi Trailer	.017		
	Semi Trailer	.017		
	Converter Gear	.017		
	Total			$.083

Vehicle maintenance records for each unit will provide cost and wear figures per mile through elapsed mileage figures, from the firm's specific transportation records. It is well documented that tire costs and wear vary according to geographic area, long versus short haul, average load, tire size, and so on. The figures shown will, therefore, vary widely from actual cost for these reasons.

If records are not currently maintained on tire and maintenance cost per unit of carrier's equipment, it is highly recommended that such records be initiated. There is no substitute for accurate records indicating size, type, and cost of tires mounted on each vehicle. If mileage readings are recorded when tires are mounted, the record will provide accurate cost per mile figures.

In the alternative method for determining tire cost illustrated in Table 6.3, it is assumed that, from the purchase of new vehicles, or from the mounting of new tires, tire wear will range from 50,000 to 95,000 miles, depending upon the type of vehicle. It is also assumed that the firm utilizes recaps on some occasions. The illustration theorizes that an average of 1.5 recaps are used for each casing, with a range of 3 to 5 recaps per vehicle. These costs are factored into the cycle of the tire cost to produce the figures indicated for cost per mile.

Maintenance Cost

The final figure needed to prepare the overall vehicle running cost is maintenance per mile. Many carriers maintain the necessary records to produce reliable figures. Some have detailed parts and labor records on each piece of revenue equipment. For those who have such records, this cost increment is relatively simple to obtain. It is recommended that maintenance costs for each vehicle be traced back 3 years. This is the minimum time frame during which major maintenance work will have occurred, such as transmission, starter, alternator, radiator, brakes, and steering repair, and the records should produce reliable results. Out-of-frame engine overhaul may well have been recorded for some equipment during the period, and should be represented in the calculations.

STOP
IMPORTANT!

Various preventive maintenance and driver inspection reports required by the U. S. Department of Transportation, state regulatory agencies, Highway Patrol safety inspections, and, perhaps, even OSHA can be used to find maintenance costs, if comprehensive records do not exist. When these reports indicate needed repairs, the analyst can trace recommendations to repair part invoices, and match repairs made against elapsed mileage.

A second reliable source for maintenance figures is from records maintained by outside repair shops. Their invoices will include dates, mileage readings, parts mounted, labor hours, and cost. Accumulation of such records in tabular form will provide maintenance cost per mile by determining the elapsed miles during the study period, and comparing those miles with total cost of parts mounted, including labor.

A third source for data is from repairs done outside to equipment under warranty. The shop performing the work keeps records similar to those of outside repair services. Some manufacturers or distributors also maintain records of warranty repairs.

Your target is to get figures for elapsed miles over a 3-year period for each vehicle in the fleet for parts installed, and the labor cost for each installation. From these figures, it is not difficult to tabulate the cost per mile for the equipment classifications under study. An example of the desired results is shown in Table 6.5.

TABLE 6.5

COMPARATIVE MAINTENANCE COST PER MILE

Line No.	Item	Local Truck	2-Axle Tractor	3-Axle Tractor	Short Semi	Long Semi	Conv Gear
1.	Maintenance Cost Per Period	$144,567	$144,899	$145,999	$16,100	$22,514	$1,440
2.	Elapsed Miles	826,097	731,813	682,238	731,818	682,238	288,013
3.	Maintenance Cost Per Mile	$.175	$.198	$.214	$.022	$.033	$.005

The preparation and maintenance of vehicle records on an individual basis are important not only for pricing trucking services, but also for use in maintaining the company management policy. The price-leader who attempts to price service at the lowest cost, and the focus competitor who concentrates on a narrow book of business, must continually monitor their operating costs. These competitors must also take action to reduce costs when records indicate problems.

Records of maintenance on individual vehicles may disclose that some units are creating unusual and unnecessary costs. Perhaps similar units by the same manufacturer and of the same vintage are not performing in the same way. Or the higher-than-normal vehicle cost may be created by a driver's poor habits. With proper record keeping, the informed manager can react on a timely basis to maintain or improve competitive position. This fast corrective action is vital to successful lowest-cost pricing.

Carriers who maintain repair shops and perform vehicle maintenance using company employees must determine which expenses are included in the direct maintenance cost per mile. Parts purchased and mechanic wages are obviously included in shop work, but these figures do not produce an accurate or total maintenance cost per vehicle. The carrier will also need to record all shop-related costs for each work order, including fringe benefits and payroll taxes for mechanics. Chapter 4 demonstrated how these costs are determined.

In addition to labor fringe costs, shop overhead, or indirect, cost should also be recorded in the work order. These items would include wages for shop foremen, parts runners, and parts inventory clerks, plus rent, utilities, and other expenses associated with the shop. If the cost per mile does not include such costs, it is understated. A brief illustration of a method to determine these costs is as follows:

	DIRECT	INDIRECT
Mechanic wages	$130,000	
Mechanic fringe benefits	15,000	
Repair parts	160,000	
Shop supervision		$ 40,000
Parts runner		18,000
Fringe benefits and payroll tax		7,000
Rent		16,000
Utilities		12,000
Total	$305,000	$ 93,000

The illustration above produces a ratio of 30% indirect to direct cost. Accordingly, costing of each work order would be increased by 30% over the direct cost of parts and labor. If mechanic wages were $15 per hour, and a repair job took 4 hours, the direct cost to complete the work is $60, not including the parts. In the same example, the parts to repair the vehicle cost $80, making direct cost to perform the work $140. When a 30% loading for indirect cost is added, the total cost recorded on the work order was $182.

IMPORTANT!

Inclusion of all shop cost in the cost-per-mile figure results in a more accurate measurement of maintenance cost, and may be easily compared with work performed on the outside where invoices include the vendor's overhead loading. Finally, decisions relative to maintenance cost will be predicated upon the actual cost per mile.

Vehicle Running Cost Summary

In this chapter, individual components of vehicle running cost have been developed. These components are not used on an individual basis in the construction of total cost. They must be summarized by vehicle type in a similar manner to the methods employed in developing labor cost and vehicle fixed cost. Table 6.6 brings fuel, oil, tire, and maintenance costs together in terms of vehicle combinations widely used in the industry.

TABLE 6.6

VEHICLE RUNNING COST PER MILE

Line No.	Item	Local Truck	2-Axle Tractor	3-Axle Tractor	Short Semi	Long Semi	Conv Gear
1.	Fuel/Oil Cost	$ .148	$ .182	$ .207	$ -	$ -	$ -
2.	Tire Cost	.036	.032	.040	.017	.029	.017
3.	Maintenance Cost	.175	.198	.214	.022	.033	.005
4.	Running Cost	$ .359	$ .412	$ .461	$ .039	$ .062	$.022

The final calculation is the preparation of running cost per mile for combinations of vehicles. The combinations become the vehicle unit operated most frequently by the motor carrier being studied. This procedure is accomplished in a table similar to Table 6.7. The combinations of vehicles prepared in connection with the vehicle fixed cost analysis must be the same combinations employed in developing the vehicle running cost per mile. If other combinations are used, there is no way to summarize direct cost for an operation. Advance study design is critical so that the results will accurately reflect the cost underlying the carrier's price structure.

TABLE 6.7

VEHICLE RUNNING COST PER MILE IN COMBINATION

Line No.	Item	Running Cost Per Unit	Running Cost Per Combination
1.	Bobtail	$ .359	$ -
2.	2-Axle Tractor and Short Semi:		
	Tractor	$ .412	
	Trailer	.039	
			$ .451
3.	2-Axle Tractor and Doubles:		
	Tractor	$ .412	
	Trailer	.039	
	Trailer	.039	
	Converter Gear	.022	
			$ .512
4.	3-Axle Tractor and Long Semi:		
	Tractor	$ .461	
	Trailer	.062	
			$ .523

Direct Cost Overview

Before continuing the process of building the blocks to total cost for specific service, a short review of the discussion's progress will be useful. Motor carrier cost is virtually all variable in nature. That is, all industry cost can be avoided, and no long term investment in assets is required to continue business. Motor carrier costs vary in one of two ways: by the individual service, such as one truckload from here to there, or by overall volume. We have discussed those costs that vary in accordance with the particular service provided, such as vehicle investment and running cost. Direct labor cost not only changes in the same way, but also varies in terms of volume. When volume increases, labor cost is added or productivity is increased. When volume slides, the reverse is true.

Chapters 4, 5, and 6 explained methods to determine the components of direct cost. In following chapters, each of the components will be utilized to prepare total cost and rates for several trucking circumstances. Table 6.8 demonstrates the format used in following chapters to combine the ingredients of direct cost into usable terms.

TABLE 6.8

SUMMARY OF DIRECT COST

Line	Item	Amount No.
1.	Labor Cost For Direct Employees	$ xxxxxxx
2.	Vehicle Fixed Cost	xxxxxxx
3.	Vehicle Running Cost	xxxxxxx
4.	Total Direct Cost	$ xxxxxxx

In following chapters, the concept of cost development in Table 6.8 is consistently used. The formula applies to all services provided by motor carriers when the various productivity measurements are included.

Indirect Cost

The objective in connection with indirect cost development is to measure operating costs incurred that cannot effectively be allocated to a particular traffic flow or book of business. Indirect Cost is just what the name implies: it is an incurred cost that is not directly involved in the transportation service, but is essential to the business. Examples of such costs are telephone, utilities, building cost or office rent, and salaries for dispatchers, clerical personnel, and management. While all of these elements are necessary to the overall operation, they are not generated by any particular service. Most industries refer to these costs as "overhead," which is also an acceptable term.

Method of Determination

IMPORTANT!

The only effective method for determining the impact of indirect cost on service requirements is by analysis of the Income and Expense Statement for a given period of time. Ordinarily the analyst will review at least the two preceding years' statements as a method of obtaining an accurate result. This process requires analysis of each expense account to determine whether any portion of it is attributable to cost already determined to be direct in nature. If, for example, an expense account entitled "Labor Cost" includes all employees, the amount included for drivers, platform workers, or other employee classifications measured in the direct analysis in Chapter 4 must be allocated between direct and indirect cost. The indirect cost portion would include all employees not included in the direct cost study. In many cases, the driver would be classified as direct, and all of the other employees would be classified as an indirect cost. The result of this individual account examination will give the ratio of indirect cost to total cost.

The demonstration and discussion in this chapter is based upon the Instruction 27 Class I and II Annual Report required by many states as well as the ICC. At this writing, it is not known whether such requirements will continue, but it is recommended that those carriers who have maintained this chart of accounts continue to do so, with the refinements discussed. It is also recommended that other carriers consider adopting this system; it lends itself nicely to the analysis that follows. As our discussion unfolds, it will become clear why a detailed Income and Expense Statement is desirable, particularly for the operator who intends to follow this cost and pricing procedure.

TABLE 7.1

DETERMINATION OF INDIRECT COST

Line No.	Item	Direct	Indirect	Total
1.	Clerical & Admin. Wages	$	$ 690,555	$ 690,555
2.	Drivers and Helpers Wages	890,750		890,750
3.	Cargo Handlers Wages	635,020		635,020
4.	Vehicle Repair Wages	243,450		243,450
5.	Owner-Operator Wages	444,900		444,900
6.	Other Labor Wages		65,470	65,470
7.	Federal Payroll Taxes	150,384	33,197	183,581
8.	State Payroll Taxes	37,590	9,195	46,785
9.	Workers Compensation	312,227	4,687	316,914
10.	Group Insurance		8,899	8,899
11.	Pension and Retirement	46,667	14,447	61,114
12.	Health and Welfare	73,440		73,440
13.	Other fringes		4,667	4,667
14.	Fuel and Oil	133,490	9,944	143,434
15.	Vehicle Parts	439,997	11,687	451,684
16.	Outside Maintenance	14,567	2,111	16,678
17.	Tires and Tubes	148,887	4,888	153,775
18.	Other Operating Supplies	6,150	44,333	50,483
19.	Tariffs and Advertising		8,844	8,844
20.	Commission and Fees		2,300	2,300

(continued)

21.	Officers and Other General Expense		16,488	16,488
22.	Gas, Diesel and Oil Tax	12,014	1,014	13,028
23.	Vehicle License Fees	16,700		16,700
24.	Other Taxes		2,890	2,890
25.	Real Estate and Personal Property Tax		6,440	6,440
26.	Fuel and Oil tax, State	21,140	1,550	22,690
27.	Vehicle Licenses, State	44,450	1,100	45,550
28.	PUC Fees		2,640	2,640
29.	Liability and Property Damage	167,990	4,300	172,290
30.	Cargo Loss and Damage Insurance		16,400	16,400
31.	All Other Insurance		4,500	4,500
32.	Communications		94,480	94,480
33.	Utilities		36,776	36,776
34.	Building Depreciation		16,500	16,500
35.	Revenue Equipment Depreciation	560,400		560,400
36.	Other Depreciation		4,500	4,500
37.	Amortization			
38.	Vehicle Rent With Driver	944,000		944,000
39.	Vehicle Rent Without Driver	4,480		4,480
40.	Other Purchased Transportation			
41.	Other Purch. Trans. Air and Water			
42.	Allowance to Shippers			
43.	Equipment Rents Credit	-2,700		-2,700
44.	Gain/Loss on Disposal	-16,750	-300	-17,050
45.	Total Expenses	$ 5,329,243	$ 1,124,502	$ 6,453,745
46.	Percent of Total	82.6	17.4	100.0

Account Analysis

The array of expense accounts in Table 7.1 might be found in any motor carrier's financial report. The individual account totals must be allocated between both direct and indirect expense. The primary criteria for the determination is whether the particular expense is measured in the preparation of direct cost. A cursory review of the allocations will disclose that some accounts are direct in nature, some include both cost increments, and some are indirect expenses.

Line 1 is the total of wage cost for clerical and supervisory employees. These wages are an indirect expense and not included in the direct cost determination for two reasons. First, clerical wages are not variable by the individual transportation service. They vary in the sense that they can be adjusted by an astute management as volumes fluctuate. The second reason why clerical wages are not included in direct cost is that there is no unit for measuring them in terms of productivity in connection with a particular service.

Line 2 indicates wages for driver and helper job descriptions that were included in the analysis in Chapter 4. In the direct cost process, the base hourly wage rate and overtime annual earnings were determined. Including the wages indicated on line 2 in the indirect allocation for the cost study would be incorrect; these wages would be included twice. The analyst should test general ledger postings to verify that the account includes only the driver and helper wages described in the account title. If the verification is conclusive, the dollar amount of expense should be posted as a direct expense.

In line 3, it becomes apparent that the hypothetical carrier is an LTL general commodities carrier. Cargo Handler is a job classification usually associated with that sub-industry. Here again, the analysis of direct labor cost included an hourly labor cost for Cargo Handler because this expense is variable with service requirements. Therefore, the expense for this wage classification is a direct cost.

Expense in line 4 requires considerable diligence to determine the proper allocation. The maintenance cost portion of the vehicle running cost included mechanic labor cost. Total maintenance cost, including the cost of parts, was developed from company individual vehicle records, outside vendor invoices, and related documentation. Use of the described methods can create difficulty in allocation of the Income Statement expense account.

If maintenance cost per mile is determined from vehicle in-house records, it is likely that the posting of labor cost included only the mechanic who actually performed the work. If this is the case, the cost of shop supervisors, parts required, lube men, etc. should be allocated as an indirect expense. On the other hand, if the maintenance cost in the direct portion of the study was from outside vendor invoices, all of the cost in the maintenance account should be allocated as a direct cost because the invoice would include the vendor's overhead cost. If repairs were done outside the firm, there would be little, if any, carrier overhead. In some cases, the motor carrier may have its own shop but prefer to farm out certain work to obtain a higher level of expertise. If this is the case, the analyst must determine the proper allocations based upon the individual circumstances. The example in Table 7.1 assumes that all of the maintenance is done on the outside.

Owner-operator Wages in line 5 are really a substitute for the direct cost of employee drivers. If the account includes only owner-operators using vehicles owned by others, the wages paid are treated the same as those for drivers. The amounts in this account are classified as direct expense because these drivers substitute for company drivers.

Other Labor Wages includes employees such as janitors, gardeners, or others who perform work not related to the trucking operation. This account contains wages of employees that cannot be classified in other categories. It should be analyzed to determine if the account has been properly posted with only indirect wages, and the result treated accordingly. Employees unrelated to trucking operations are classified as indirect for the purposes of cost-based pricing.

Federal payroll taxes include FICA and Federal Unemployment Insurance for all employees. The amounts paid for drivers, helpers, packers, platform workers, and other employees for whom labor cost is determined in the direct portion of the study are treated as a direct expense in this analysis. Taxes paid on all other employee classifications are classified as indirect. The preparation of employee total hourly labor cost in the direct portion of the study included the cost of payroll taxes (See Table 4.15) for all employees. This account must be analyzed, and the totals of both direct and indirect expense distributed accordingly.

State payroll taxes are allocated in the same fashion as Federal payroll taxes. The account must also be analyzed, and the results distributed between direct and indirect expenses.

Workers compensation also includes expense for all employee classifications (see Table 4.15 of the direct cost study). The analyst must determine the proper allocations according to the employee classification found in the direct cost analysis. Clerical and management personnel are included as an indirect expense; the employees for whom direct cost is determined are allocated as a direct expense.

Group Insurance usually includes the cost of insurance for clerical and management employees. If this is true, the expense must be allocated as an indirect expense. The group insurance expense of other wage earners included in the direct portion of the study is treated as a direct expense.

Pension and Retirement, Health and Welfare, and Other Fringes expenses are allocated in the same way as other fringe benefit and payroll tax accounts. Contributions for direct wage earners are direct; others are indirect.

Fuel and Oil must be analyzed to determine the amount of fuel expense incurred by company sales and management cars, yard goats, and other auxiliary vehicles. All of these vehicles are treated as an indirect expense. The only direct expense in this account is for the fuel purchased for revenue equipment. This is because the direct portion of the study included only fuel and oil cost of such vehicles.

Vehicle parts, outside maintenance, and tire expenses receive the same treatment as fuel and oil expenses. Maintenance and tire cost connected with auxiliary vehicles are allocated to indirect expense, and revenue equipment expense is allocated to direct expense.

Other Operating Supplies is a catchall account that includes general supplies, some of which may be direct in nature. For example, if the account includes small items used either in the maintenance shop or on revenue equipment, the total must be included in direct cost if the carrier loads its in-house work orders with overhead cost. The majority of expenses in this account, however, are expected to be indirect.

Tariffs, advertising, commissions, and officer and other employee general expenses are indirect because none of them are determined in the direct analysis, nor can they be allocated to the direct cost of any particular flow of traffic.

Federal and state fuel taxes, vehicle license fees, and other vehicle fees are usually allocated as a direct expense because they are included in either the determination of vehicle fixed cost or vehicle running cost. The only exception is when the costs are allocated to auxiliary vehicles, at which time they become an indirect expense.

In preparation of vehicle fixed cost in Table 5.7, the cost of public liability and property damage insurance coverage for revenue equipment is determined. This determination also includes comprehensive and collision coverage. All other insurance expense, such as real estate insurance and blanket liability coverage, is considered as an indirect expense.

Communications and utilities are classified as indirect expenses. The only rare exception would be the installation of radios at the time new or used revenue equipment is purchased. The cost of the radios, for example, would be included in the vehicle fixed cost unless that particular cost was removed from the acquisition cost at the time of purchase.

Depreciation has been described as the periodic write-down of an asset. In the determination of vehicle fixed cost, the study makes an analysis of economic value, vehicle life, and salvage value of revenue equipment. These calculations take the place of depreciation expense in the cost study for these vehicles. Therefore, depreciation expense for revenue-producing vehicles is allocated as a direct expense. All other depreciation is indirect.

Amortization expense of leasehold improvements is always an indirect expense.

Vehicle rents of revenue equipment are direct expense because these costs are determined for driver labor, vehicle fixed cost, and vehicle running cost in the study of direct cost. It may be argued that the precise cost trade-off between company drivers with company vehicles and rented vehicles with or without drivers is not exactly the same. This may be true in some instances, but our objective is to demonstrate a cost-finding system that portrays the cost to provide transportation by truck. Whether the service is provided by company employees and vehicles or with rented equipment is not material. For purposes of allocation, the objective is to include all cost increments without overlapping any of the elements. In the next chapter, we provide an analysis of the ownership of vehicles with employee drivers, which can be utilized to compare with rental vehicles or sub-haul systems.

Equipment rents credit is really income from rental of equipment. In the example, this cost was considered to be rental of revenue equipment. If income is received for other equipment rentals, it would be an indirect income.

Gain or loss on the disposal of assets is, in reality, an overstatement or understatement of depreciation expense. If the disposed asset is revenue equipment, the expense, or income, is direct, and other asset disposal is indirect.

General Discussion of Indirect Cost

The chart of expense accounts in the example reflects a strict trucking operation. In practice, other business opportunities may be included in financial statements, even though the prescribed system of accounts precludes their inclusion as operating expenses. When this is true, the expense of unrelated activities, such as the buying and selling of a product, must be excluded from both the total expense and the individual allocation determination. The concept in the cost analysis, and the result to be achieved, is to determine prices only for trucking services. The commingling of expenses will not accomplish that objective.

The example in Table 7.1 is an analysis of corporate expense. If the company is a proprietorship or partnership, the analyst must impute a wage for ownership. In typical accounting systems, the expense of corporate management and ownership is included in the corporation's expense accounts, but the cost of individual entrepreneurs is not. If owners of proprietorships have determined that proprietary wages should be included in the Income and Expense Statement, then no input is required. In either event, the cost is indirect, and must be included so that the rate assessed to buyers will recover that cost.

Finally, smaller firms may not maintain accounting records as detailed as the example in Table 7.1. The described procedure can still be achieved with fewer expense accounts. Each account should be analyzed in detail to determine the indirect ratio. After the analysis recommended in Table 7.1 is completed, the expense distribution in the accounting system should be modified on a permanent basis to consider the discussions in this chapter for each account. The purpose of these adjustments is to create an array of accounts that will automatically determine the indirect ratio without the time and cost necessary to complete the described analysis. Postings from journals can be constructed to detail whether an entry is direct or indirect.

Now that regulatory agencies have less control over carrier activities, it is anticipated that motor carriers will give more consideration to their individual needs, and to the needs of their buyers, than to government requirements. The carrier genuinely interested in monitoring operating cost will make the necessary accounting adjustments to facilitate the determination of the indirect ratio. Such adjustments will not impact upon the carrier's ability to determine income taxes or to make other managerial decisions.

Some interesting comparisons of expense relationships can be made in studies of this type. The result in the example indicates that nearly 83% of the total cost is incurred in expenses related to traffic flow. The other 17% is variable in accordance with volume. Is there one expense that is fixed, and not adjustable by traffic flow or volume? If your response is ownership of terminals, shops, or office buildings for the trucking operation, you are incorrect. A partial definition of a fixed cost is a cost that cannot be substituted, such as railroad track beds. In the case of a motor carrier's real estate, it can be substituted with real estate buyers in the same industry or by firms in other industries. Motor carriers incur no expense that is truly fixed.

Other interesting comparisons are that labor costs are just under 72% of the total cost, and that the total of all labor cost and direct vehicle cost makes up 95% of the total cost. Of course, these figures do not reflect the operation of the industry as a whole, but they are believed to be indicative of existing relationships.

The numbers also support the conclusion that nearly all trucking cost is variable. This condition creates competitive problems because no operator is required to be in business for the long term. Almost anyone can acquire a piece of revenue equipment and walk away if the business fails. On the other hand, the responsible carrier will prepare costs in detail, price services accordingly, and act responsibly to provide necessary industry stability.

In summary, the analysis of indirect cost in the illustration indicates that the ratio of indirect cost to total cost is 17.4%. This figure will be the basis for all ensuing demonstrations of total cost, except in the chapter that discusses household goods transportation. The figure of 17.4% is representative of the cost relationship found in the overall industry. However, the ratio of indirect cost varies widely in sub-industries. Some examples provide perspective on this point. In the dump truck area, the indirect ratio using this method is expected to be just under 10%. This low ratio is obtained because many participants are one-truck operators who maintain no sophisticated records. Owners may do their own dispatch, bill only a few buyers, and generally subhaul for other carriers. Overlying carriers work with few contractors, and their billing procedures do not require sophisticated computer systems or significant communication expenses in relation to total cost.

At the other end of the indirect spectrum is the local household goods carrier who is an agent for a major van line. In this case, the carrier's primary difficulty is government regulation and the costs incurred to comply with it, such as estimating the cost of shipments for householders, a lengthy and detailed document. The documents, required in response to almost every inquiry, incur cost with little return because the buyer often chooses another carrier.

Another high cost for this type of carrier is the transportation agreement documentation required by the government. A shipping document can be several pages in length to cover all of the regulatory conditions, and is generally so intricate that it does not lend itself to data processing. It is common for indirect cost in the household goods industry to be 35% of total cost.

Historically, implementation of new regulations governing the service standards of the household goods carrier industry has not included a cost/benefit analysis to determine whether the cost of added regulation produces economical results. Consequently, the level of indirect cost as a ratio to total cost has outstripped the remainder of the industry.

In most specialized segments of the industry, such as bulk transportation of cement and liquid products, the indirect ratio is expected to be about 15%. These operations are heavily influenced by vehicle fixed expense in relation to total cost. Bulk trailers, such as pneumatic hoppers, and stainless steel liquid food, or chemical trailers, are very expensive, and produce a higher cost relationship to total cost. The indirect cost is less, however, because billing and sales costs are less than, for example, the LTL carrier. These carriers generally deal with fewer buyers, the product is transported in repetition, and computer systems readily accommodate billing. All of these conditions tend to keep indirect cost relatively low.

In the LTL transportation of general commodities, the indirect ratio to total expense should be 19-20%, largely because indirect labor is such a high cost of operation. Carriers in this industry incur higher indirect cost because they employ claims clerks and a larger number of dispatchers, and they require more management personnel than other carrier groups. This sub-industry also requires higher sales expense because it relies on a high volume of small shipments from many buyers. Finally, LTL carriers operate more than one terminal, a condition that creates a higher indirect expense for real estate.

After completing the indirect study, the analyst is ready to consider the compilation of the elements discussed previously. Specifically, the analyst can now consider the methods of total cost determination for various motor carrier activities. It is suggested that the analyst now review the cost construction in Tables 4.15, 5.9, and 6.7. These tables reflect total cost for each of the three direct cost increments necessary for determining the total cost. The only missing ingredients are productivity measurements to perform the operational processes. Time and/or speed are required to convert the running cost per mile to the running cost per hour, the labor cost per hour to the labor cost to trip, and the vehicle fixed cost per hour or per mile to the cost per trip.

Where the objective is to determine an hourly rate, the running cost must be converted to the cost per hour by finding the running speed for the overall operation under study. For example, a bobtail travels 45 miles per hour while running for 2 hours, and loads in a half-hour and unloads in a half-hour. The 90-mile round trip takes 3 hours. Using these hypotheticals, the running distance for the trip was 90 miles divided by 3 hours, or 30 miles per hour.

The hypothetical figures in the preceding paragraph produce an hourly cost summary and hourly rate in tabular form, as shown in Table 7.2.

TABLE 7.2

CALCULATION OF HOURLY COST AND RATE

Line No.	Item	Amount
1.	Bobtail Driver from Table 4.1	$ 17.141
2.	Bobtail Vehicle Fixed Cost From Table 5.9	4.697
3.	Bobtail Running Cost Per Mile from Table 6.7, ($.359 x 30 mph)	10.770
4.	Direct Cost Per Hour	$ 32.608
5.	Indirect Cost Per Hour	6.869
6.	Total Cost at 100 O. R.	$ 39.477
7.	Rate at 93 O. R.	$ 42.24

If the figures used in our example represented a particular transportation service, the cost per hour to the buyer for that service would be $42.24. Direct cost per hour must be expanded to include indirect cost. In Table 7.1, the indirect ratio of 17.4% was calculated in terms of total cost. This concept must be carried forward to the cost function by dividing the complement of the indirect cost ratio into the direct cost. In the example, the direct cost per hour of $32.608 is divided by .826, which produces the total cost at a 100 operating ratio.

In Table 7.2, the result is an indirect expense of $6.869, which is 17.4% of the total cost at an operating ratio of 100. As a practical matter, the figure for the total cost at a 100 operating ratio is determined by calculation, and the indirect cost is determined by subtraction ($39.477 - $32.608 = $6.869). Application of the indirect ratio is necessary to obtain the total cost, both direct and indirect. When the ratio was developed, it was determined as a ratio of indirect cost to total expenses. If that ratio were multiplied by the direct cost, the result would understate the total cost. For example, Table 7.2 indicates a direct cost of $32.608 and an indirect ratio of 17.4%. Multiplying these figures produces $38.282, which is not the total cost. If prices were constructed using this method, the carrier would incur losses.

If the analyst prefers to multiply direct cost by a factor rather than using the illustrated method, he or she can find the ratio of indirect cost to direct cost rather than to the total cost. The total in Table 7.1 for indirect cost is $1,124,502, and the total for direct cost is $5,329,243. The ratio of indirect to direct cost is 21.10%. Accordingly, multiplying the direct cost in Table 7.2 of $32.608 by 121.10 produces $39.488, the same result as that determined in Table 7.2. If the indirect ratio was carried to three decimal places, the dollar amounts would be identical. Both methods produce cost at a 100 operating ratio.

If the firm assessed its buyer at the same rate as the cost at an operating ratio of 100 ($39.477), it would break even on the price, receiving only the revenue necessary to cover the cost. To produce profit, it must set a rate higher than the cost. Table 7.2 employs a profit margin of 7%. This is the level most regulatory agencies have recognized as appropriate. As a practical matter, the firm can choose any profit margin it believes necessary, given the company's financial needs and the competitive conditions.

The method demonstrated above does not include the cost of borrowed money or income taxes. Historically, in regulatory rate-making, these costs have been borne in the profit margin. Accordingly, the profit margin of 7% must cover interest expense and income tax as well as net return to ownership. Another reason for exclusion of these two items in the direct or indirect cost illustrations is that each carrier has different financial needs and tax considerations. It is conceivable and, perhaps, appropriate that an individual carrier adopting the cost methods described will include these two components in indirect cost.

Before making that judgment, however, the carrier should recognize that tax consequences in the Income Statement are historical, and not prospective. Tax liability is predicated upon past results, and price-setting considers future economic expectations as well as incurred expenses. If the carrier accounted for interest expense and income tax as an operating expense, it risks understatement of cost for pricing purposes. When these items are included in profit margins, however, the analyst can make timely adjustments in the price structure. When interest expense and income taxes are shown on the Income Statement as an operating expense, and the analyst chooses to include them in the profit margin for pricing purposes, both items must be removed from an indirect cost worksheet such as that in Table 7.1.

The remainder of this book will discuss practical applications of the various cost components presented so far, using productivity measurements and functional operations.

Vehicle Rental and Leasing

Vehicle rental and leasing is a major component of the trucking industry. Almost all trucking operations rent vehicles. We have two reasons for discussing the subject at this point. We recognize its importance to the overall scheme of product distribution, and our discussion here provides an opportunity to bring together the concepts and illustrations mentioned earlier in this book without typical complications in activities of other trucking operations. Such complications arise in connection with measurement of speed, distance, and freight handling as productivity factors. Vehicle rental and leasing do not involve productivity measurements because they are largely driven by time increments. Vehicles are rented for a specified time period, and productivity during the period is the responsibility of the buyer.

Discussion of vehicle rental and leasing goes far beyond the 1-day truck rental from a local agency. Our use of the term "rental and leasing" does include this 1-day unit, but it also includes leasing of vehicles to shippers for long periods, rental of owner-operator power units for a specific purpose, rental by overlying carriers of units with driver from underlying carriers, and vehicle leasing as a source of acquisition in place of traditional purchases. The last type of leasing can apply to carriers as well as shippers.

Theories of Rate-making

For the first time in this book, the reader will be able to convert raw cost to a usable rate, or price. Discussion of motor carrier economics in earlier chapters indicated that all costs incurred by the industry are variable. They vary either by the individual transportation service and the flow of traffic or by the over-all revenue and shipment volume of the firm. As you begin to create rate structures, the significance of this economic theory upon practical applications begins to take shape.

The underlying premise of cost determination is that prices determined must include all of the cost incurred whenever possible. Variable cost and fully allocated cost are the same in terms of motor carrier economics. When the price assessed to buyers does not cover the fully allocated cost, and all of the cost is variable, the firm will lose money on that book of business. Accordingly, the rates in this book are constructed to include both direct and indirect costs, with an increment of overhead cost recovered in each rate. This method is equal to the fully allocated cost method of price structuring. When all rates recover full cost, the firm generates profits.

The second aspect of this scenario is that when all costs are variable, they are also dynamic, in the sense that they are always changing. Overall maintenance cost, for example, changes according to the terrain, the driver's ability, the vehicle configuration, traffic congestion, and other factors. As a result, measured maintenance cost during a 2-year historical period may not be the same as that experienced over the next annual period because the conditions surrounding it change.

Cost-finding for motor carriers must be a continuing process, to assure that the cost and the rate remain in the proper relationship. There is often temptation to reduce rates to meet competition, and, to remain viable, that strategy may have to be employed. However, the carrier must realize that reductions may impair profits, and that it will be necessary to generate additional net income from other sources. Certainly, all rates do not return full cost, even though it is always desirable that they do, but the demonstrations in this and succeeding chapters are predicated upon full cost recovery in each rate. The firm must determine where, and when, to price its service upon considerations other than cost. It is essential, however, that the cost be known in advance of the price quotation.

Another aspect of the pricing scenario is productivity. In considering whether to reduce prices below fully allocated cost, the firm should first determine if all levels of the operation are as productive as possible. If not, it should reduce cost through increased productivity before reducing prices below existing cost. Here, the cost study goes beyond mere price-setting. Cost studies using the procedures in this book will produce productivity measures in all areas of direct cost. Astute managers can study the measurements, and take any appropriate corrective action.

In summary, motor carrier prices should always be predicated upon total variable cost (fully allocated cost). When this is not possible because of competition, the firm should review cost and productivity levels in each of the categories set forth in this book. Before reducing price to meet competition, cost should be reduced and productivity increased to acceptable levels consistent with safe and legal operations. Once this is accomplished, the operator can reduce prices further with confidence that all of the elements of pricing have been addressed. Although not based upon any particular set of circumstances, cost levels selected as examples and illustrations in this book should be considered as the lowest possible efficient cost.

Vehicle Rental Without Driver

Rental without a driver can be a long- or short-term proposition, but when the buyer rents a vehicle including the driver, it is generally a long-term agreement. Short-term arrangements occur for a variety of reasons, and are similar to the retail truck rental operations of Ryder, Penske, and other vehicle rental businesses. Such agreements generally occur when the buyer needs additional vehicles to cover overflow or to compensate for equipment failure in the for-hire or private fleet.

Another reason for vehicle rental without driver is a private carrier's belief that it can more effectively distribute products with its own employees. In this rental arrangement, the buyer elects not to invest in the acquisition of vehicles. Rental agencies have developed systems by which they can capture the entire distribution system of selected buyers on a long-term basis under this scenario. They enter into agreements for long-term rental that often include a commitment to provide vehicle maintenance during the lease term.

IMPORTANT!

This is an area that for-hire motor carriers should examine as a method to increase market share in the current competitive environment. A large volume of business is available from shippers who perform route service between their manufacturing facilities and distribution points. These systems often require several vehicles on a daily basis, with the buyer operating the fleet but avoiding vehicle acquisition. An astute motor carrier might step in and provide vehicles on a long-term lease, either with or without drivers, to preclude the entire loss of the book of business.

Vehicle Rental With Driver

Vehicle rental with driver occurs when the customer believes it can distribute its products more efficiently by controlling the carrier's vehicle and driver. It avoids vehicle acquisition cost as well as administrative problems connected with employee drivers. The buyer controls the dispatch and coordinates the flow of distribution, and the carrier incurs the cost of both the employee and the vehicle. These agreements are generally long term, often extending as long as a year. Vehicle rental with driver bodes well for the carrier when a shipper is considering other distribution methods to replace carriers on a single-shipment basis.

Under past regulatory systems, truck rental agencies, such as Ryder and Penske, have been precluded from providing vehicle rental with driver because of the need for entry requirements as for-hire carriers. Vehicles rented with driver have been considered as for-hire transportation that requires operating permits from the ICC, state agencies, or both. Accordingly, for-hire carriers have enjoyed almost an exclusivity in this market. In a deregulated environment, however, the rental agencies are free to enter into these agreements, and it is expected that competition in rental and leasing will become more acute. Motor carriers with access to this type of distribution should consider more active participation as a method of increasing revenue and improving equipment utilization.

The second rental and leasing system with driver is a carrier-to-carrier relationship where vehicle rental consists of the overlying, or prime, carrier splitting the activity with another entity, such as the power unit owner-operator. This system is found primarily in long-haul truck transportation where the overlying carrier provides the trailers, and hires the tractor and the driver. The operation fits nicely with intermodal service, such as piggyback and other containerized systems.

Certain specialized carrier sub-industries also utilize the tractor and driver rental system. It is particularly popular in the dump-truck field where larger carriers contract with the shipper for trucking service, provide trailing equipment, and rent the tractor and driver from entities the industry calls "pullers." This system is critical to the provision of service for large construction jobs, such as highway improvement. Massive highway construction requires the commitment of large numbers of vehicles over a short period of time. As a rule, the overlying carrier cannot provide sufficient numbers of vehicles, so it supplements its fleet with pullers and/or sub-haulers.

Sub-hauling is the third type of vehicle rental with driver. All sub-industries within the trucking environment use the sub-haul system to some extent. In this concept, the overlying (prime) carrier employs another full-service carrier to assist in producing the transportation product. Sub-hauling contributes to industry fragmentation, and helps create additional competitive conditions if the underlying carrier (sub-hauler) competes with the overlying carrier for other business on an equal basis.

In previous chapters, industry fragmentation was discussed at length. In both the owner-operator and sub-hauling relationships described here, this fragmentation is clearly visible. The owner-operator rental relationship often becomes a competitive situation when the underlying entity becomes a full-fledged carrier. Similar conditions are created in the sub-haul relationship when the sub-hauler becomes informed on the economics of transportation, and chooses to become a full-fledged carrier servicing shippers and other carriers. Once again, fragmentation creates additional competitive burdens.

Vehicle Rented to Shipper Without Driver

Discussion of carrier rental to a shipper will be limited to pricing concepts. Circumstances that induce this relationship vary widely, but the economics supporting the activity are constant. It is sufficient to say that carriers should become well informed on the pricing concepts so that the marketing plan may include this system in the overall service provided.

Those familiar with pricing practices of truck rental companies, such as Penske and Ryder, recognize the construction of rates to be a fixed price-per-time period with an additional price based upon miles operated during the rental period. The underlying economics of vehicle usage discussed in earlier chapters demonstrate why these rental prices are so constructed. Vehicle investment cost (fixed cost described in Chapter 5) is recovered by the lessor in the time price, and vehicle operating cost (running cost described in Chapter 6) is recovered in the mileage price. Each of the rates includes an increment of indirect cost as well as profit. Every rate developed in this book contains both of these recoveries for the carrier so that no rate subsidizes another, from a cost perspective. The illustration in Table 8.1 depicts the structure used in vehicle rental on an annual basis.

TABLE 8.1

ANNUAL BOBTAIL RENTAL WITHOUT DRIVER

Line No.	Item	Amount
	TIME RATE:	
1.	Vehicle Fixed Cost Per Year (Table 5.7)	$ 7,515
2.	Indirect Cost Per Year (Table 7.1)	1,583
3.	Cost at 100 O. R.	$ 9,098
4.	Rate at 93 O. R.	$ 9,735
	MILEAGE RATE:	
5.	Vehicle Running Cost Per Mile (Table 6.6)	$ .359
6.	Indirect Cost Per Mile (Table 7.1)	.076
7.	Cost at 100 O. R.	$ .435
8.	Rate at 93 0. R.	$ .465

The time rate and vehicle fixed cost in Table 8.1 are designed to recover the cost to acquire a bobtail, including licensing and insurance. This figure was determined in our earlier discussion of vehicle fixed cost in Table 5.7. Indirect cost is the ratio determined in Table 7.1, which was 17.4% of total cost in Table 8.1. We used that figure for illustration even though the indirect ratio in vehicle rental and leasing should be significantly less.

Many of the indirect costs found in motor carrier operations do not exist in connection with leasing. These include dispatch, utilities, communications, clerical support, and wages for other supervisory personnel. When developing the leasing cost for pricing purposes, the analyst must determine the anticipated indirect ratio in a particular situation.

Cost at a 100 operating ratio is the break-even point, and the selected operating ratio of 93% is the same as the rate to be assessed over an annual period. In accordance with previous discussion, the 7% profit margin includes the cost of money, income taxes, and retained earnings, and is simply a figure selected for illustration. The analyst must consider the carrier's particular tax implications, financial resources, and competition in setting the targeted profit margin.

The mileage rate is determined using the same considerations except, of course, the objective is to recover the running cost incurred during the lease period. Terms of the lease will specify what elements of running cost are to be paid by the parties. For example, if fuel cost is paid by the lessee, it must be removed from the mileage rate assessed by the lessor.

In our example, rates for an annual vehicle lease are assessed and collected monthly to provide cash flow to the lessor. When the lease covers a 1-year period, the periodic payment would be $811.25 ($9,735 ÷ 12). In addition to the monthly fee, the carrier must also recover the vehicle operating cost per mile shown in Table 6.7. That table indicated a cost per mile for fuel, oil, tires, and maintenance of $.359 for a bobtail. Using the same calculation method and cost levels described in connection with vehicle fixed cost recovery in Table 8.1, the rate to be assessed is $.465. The analyst must also consider expected indirect cost and net income from a specific lease when setting the mileage rate.

In the example in Table 8.1, the rate to be assessed per month is $811.25 for 12 months plus $.465 per mile for each mile operated during the month by a straight truck, or bobtail. The same procedure may be followed to determine rates for the rental or leasing of any vehicle type or combination. The final objective should be to set up a price schedule for all vehicle types available for lease. Such a schedule can then be distributed to the sales force for marketing guidance.

In the next example, the buyer and the seller enter into a monthly rental agreement that differs from the annual arrangement in that the buyer is free to reject the agreement at the end of each month. The seller owns a fleet of vehicles reserved for rental, and offers these units on any time basis required by customers. Because it is unlikely that the vehicle will be rented for all 12 months, the monthly agreement changes the calculation of cost. Table 8.2 illustrates the difference.

TABLE 8.2

MONTHLY BOBTAIL RENTAL WITHOUT DRIVER

Line No.	Item	Amount
	TIME RATE:	
1.	Vehicle Fixed Cost Per Year (Table 5.7)	$ 7,515
2.	Indirect Cost Per Year (Table 7.1)	1,583
3.	Annual Cost at 100 O. R.	$ 9,098
4.	Annual Use Months	11
5.	Cost at 100 O. R. Per Month	$ 827
6.	Rate at 93 O. R. Per Month	$ 885
	MILEAGE RATE:	
7.	Vehicle Running Cost Per Mile (Table 6.7)	$ .359
8.	Indirect Cost Per Mile (Table 7.1)	.076
9.	Cost at 100 O. R.	$ .435
10.	Rate at 93 O. R.	$ .465

IMPORTANT!

The rate on a monthly basis is higher than on a yearly basis because the expected use is lower. Also, by assessing a higher base rate for a monthly lease, the carrier is attempting to induce the buyer to enter into an annual lease. From the carrier's point of view, a yearly lease is preferable because it guarantees equipment utilization over a longer period of time; the same number of dollars are returned in the rate over the annual life of the lease. The mileage rate stays the same because the consumption of fuel, oil, tires, and maintenance does not change with the lease period.

In addition to annual and monthly rentals, shippers may also require weekly rentals. The same cost concepts apply to these rentals as applied to rentals for longer periods. In constructing weekly rates, the analyst will determine the number of weeks the bobtail fleet can be expected to be used in that service each year. Though the exact number varies, the industry has found that number to be approximately 40 weeks for each annual period. The example in Table 8.3 utilizes 40 weeks to recover the vehicle fixed cost on an annual basis.

TABLE 8.3

WEEKLY BOBTAIL RENTAL WITHOUT DRIVER

Line No.	Item	Amount
	TIME RATE:	
1.	Vehicle Fixed Cost Per Year (Table 5.7)	$ 7,515
2.	Indirect Cost Per Year (Table 7.1)	1,583
3.	Cost at 100 O. R.	$ 9,098
4.	Annual Use Weeks	40
5.	Cost at 100 O. R. Per Week	$ 227
6.	Rate at 93 O. R. Per Week	$ 243
	MILEAGE RATE:	
7.	Vehicle Running Cost Per Mile (Table 6.7)	$ .359
8.	Indirect Cost Per Mile (Table 7.1)	.076
9.	Cost at 100 O. R.	$ .435
10.	Rate at 93 O. R.	$ .465

It might be argued that, if the firm expects to lease the vehicle only 40 weeks, but expects to recover the vehicle fixed cost for a full year, the price is over-stated. This may be true if the firm has other work available for the unit during the 12-week period it is not employed under a weekly rental agreement. When this is the case, an adjustment must be made in the annual cost to be recovered. The analyst needs to be well informed on this subject before adjustments are made. The ultimate objective is to produce adequate net income results for the firm by improving equipment utilization.

Daily and hourly rates are also available in the rental market for vehicles without driver. Again, the cost determination concepts are similar. Daily rates are based upon 8 hours per day, 5 days per week, as compared with the weekly rate which is based on 40 weeks per year, 7 days per week. To convert a weekly rate to a daily rate, divide the weekly rate by 5 days. Hourly rates are applied for weekend work. Table 8.4 shows how to find the weekly rate and divide it by 5 days.

TABLE 8.4

DAILY BOBTAIL RENTAL WITHOUT DRIVER

Line No.	Item	Amount
	TIME RATE:	
1.	Vehicle Fixed Cost Per Year (Table 5.7)	$ 7,515
2.	Indirect Cost Per Year (Table 7.1)	1,583
3.	Cost at 100 O. R.	$ 9,098
4.	Annual Use Weeks	40
5.	Cost at 100 O. R. Per Week	$ 227
6.	Cost at 93 O. R. Per Week	$ 243
7.	Rate Per Day	$ 48.60
	MILEAGE RATE:	
8.	Vehicle Running Cost Per Mile (Table 6.6)	$ .359
9.	Indirect Cost Per Mile (Table 7.1)	.076
10.	Cost at 100 O.R.	$ .435
11.	Rate at 93 O.R.	$ .465

The analysis in Table 8.4 produces a rate structure of $48.60 per day plus $.465 per mile.

Cost of borrowed money, or interest expense, is a significant consideration in the determination of prices. We have not dealt with it extensively because all motor carriers are familiar with the cost concepts. Though our examples consistently include interest expense in the profit margin, other methods may be used. In many instances, the interest expense for individual vehicles is known, or can be determined. In such cases, the cost of money may be allocated as a direct cost, and included in the determination of vehicle fixed cost.

Carrier Vehicle Rented to Shippers With Driver

Cost determination for this service is similar to that described in vehicle rental without driver except that labor cost considerations are required for fully allocated cost pricing. Table 4.13 illustrated development of hourly labor cost including fringe benefits, payroll taxes, and workers compensation insurance on a straight time basis. That table used $17.327 per hour as the cost for a line driver. Even though a bobtail rental would not include the labor cost for a line driver, that cost is used for demonstration purposes so that the reader can track the process. In addition, Table 4.12 provided a cost for overtime work of $23.235, with the overtime rate at 1.5 times the straight time rate. A double time rate may be necessary if work is performed on Sunday or holidays. In this event, the analyst may determine that cost using the same concepts as those applied to the 1.5 times the straight time cost development.

When vehicles including the driver are leased to a buyer on an annual basis, the cost analysis must include both vehicle fixed cost and labor cost on an annual basis. For this purpose, the driver of the vehicle works 8 hours per day, 21 days per month, 12 months per year. It does not matter if the same driver is used all year; the vehicle is in service for that period. The 21 days per month is determined by subtracting 104 weekend days and 8 holidays from 365 annual days. The resulting 253 days are divided by 12 months to obtain 21 days per month. This method results in the cost and the rate for a vehicle with driver on a 5-day work week of 8 hours. Overtime rates must be calculated to offer the buyer a full range of price structures. Table 8.5 indicates the straight time monthly rental rate determination for an annual lease.

TABLE 8.5

ANNUAL VEHICLE RENTAL WITH DRIVER

Line No.	Item	Amount
	TIME RATE:	
1.	Vehicle Fixed Cost Per Year (Table 5.7)	$ 7,515
2.	Vehicle Fixed Cost Per Month	$ 626
3.	Driver Labor Cost Per Month:	
4.	Hourly Rate (Table 4.13)	$ 17.327
5.	Hours Per Day	8
6.	Days Per Month	21
7.	Monthly Cost	$ 2,911
8.	Direct Cost Per Month (Line 2 + Line 7)	$ 3,537
9.	Indirect Cost Per Month (Table 7.1)	745
10.	Total Cost at 100 O. R.	$ 4,282
11.	Rate at 93 O. R.	$ 4,582
	MILEAGE RATE:	
12.	Vehicle Running Cost Per Mile (Table 6.6)	$ .359
13.	Indirect Cost (Table 7.1)	.076
14.	Cost at 100 O. R.	$ .435
15.	Rate at 93 O. R.	$ .465

An annual bobtail rental with driver would cost the buyer a rate of $4,582 per month plus $.465 per mile. To find the cost per month for the vehicle fixed cost, we divided the annual direct cost by 12 months. The monthly labor cost is determined by multiplying the total hourly labor cost by 8 hours per day and 21 days per month. The total direct cost per month is then expanded to include indirect cost and profit margin.

The overtime rate to be assessed requires additional calculation. The only portion of direct cost in this instance is overtime labor cost. The annual vehicle fixed cost is recovered in total. Using the method in Table 8.5, the annual vehicle fixed cost is divided by 12 months to recover the full cost. Accordingly, the overtime rate is determined by including overhead and profit margin as an additive to the hourly overtime total labor cost only. Recovery of annual vehicle fixed cost in the base monthly rate and vehicle running cost in the mileage rate, leaves only the additional cost of overtime labor to be recovered in the overtime rate. This is illustrated in Table 8.6.

The exception to this method is where the transportation to be conducted under the lease routinely requires an inordinate number of hours per day. In these conditions, the vehicle fixed cost should be constructed using a shorter life for the vehicle. A shorter life compensates for additional use that may not have been contemplated in the overall fleet. The analyst, when establishing annual vehicle rates, should have knowledge of operating conditions in the particular circumstances.

TABLE 8.6

OVERTIME HOURLY RATE — ANNUAL VEHICLE RENTAL WITH DRIVER

Line No.	Item	Amount
1.	Hourly Labor Cost (Table 4.12)	$ 23.235
2.	Indirect Cost (Table 7.1)	4.895
3.	Hourly Cost at 100 O. R.	$ 28.130
4.	Hourly Rate at 93 O. R.	$ 30.10

The price structure for annual rental of a bobtail with a driver is now complete, including work accomplished at overtime rates. Monthly, weekly, and daily prices may be determined using the concepts set forth in connection with rental without driver. Periodic driver cost is predicated upon the hourly rate multiplied by the hours worked in the various types of service. Consequently, a carrier would lease a bobtail to a lessee on an annual basis of $4,582 per month plus $.465 per mile for all miles traveled. Time worked during periods other than Monday through Friday between 8:00 a.m. and 5:00 p.m. would be assessed at a rate of $30.10 per hour plus $.465 for each mile traveled.

Carrier-to-Carrier Vehicle Rental

Previous discussion in this chapter outlined the general conditions that spark carrier-to-carrier rental. This rental is found in sub-industries where the prime carrier does not provide the entire vehicle combination to perform high-volume, long-haul traffic or the high-volume, short-time frame transportation typical of dump truck operations. In essence, this rental amounts to no more than revenue sharing, with the owner-operator receiving payment for direct cost, and the prime carrier being paid for the overhead cost incurred in sales and billing. Owner-operator compensation is generally expressed in terms of price per mile or as a percentage of revenue. Our examples break down the various cost increments discussed in previous chapters to obtain a sense of cost allocation between carriers.

In the first example, it is assumed that the prime carrier books the shipper's business; that is, it obtains business through sales expense. It also provides trailing equipment and does billing to the customer. The underlying owner-operator provides the labor and power unit. The overlying (prime) carrier determines the price split between the owner-operator and itself, and the owner-operator determines whether the split will be profitable.

To assess cost allocation between the parties in this operation, it is necessary to return to the basic formula discussed earlier: total motor carrier cost equals direct cost, which is made up of labor, vehicle fixed and running costs, indirect cost, and profit. The examples will reflect these cost elements and the cost allocations necessary. Before a detailed examination of cost allocation between the parties is begun, the analyst must determine the price to be assessed to the shipper. This is the basis used to determine whether the splits will be profitable for both the prime carrier and the owner-operator.

In Table 8.7, cost considerations are predicated upon the cost of a line driver and a three-axle tractor and long semi combination.

TABLE 8.7

DETERMINATION OF COST/RATE PER MILE

Line No.	Item	Amount
1.	Vehicle Fixed Cost (Table 5.9)	$ .257
2.	Vehicle Running Cost (Table 6.7)	.523
3.	Labor Cost (Table 4.14)	.361
4.	Direct Cost	$ 1.141
5.	Indirect Cost (Table 7.1)	.240
6.	Cost at 100 O. R.	$ 1.381
7.	Rate at 93 O. R.	$ 1.48

Revenue for motor carrier transportation at a distance of 1,000 miles is $1,480, based upon the incremental cost included in the earlier tables. This revenue must be allocated between the prime carrier and owner-operator in a manner that will return profit to both parties.

In the process of cost distribution, our analysis begins with the owner-operator furnishing both the power unit and direct labor.

TABLE 8.8

DETERMINATION OF OWNER-OPERATOR REVENUE

Line No.	Item	Amount
1.	Labor Cost:	
2.	Base Mileage Rate (Table 4.14)	$ .230
3.	Self Employment Tax (15.3%)	.035
4.	Medical Insurance ($250 month)	.038
5.	Labor Cost Per Mile	$ .303
6.	Vehicle Fixed Cost for Tractor (Table 5.7), ($16,035÷85,000)	.189
7.	Vehicle Running Cost for Tractor (Table 6.6)	.461
8.	Direct Cost	$ .953
9.	Indirect Cost (Table 7.1)	.201
10.	Cost at 100 O. R. (17.4% Indirect)	$ 1.154
11.	Rate at 93 O. R.	$ 1.23

TABLE 8.9

DETERMINATION OF PRIME CARRIER REVENUE

Line No.	Item	Amount
1.	Vehicle Fixed Cost for Trailer (Table 5.7), ($5,805 ÷ 85,000)	$ .068
2.	Vehicle Running Cost for Trailer (Table 6.6)	.062
3.	Direct Cost	$ .130
4.	Indirect Cost (Table 7.1)	.027
5.	Cost at 100 O. R. (17.4% Indirect)	$ .157
6.	Rate at 93 O. R.	$ .17

The total cost at a 93 operating ratio for both of the operators totals $1.40, which is $.08 less than fully allocated cost for the operation in the total set forth in Table 8.7. The difference results from exclusion of vacation, holidays, sick leave, and workers compensation in the calculation of the amount due the owner-operator. The analysis assumes the owner-operator does not factor this cost into its cost per mile. The combination of prime carrier and owner-operator operation reduces the total cost from the cost incurred by the prime carrier alone because of the elimination of labor cost elements. Accordingly, the rate per mile could be reduced by this amount for competitive purposes.

The method of cost distribution provided in Tables 8.7 through 8.9 illustrates that the very nature of indirect or overhead cost precludes it from being allocated to specific transportation situations. Such costs are not directly attributable to a particular service, one reason they are labeled "indirect." It will be observed in the illustrations that the owner-operator indirect cost is $.201 per mile, while the prime carrier gets just $.018.

In terms of shipment cost distribution, the owner-operator would receive $201 for indirect cost on a 1,000-mile haul and the prime carrier would receive only $18. This distribution of cost is in reverse of the actual cost borne by each because the analysis is based on the prime carrier providing the trailer and doing the billing and sales work, and the owner-operator providing the bulk of the remaining direct cost. In reality, the indirect cost should be distributed at approximately \$201 to the prime carrier and \$18 to the owner-operator. Clearly, indirect cost does not always follow direct cost.

Where the revenue will be split, it is first necessary to determine the revenue required to perform the service, and then to allocate direct cost in accordance with the incremental cost of service provided by each participant. The indirect cost should be allocated to the party who incurs the cost. In Tables 8.7 through 8.9, the owner-operator incurs a direct cost of \$.953 for vehicle fixed cost, vehicle running cost, and the labor cost for driving the vehicle. It will also need to recover some indirect cost for telephone calls to the dispatch office and the receiver of freight to coordinate delivery. In addition, it is required to obtain signatures and perhaps perform other duties such as checking freight. Finally, the owner-operator must receive a profit from the operation. The prime carrier and owner-operator should agree, or the prime carrier should determine, that the owner-operator will receive compensation for overhead of some figure, such as the \$.027 per mile shown in our example. As a result, the owner-operator cost at break-even would be \$.980. The amount it should receive, including profit, would be \$1.049.

The prime carrier can make this determination in accordance with a detailed analysis of the indirect cost it incurred in obtaining the book of business. These costs would include sales costs and other overhead costs, such as communications, rent, utilities, and so on. The only substantial overhead costs avoided by the prime carrier in the transaction are dispatching and communicating with drivers; the owner-operator is expected to handle the shipment from start to finish, once loaded. Of course, each relationship is unique, and each must be evaluated within the particular circumstances involved.

The prime carrier would receive a direct cost of \$.13 for trailer rental plus an indirect cost of \$.201. These costs, including profit, would generate a revenue split for the prime carrier of \$.354. In this scenario, the owner-operator would receive 74.8% of the revenue, and the prime carrier would receive 25.2%.

It is important to remember that our figures are brought forward from earlier examples, and that such determinations are not representative of a particular service. This is particularly true of indirect cost. In an operation of this type, the overall ratio would be significantly less than the 17.4% developed in table 7.1.

Previously we discussed another motor carrier situation where revenue sharing is prevalent. Dump truck operations often use "pullers" to pull prime carrier trailers during large construction jobs. The procedure for developing revenue splits is similar to that discussed in connection with long-haul operations, although the various factors connected with the traffic are different. Revenue splits in dump-truck operations are predicated upon a percentage of revenue distributions. To demonstrate this concept, we again return to earlier calculations so that the reader can easily follow the development.

TABLE 8.10

DETERMINATION OF DUMP-TRUCK RATE PER HOUR

Line No.	Item	Amount
1.	Labor Cost (Table 4.15, Local driver)	$ 17.141
2.	Vehicle Fixed Cost (Table 5.9)	12.530
3.	Vehicle Running Cost (Table 6.7, 35 mph)	17.150
4.	Direct Cost Per Hour	$ 46.821
5.	Indirect Cost (Table 7.1)	9.863
6.	Cost at 100 O. R.	$ 56.684
7.	Rate at 93 O. R.	$ 60.65

Determination of vehicle running cost per hour involves cost per mile times the number of miles traveled per hour. The calculation does not involve running speed only while traveling; it is predicated upon miles traveled per hour during the entire trip, including loading and unloading times. For example, a round-trip service takes a half-hour to load and a half-hour to unload. Running speed while traveling is 55 miles per hour. Given these conditions, loading and unloading time is 1 hour and travel time is 1.82 hours, or 2.82 hours for the entire trip. In 2.82 hours, the vehicle traveled 100 miles, which is 35.5 miles per hour. Accordingly, in each hour, the vehicle traveled 35 miles at a cost of $.512 per mile.

The purpose of Table 8.10 is to illustrate the methods to produce an hourly rate for dump-truck service. From this table, underlying increments may be allocated to the carriers involved. The demonstration describes the situation where the overlying (prime) carrier hires a puller who furnishes the power unit and driver. Table 8.11 develops the proper split for the puller, using the illustrated costs.

TABLE 8.11

DETERMINATION OF "PULLER" REVENUE

Line No.	Item	Amount
1.	Labor Cost (Table 4.15, Local Driver)	$ 17.141
2.	Vehicle Fixed Cost (Table 5.7 and 5.8, tractor only)	7.369
3.	Vehicle Running Cost (Table 6.7, tractor only 35 mph)	14.420
4.	Direct Cost Per Hour	$ 38.930
5.	Indirect Cost	2.049
6.	Cost at 100 O. R. (5%)	$ 40.979
7.	Revenue Split at 93 O. R.	$ 43.85

Vehicle fixed cost in Table 5.7 for the tractor only was $13,265 per year. Annual use hours for this vehicle classification in Table 5.9 was 1,800 per year. Annual vehicle fixed cost divided by annual use hours produces the figure on line 2 of Table 8.11.

The prime carrier receives payment for trailer rental in the form of vehicle fixed cost and vehicle running cost for the trailer only. It also receives payment for its indirect cost, as shown in Table 8.12.

TABLE 8.12

DETERMINATION OF PRIME CARRIER REVENUE

Line No.	Item	Amount
1.	Trailer Fixed Cost Per Hour (Table 5.7 & 5.8)	$ 5.161
2.	Trailer Running Cost Per Hour (Table 6.7, 35 mph)	2.730
3.	Direct Cost Per Hour	$ 7.891
4.	Indirect Cost	7.811
5.	Cost at 100 O. R.	$ 15.702
6.	Revenue Split at 93 O. R.	$ 16.80

Both vehicle fixed cost on line 1, and vehicle running cost on line 2 use the cost for two short trailers in Table 5.7 because dump-truck units do not use a converter gear.

If the hourly rate to the shipper was $60.65, and the other assumptions were correct, the puller would receive 72.3% of the revenue, and the prime carrier would receive the other 27.7%.

The handling of indirect cost is similar to that utilized in connection with the owner-operator situation. The overlying carrier and the puller must determine the proper indirect cost incurred by the puller by analyzing the overhead items the "puller" will incur. Once that ratio is determined, the overlying carrier receives the remaining dollar amount to cover its indirect cost. The example in Table 8.11 assumed that the puller would need 5% to cover its cost of paperwork and communications. The dollar amount was calculated based upon the direct cost, and this amount was subtracted from the indirect dollar amount included in the rate in Table 8.10. This remainder is a part of the overlying carrier revenue split. Both the puller and overlying carrier receive a 7% profit based upon incurred cost. This method covers the cost of indirect items incurred by both parties as well as distributed profits.

Sub-hauling

The final component in the vehicle rental or leasing discussion is commonly called sub-hauling. Here, the prime carrier hires another carrier to perform the actual transportation. Before the prime carrier can hire another carrier, it must determine the cost and the rate that will be incurred for the transportation service. Where the direct cost is high in relation to the total cost, the prime carrier will receive less in terms of total cost recovery in the rate. Generally, the prime carrier will receive the indirect cost, and the sub-hauler will receive the direct cost. The prime carrier sells the service, bills the customer, dispatches the equipment, takes responsibility for the transportation, and oversees the overall performance; the sub-hauler provides the transportation itself.

By analysis of its own expected cost to provide service, a prime carrier can determine the split to be paid the sub-hauler. The prime carrier can expect the sub-hauler to incur substantially the same direct cost because it will expect its sub-haulers to perform to the prime carrier's level. In other words, the prime carrier knows its cost and productivity standards and demands the same level of service from its sub-haulers. The volume of business is reduced for sub-haulers who do not perform to these standards. However, if the prime carrier sets too high a standard, it may find difficulty in obtaining sub-haulers. The final test is, of course, dollars. If the prime carrier does not pay its sub-haulers in a timely fashion, the service will ultimately suffer.

A final caution on prime carrier responsibility: it cannot supervise the methods by which a sub-hauler performs its work. If the sub-hauler is truly an independent contractor, the prime carrier cannot prescribe operating methods. It can, however, discontinue using unsatisfactory sub-haulers.

A prime carrier will perform the same analysis as that shown in Tables 8.7 through 8.9, modified for existing conditions, to properly price its product and fairly treat its sub-haulers. The sub-hauler should be paid for direct cost to provide the service plus a small increment of indirect cost and an appropriate profit margin. The overlying, or booking, carrier should receive its indirect cost and a similar increment of profit.

Rental and Leasing Summary

Many shippers and receivers of freight who elected to purchase and operate trucks to distribute their own products will soon begin to prepare new evaluations of those earlier decisions. Many of those decisions were made in the 1970s and 1980s when it was fashionable to believe that the for-hire trucking industry was out of step in terms of pricing. With expected price competition in the new environment, astute traffic or transportation managers operating a private company fleet should begin to search for alternate distribution strategies. Such evaluations will include an analysis of carrier cost methods, such as those described in this book, to compare private and for-hire fleets.

Private operations can make the same use of this material because direct cost preparation in the operation of motor vehicles is no different in the private fleet. Additionally, equipment rental firms will more aggressively sell their products and expand their existing markets to include vehicle-with-driver leasing agreements. With all of these sources available, many vehicle-owned private fleets will cease to exist, and shippers will concentrate financial resources on product manufacturing.

Carrier relationships in the new environment may become strained as participants jockey for position. Overlying carriers will attempt to extract a larger share of the revenue in carrier-to-carrier arrangements that include owner-operators, pullers, and sub-haulers. Owner-operators will find it absolutely essential to know their operating cost before negotiating terms with overlying carriers. We cannot overemphasize the fact that owner-operators must include in their cost analysis the vehicle fixed cost methodology described in this book. To do otherwise could mean that a tractor could become worn out with no funds available for its replacement!

 # Specialized Motor Carriers

Until now, our discussion of cost-finding techniques has been associated with rate assessments on an hourly or other time period. Of all trucking price structures, these rates are the least complicated. In this chapter, we will discuss productivity measurements and their impact upon rate-making. First, however, a brief exploration into the types of carrier we call "specialized" will be helpful.

Specialized carriers are those that operate in a radial fashion from one yard or terminal, transporting shipments in truckload quantities. Vehicles leave the point of domicile and return to that same point at the end of the work period. The other common characteristic is that they specialize by commodity or groups of commodities. For cost-finding purposes, all such carriers operate in much the same fashion, transporting commodities in truckload quantities and incurring costs for loading, transporting, and unloading one shipment at a time. Direct cost development generally involves only a single employee, the driver, as opposed to household goods carriers or LTL general freight carriers which use several employee classifications in direct operations.

Finally, these carriers generally provide service for a limited number of shippers, which means the transportation lends itself to a contract-type service rather than a common carriage service. A tank truck carrier, for example, may transport only petroleum products, or it may transport petroleum and other chemical mixtures compatible with petroleum products and tank construction. Such commodities may include fertilizers, pesticides, and fungicides, among others. Tank carriers of caustics and other highly specialized liquid products operate more exotic trailers, and incur costs different from normal tank operations because of their higher trailer cost and different loading characteristics. By "normal tank operations," we refer to the transportation of refined petroleum products from the refinery to bulk purchasers such as other motor carriers, automobile service stations, and bulk distribution plants. Asphalt carriers are also included in this category although they have different transportation characteristics.

Bulk food-grade carriers that transport liquid sugar, molasses, and other food products are a significant part of the specialized carrier group. Also included in this category are bulk carriers of sugar, flour, and other bulk dry food products. These carriers provide specially designed trailers constructed of high-grade stainless steel. Most adhere to high specifications for cleanliness.

Bulk cement carriers transport products such as flyash and specialty sand in addition to cement. These carriers incur a different set of cost conditions due to trailer construction, location of points of origin, and length-of-haul peculiarities. In some geographic areas, marketing of cement by producers is a highly competitive industry. The competition occurs between several producers located at a distance from the market. One cement mill may be located 50 miles from a metropolitan area; another competitor may be 20 miles away.

Historically, the transportation cost has been used as one method to equalize the distribution cost. For example, the mill located 50 miles from the market may request that its servicing carrier reduce its rate for 50 miles in return for some shorter-haul traffic at a relatively higher rate. This practice allows the mill to compete in a distant market by equalizing the distribution cost in the closer market.

These circumstances can spell trouble for the uninformed carrier. If the carrier has not properly distributed its operating cost through mileage brackets served, or if the shipper tenders an imbalance of shipments by length of haul, the unsuspecting carrier can find itself in financial difficulty. When the carrier grants long-haul price concessions in return for relatively higher short-haul rates but receives no short-haul loads, it suffers a net loss. Transportation of cement requires a higher degree of shipper/carrier cooperation and a better understanding of transportation needs than in most other relationships.

Dump-truck transportation is another specialized service with unique operating characteristics. Dump-truck carriers conduct operations in two major circumstances: construction or inter-plant hauls. Construction hauling is often vehicle-intensive in that a large number of vehicles may be required for a short period of time. For example, when hot mix is laid during highway construction, dump trucks must be in line at the site to drop the mix as the laying machines work. Delays one way or the other can create significant losses to contractors. Inter-plant hauling which involves repeated pickup and delivery from the production area to the final manufacturing plant is more routine.

Flatbed carriers make up a large portion of specialized carrier service. They transport products other than bulk in truckload quantities for any length of haul. Short-haul flatbed carriers do not usually split revenue among overlying and sub-hauling entities, but they may use the owner-operator concept in long-haul service.

Household goods carriers are obviously specialized, but that industry differs from those under discussion primarily because of carrier relationships and the nature of the goods transported. The household goods industry consists of van lines and agents who interact in the production of overall service. Economics of this very personal and highly regulated service will be discussed in following chapters.

The purpose of this introductory discussion of truckload specialized transportation is to illustrate the similarities in the various operations. There are, however, enough significant differences to keep from lumping all of these systems into one cost study. For example, if a carrier operates regular tank trailers for liquid products and pneumatic hoppers for dry bulk products, it should not assess one rate for both operations because the operating costs are not the same. Average load, trailer cost, load and unload times, and other characteristics warrant separate cost and rate development. From a pricing perspective, all specialized carriers except household goods develop identical operating circumstances. That is, they all transport truckload shipments moving various lengths of haul.

Following our previous discussion of determining labor, vehicle fixed cost, and vehicle running cost as they relate to direct operating cost, and of determining indirect cost, we now move on to the more refined concepts used in carrier pricing.

Up to now, our discussions have been limited to an hourly or other basis of pricing. However, specialized carriers offer three different price structures: rates expressed in terms of incremental distances (commonly called distance rates); rates that apply between specified points (often called point-to-point rates); and volume-incentive rates. Once the carrier has prepared the cost and the rate for each of these structures, it is prepared to offer transportation normally required by all shippers using specialized truckload motor carriers.

The introduction of distance into the pricing of motor carrier service means that we must measure some productivity elements. Two of these measurements can be prepared from a field study of actual company operations: loading and unloading time per shipment, and running speed by length of haul. To make these measurements, the driver, or an observer, must complete trip reports similar to that provided in Appendix A, Form 5. From the information produced during a sample period reflecting the scope of transportation under study, the analyst can develop the productivity factors.

To discover the average loading time, the analyst would need to compile all loading times, and divide that result by the number of observations. The end result would be average loading time for the product transported. This procedure is repeated to determine the figure for unloading time. These two figures produce the time to be used in the cost formula.

The productivity measurement to determine travel time is running speed. For each trip in the sample, the running speed from the shipment point of origin to its point of destination is determined. The speed at each point-to-point measurement is marked on a scattergram showing distance on the horizontal plane and speed on the vertical plane (see Graph 9.1). Once all the speed observations are indicated in the graph, the analyst draws a trend line that represents their dispersal. The line should be a smooth curve, not a point-to-point line.

GRAPH 9.1

RUNNING SPEED SAMPLE

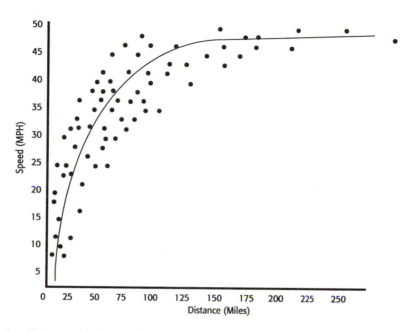

It will be noted that as distance increases, the rise in speed is reduced. This is caused by traffic conditions, vehicle configuration, and speed laws. It is generally conceded that, if a driver obeys speed laws, the highest trip speed from point of origin to point of destination will be 46 to 48 miles per hour. Short haul, on the other hand, is more heavily impacted by traffic congestion.

If sample trips are representative of the scope of business, a curve, such as that illustrated, will be produced. From time to time, the analyst may observe a trip that does not conform to the overall sample. For example, if a speed of 10 miles per hour is observed for a 100-mile trip, the observation should be discarded. The driver may have entered faulty data; the trip may have involved some unusual condition such as breakdown; or some other situation occurred that rendered the observation unusable.

In most regulated environments, agencies have permitted rates to be set based upon a round-trip cost for a one-way haul. That is, while the outbound load receives no return load, the equipment must be returned to the original loading point or to the point of domicile. There is considerable merit to this philosophy. Historically, cost studies prepared by regulatory agencies or outside petitioners to establish trucking rates have demonstrated that specialized carriers do, in fact, transport only one way, with some exceptions. The major exception is flatbed trucking where carriers are frequently able to obtain return loads.

We classified these carriers as "specialized" because many of these operations are radial in nature; they transport truckload quantities, and they use a single employee, the driver. There are many reasons for a specialized carrier to load only one way. The trailing equipment may be designed to transport only a limited family of commodities, making back-haul or cross-haul extremely difficult to obtain. Shippers of specialized commodities may be located in areas where no return traffic is available. No return shipments may be available for dump-truck carriers in construction work, or, if they are available, the carrier cannot coordinate them with the tight outbound schedule.

The concept of round-trip cost for one-way transportation provides a clear demonstration of cost analysis for distance rate-making. In Table 9.1 we have randomly selected conditions that might be found in the round-trip operation of a tank truck, a pneumatic hopper, and a dump-truck carrier or other similar operation.

TABLE 9.1

DEVELOPMENT OF TRIP COST — BY LENGTH OF HAUL

Line No.	Item	Length of Haul (Miles)				
		10	25	50	100	250
1.	Load Time	.75	.75	.75	.75	.75
2.	Unloading Time	1.00	1.00	1.00	1.00	1.00
3.	Loading/Unloading Time	1.75	1.75	1.75	1.75	1.75
4.	Running Speed (Graph 9.1)	15	23	34	43	47
5.	Running Time (Round trip)	1.33	2.17	2.94	4.65	10.64
6.	Trip Time	3.08	3.92	4.69	6.40	12.39
7.	Labor Cost (Table 4.15 Line Driver $18.051)	$ 55.597	$ 70.760	$ 84.659	$115.526	$223.652
8.	Vehicle Fixed Cost (Table 5.9, $12.828)	39.510	50.286	60.163	82.099	158.939
9.	Vehicle Running Cost (Table 6.7, $.512)	10.240	25.600	51.200	102.400	256.000
10.	Total Direct Cost	$ 105.347	$146.646	$196.022	$300.025	$638.591
11.	Indirect Cost (Table 7.1)	22.192	30.892	41.293	63.201	134.522
12.	Total Cost at 100 O. R.	$ 127.539	$177.538	$237.315	$363.226	$773.113
13.	Revenue at 93 O. R.	$ 136.47	$ 189.97	$253.93	$ 388.65	$ 827.23
14.	Average Load	52,000	52,000	52,000	52,000	52,000
15.	Rate Per 100 Pounds	$ .262	$ .365	$ .488	$ .747	$ 1.591

Trip time is comprised of loading, unloading, and running time, all of which are determined by compiling data from a field survey of representative trips. Loading and unloading time is not affected by speed and, therefore, does not change as distance changes. Running time, on the other hand, is a function of speed that does change with distance. Table 9.1 demonstrates the methodology used for determining the final cost and the rate at specific distances.

Once the trip time is determined, it is related to the various direct cost elements necessary to provide the service. The cost per hour for labor and vehicle fixed cost are multiplied by.the round-trip hours required for each trip length of haul. The running cost per mile is multiplied by the round-trip miles at each cost point. The illustration assumes that there is no return load. Direct cost is expanded by a factor of 17.4% to include indirect cost, as illustrated in Table 7.1.

In summary, Table 9.1 represents full cost per trip and a rate per 100 pounds by length of haul. The rate is predicated upon an operating ratio of 93 to produce a profit of 7%. (For discussion of this concept, see Chapter 7.) For demonstration purposes, it does not matter whether the vehicles are pneumatic hoppers, flatbeds, dump trucks, or tank trucks. Cost by length of haul is determined in the same fashion for all specialty carriers discussed in this chapter. The numbers would change, of course, because our examples do not represent a particular set of conditions. In practice, the analyst would substitute the proper figures for the service studied. Finally, if the analyst were to plot the rate per 100 pounds at each mileage point on a line graph, he or she would find a straight line progression.

The field study necessary to compile the trip times and their components relies upon data collected in Form 5, Appendix A. The form is designed to provide the load and unload times, running speed, length of haul, and other data necessary to measure specific transportation cost. Once compiled, the various time increments are brought forward to schedules, such as that set forth in Table 9.2.

TABLE 9.2

SUMMARY OF DRIVER TRIP REPORTS

Trip #	Veh #	Lv/Ar. Time	Yard Odo.	#	Arrive Origin Time	Odo.	#	Depart Origin Time	Odo.	#	Arrive Destination Time	Odo.	#	Depart Destination Time	Odo.	Weight
1	320	0730	200	1	0815	225	1	0850	225	1	1010	277	1	1100	277	51,200
1				2	1130	302	2	1215	302	2	1420	387	2	1500	387	51,100
1		1630	462													
2	320	0730	462	1	0930	542	1	1005	542	1	1040	562	1	1135	562	52,200
2				2	1345	659	2	1415	659	2	1500	682	2	1550	682	51,600
2		1635	708													
3	320	0730	708	1	1000	819	1	1130	819	1	1415	924	1	1510	924	50,600
3		1650	1007													
4	320	0800	1007	1	0830	1022	1	0945	1022	1	1045	1060	1	1115	1060	51,140
4				2	1200	1093	2	1230	1093	2	1300	1113	2	1350	1113	50,000
4				3	1415	1123	3	1500	1123	3	1530	1140	3	1600	1140	51,420
4				4	1645	1165	4	1715	1165	4	1730	1168	4	1745	1168	51,100
4		1815	1188													
5	320	0715	1188	1	1130	1380	1	1215	1380	1	1300	1396	1	1400	1396	52,000
5		1830	1594													

Table 9.2 is a hypothetical summary of the field survey of each day's work for one unit of carrier's equipment for one 5-day week. Similar reports should be prepared for each unit of equipment (in combination) used during the test period. The format of Table 9.2 can be achieved in Lotus, Excel or other software to facilitate data processing applications. The test period should be sufficiently comprehensive to produce results that will reflect the entire operation under study. Two summaries should be made for bulk and sack cement, for example, as the transportation characteristics of these two commodities are quite different. Sack cement transportation requires longer load and unload times than bulk cement because sacks are loaded a pallet at a time. Differences in vehicle fixed cost exist as well. Flatbed trailers for sack cement are much less expensive than pneumatic hopper trailers for bulk cement. For accuracy, the two operations should be rated as separate commodities.

From Table 9.2, we can extract trip performance information to be used in preparation of tables similar to Table 9.3. It may be observed that all times and mileages for each leg of each trip are recorded in Table 9.3. The purpose is to isolate each of these legs in a fashion that will provide elapsed time and distance for each function. From the analysis of each function, we may draw some conclusions about ways to improve carrier operations to maximize profits and efficiency.

TABLE 9.3

ELAPSED TIME AND DISTANCE REPORT

Trip #	Veh. #	Stem Time	From Miles	Stem Time	To Miles	Total Time	Stem Miles	Load Time	Unload Time	Run Time	Loaded Miles	Run Time	Empty Miles	Weight
1.1	320	.75	25	-	-	.75	25	.58	.83	1.33	52	.50	25	51,200
1.2	320							.75	.67	2.08	85	1.50	75	51,100
2.1	320	2.00	-	-	80	2.00	80	.58	.92	.58	20	2.17	97	52,200
2.2	320							.50	.83	.75	23	.75	26	51,600
3.1	320	2.50	111	-	-	2.50	111	1.50	.92	2.75	105	1.67	83	50,600
4.1	320	.50	15	-	-	.50	15	1.25	.50	1.00	38	.75	33	51,140
4.2	320							.50	.83	.50	20	.42	10	50,000
4.3	320							.75	.50	.50	17	.75	25	51,420
4.4	320							.50	.25	.25	3	.50	20	51,100
5.1	320	4.25	192	-	-	4.25	192	.75	1.00	.75	16	4.50	198	52,000

Table 9.3 changes the incremental times in Table 9.2 to hundredths of an hour for each trip function. The average of the loading and unloading times can be determined by adding the appropriate column and dividing the result by the number of observations. From the distance and time indicated for the loaded portion of each trip, the running speed in miles per hour can be determined and plotted on a scattergram. Speed at the predetermined cost study points are then read from the line drawn to represent the points on the scattergram. This procedure is illustrated in Graph 9.1.

The analyst must determine which lengths of haul will be studied as most representative of the firm's distribution pattern. There should be enough selected points to provide a track of cost through all mileage brackets. For the illustration, we selected haul lengths of 10, 25, 50, 100, and 250 miles. With the data accumulated for the service under study, a table similar to Table 9.1 may be prepared. If the carrier operates longer hauls, the analyst should add a cost point at 500 miles, or farther. The selection of cost points is subjective, but at least four should be used to assure that a track will be produced. The purpose of the track will be discussed later in this chapter in connection with the final rate-making.

It will be observed that continuity of numbers does not exist between Tables 9.1, 9.2, and 9.3. The time measurements in Table 9.1 were randomly selected, and are not consistent with the brief analysis in the other two tables. The purpose of Tables 9.2 and 9.3 is to set up a worksheet that you can use to determine your own average productivity per trip by length of haul.

There are significant differences between the regulatory concept of round-trip cost for a one-way haul and actual practice. If the carrier recovers a round-trip cost from the point of origin to the point of destination, such cost may or may not cover all of the costs incurred. Also, if the carrier can obtain back-hauls or cross-hauls, it will be in position to offer significant concessions to shippers. These two concepts have substantial impact upon rate structures.

A major characteristic to consider is what we term "stem time and miles." These are miles and time incurred by the carrier that cannot be charged to the shipper. Carriers who attempt to extract a charge from a shipper for the cost of getting the carrier's vehicles to the shipper's facility, or of returning them, may experience some difficulty in attracting repeat business! This cost, however, must be recovered in the rate structure to prevent net operating losses.

Included in stem miles and time are the costs of traveling from the carrier's point of domicile to the first point of origin, and from the last point of destination to the point of domicile. The costs of both driver non-revenue time and stem time and miles are real costs of doing business in for-hire trucking. However, these elements of the operating cost must be closely scrutinized so that rates can be reduced by improving productivity. Reducing driver non-revenue time and stem cost will increase productivity, reduce rates, and improve the competitive position.

In the labor cost discussion, it was pointed out that drivers on the carrier payroll perform functions that cannot be charged to a shipper as a separate rate. These may include vehicle maintenance and safety checks, that, while an absolute necessity to the operation, cannot be applied to a particular shipment. We also asserted that if the carrier incurs higher non-revenue cost for its drivers than its competitors, it will not be competitive.

Stem cost can be regarded in the same light. Simply put, the farther a carrier is located from its market, the less competitive it is in terms of price. If a carrier must travel 40 miles to the point of origin each day, and its competitor travels only 10, the carrier is at a disadvantage. That travel distance is an incurred cost that must somehow be recovered in revenue, or the carrier will suffer a loss. The method used to include this cost in the rate structure is termed "the ratio of loaded to total miles." We must determine how many miles and how much time is used in getting to and from the job, and relate that result to the performance factors described in Table 9.1.

A straightforward example will suffice. The carrier is to provide transportation for a 100-mile haul, and all other performance factors are as those shown in Table 9.1. The carrier's equipment is domiciled 15 miles from the loading facility, and 115 miles from the point of delivery. The equipment must travel 15 miles to load, 100 miles loaded, and 115 miles back to its point of domicile. Instead of the 200 miles traveled in the round trip in Table 9.1, the equipment must travel 230 miles to perform the same transportation. The 100-mile haul in Table 9.1 would, therefore, appear as set forth in Table 9.4.

TABLE 9.4

TRIP COST FOR 100 MILE HAUL

Line No.	Item	Length of Haul 100 Miles
1.	Load Time	.75
2.	Unload Time	1.00
3.	Load/Unload Time	1.75
4.	Running Speed	43
5.	Running Time (230 miles)	5.35
6.	Trip Time	7.10
7.	Labor Cost (Table 4.15, 18.051)	$ 128.162
8.	Vehicle Fixed Cost (Table 5.9, $12.828)	91.079
9.	Vehicle Running Cost (Table 6.7, 230 miles)	117.760
10.	Direct Cost	$ 337.001
11.	Indirect Cost	70.991
12.	Total Cost at 100 O. R.	$ 407.992
13.	Cost at 93 O. R.	$ 436.55
14.	Average Weight per Shipment	52,000
15.	Rate per 100 Pounds	$ .840

Location away from the points of origin and destination in the hypothetical example create an additional 30 miles, adding .7 of an hour to the trip time, and requiring the carrier to charge the shipper an additional $47.90 for each trip in comparison with a 100-mile trip in table 9.1. Put another way, if the carrier does not include the $47.90 in its price structure, it breaks even or operates at a loss.

Accordingly, if a competitor is located closer to the shipper's or receiver's facilities, the firm in our example would find it difficult to compete. In truck transportation, the carrier's location in relation to the market it serves is critical. Empty miles to or from the carrier's domicile create competitive disadvantages difficult to overcome. On the other hand, carrier facilities strategically located in terms of market produce significantly lower cost and related pricing.

Our example of the 100-mile haul in Table 9.4 illustrates the importance of desirable carrier location in terms of market. The example is overly simple, however, because carrier equipment is not normally dispatched as shown. Good dispatch would attempt to combine loads to improve the productivity of both vehicle and driver. In that event, cost of stem miles and time are distributed equally among shipments transported in the same unit of equipment.

If, after performing a second load, the stem time and miles remained unchanged in Table 9.4, each shipment would include 15 miles and .35 of an hour, with corresponding reductions in trip cost and rate. Each shipment would bear its fair share of stem cost.

The second issue in connection with the ratio of loaded to total miles is back-haul or cross-haul. We define back-haul as a return load from or near the point of delivery of the outbound shipment. Cross-haul is defined as a return load obtained in such a manner that the distance and cost would be less than if the unit returned empty. The ratio of loaded to total miles considers both stem miles and time as well as the back-haul. If carrier dispatch is efficient, the ratio will always be more than 50, which means that the unit of equipment is loaded more than half of the time, including stem miles. Analysis similar to that provided in Tables 9.2 and 9.3 will provide the data necessary to determine the ratio of loaded to total miles at the cost points in the study. The analyst should treat each load as a single trip, from the time the equipment is loaded, travels to the unload point and unloads, to the time it travels to the point of domicile, or next loading point. A shipment ends upon reaching the reloading point or return to the point of domicile.

For recording purposes, each trip must be categorized according to length of haul so that a table similar to Table 9.1 may be prepared. The loaded length of haul determines the mileage point to which each shipment should be posted. Accordingly, all shipments moving loaded for distances up to 17.5 miles would be included in the 10-mile trip performance. The 25-mile trip performance would include loads moving between 17.5 and 37.5 miles, and so on.

The ratio of loaded to total miles in each bracket is determined from the total miles, including stem miles and loaded and empty miles posted from the trip reports. The analyst should recall that stem miles are apportioned equally to each load transported by each unit of equipment. The illustration in Table 9.3 included 433 stem miles and 10 loads in the 5-day period. The stem miles allocated to each shipment would be 43.3, with each one bearing its fair share of the cost.

A third worksheet summary of trip reports is necessary to properly construct the ratio of loaded to total miles. This worksheet determines the ratio for each vehicle during the study period. During the day each vehicle is dispatched to transport several loads of different lengths. The analyst should set up a worksheet that will show the overall ratio of loaded to total miles for each unit, each day during the study period. It should also indicate the same ratio for each load transported, by length of haul.

To find the overall ratio of loaded to total miles, the number of empty miles, including stem miles, are determined. The number of loaded miles are also found. The total of these two figures is the number of miles traveled by the unit during the day. A ratio of the loaded miles to the total miles is determined by dividing the number of loaded miles by the number of total miles. The ratio is then posted to each length of haul transported within the mileage brackets previously selected. Examples of cost study points by length of haul in this chapter have been 10, 25, 50, 100, and 250 miles. A randomly selected set of numbers will illustrate the procedure.

TABLE 9.5

DETERMINATION OF RATIO OF LOADED TO TOTAL MILES

Line No.	Item	Total	Length of Haul (Miles)				
			10	25	50	100	250
1.	Day 1, Vehicle #1	55.3		55.3		55.3	
2.	Day 1, Vehicle #2	54.6	54.6	54.6			
3.	Day 1, Vehicle #3	56.4					56.4
4.	Day 1, Vehicle #4	55.8			55.8		
5.	Day 1, Vehicle #5	52.2		52.2			
6.	Day 2, Vehicle #1	54.5	54.3				
			54.5				
			54.6				
7.	Day 2, Vehicle #2	56.4		56.5			
				56.3			
8.	Day 2, Vehicle #3	56.6					56.6
9.	Day 2, Vehicle #4	56.6				56.6	
10.	Day 2, Vehicle #5	55.2			55.2		
	Average	55.4	54.5	55.0	55.5	56.0	56.5

This table shows that 55.4% of the time the vehicles were operating with loads. It also shows the ratio for each loaded trip during the work period. The individual ratios are averaged to obtain the ratio by length of haul.

This procedure may also be used when the carrier is preparing a job bid. If the carrier has other work to blend with the proposed bid, it can determine the proposed rate using the ratio of loaded to total miles.

The ratio should always be greater than 50; anything less indicates that more than half of the miles are empty ones. As the ratio increases, empty miles decrease, resulting in higher productivity and lower rates. Studies have indicated specialized carriers have ratios of approximately 56. Studies also indicate that the ratio of loaded to total miles increases slightly as the outbound length of haul increases. Carriers resist running equipment empty for long distances, and tend to hire good dispatchers who coordinate long-haul shipments with return loads.

To illustrate the impact of the ratio upon rates, we have duplicated the figures in Table 9.1, and added the ratio. This table employs the same productivity measurements as the earlier table, and it also indicates the reduction in rate that may result from applying the ratio of loaded to total miles.

TABLE 9.6

DEVELOPMENT OF TRIP COST AND RATE BY LENGTH OF HAUL

Line No.	Item	Length of Haul (Miles)				
		10	25	50	100	250
1.	Load Time	.75	.75	.75	.75	.75
2.	Unload Time	1.00	1.00	1.00	1.00	1.00
3.	Load/Unload Time	1.75	1.75	1.75	1.75	1.75
4.	Running Speed	15	23	34	43	47
5.	Ratio of Loaded to Total Miles	.545	.550	.555	.560	.565
6.	Trip Miles	18.3	45.5	90.1	178.6	442.5
7.	Trip Running Time	1.22	1.98	2.65	4.15	9.41
8.	Trip Time	2.97	3.73	4.40	5.90	11.16
9.	Labor Cost (Table 4.15, Line Driver $18.051)	$ 53.611	$ 67.330	$ 79.424	$106.501	$ 201.449
10.	Vehicle fixed cost (Table 5.9 $12.828)	38.099	47.848	56.443	75.685	143.160
11.	Vehicle running cost (Table 6.7 $.512)	9.370	23.296	46.131	91.443	226.560
12.	Total Direct Cost	$101.080	$ 138.474	$181.998	$273.629	$ 571.169
13.	Indirect Cost	21.293	29.170	38.339	57.641	120.319
14.	Total Cost at 100 O. R.	$122.373	$ 167.644	$220.337	$331.270	$ 691.488
15.	Revenue at 93 O. R.	$130.939	$ 179.379	$235.761	$354.459	$ 739.892
16.	Average Load	52,000	52,000	52,000	52,000	52,000
17.	Rate per 100 Pounds	$ .252	$ .345	$ .453	$ .682	$ 1.423
18.	Rate per 100 Pounds Table 9.1	$ .262	$ .365	$ .488	$ .748	$ 1.588
19.	Percent Reduction	3.8	5.5	7.2	8.8	10.4

The two additional lines in Table 9.6 measure the impact of a change in loaded miles resulting from stem miles and return loading. When the ratio of loaded to total miles is imputed into the cost formula, the number of miles that can be charged to individual shipments is reduced. In Table 9.1 we used round-trip miles for each length of haul, employing the theory that truckload specialized carriers cannot obtain return loads. In Table 9.6, miles and time were reduced because of a higher loaded ratio, even though stem miles were also added. Trip miles are determined by dividing the figures in line 5 into the one-way miles at each length of haul. This clearly demonstrates in line 19 that when carriers obtain back-haul or cross-haul loads, rates are reduced, even when stem miles are included.

Throughout this chapter we have examined productivity characteristics found in specialized truck transportation. The average load, or load factor, is one of the productivity elements not discussed because it is characteristic of this transportation that all shipments be loaded to vehicle maximum weight. However, the average load is the divisor used to convert a cost per trip to a cost per 100 pounds. Not the vehicle maximum load capacity.

The running speed is similar for all specialized carriers; competitors rarely receive an edge, although running speed can be affected if drivers tend to stop frequently, or have poor skills. Both the load factor and the running speed can be monitored by reading driver trip reports. The analyst can readily determine when a driver consistently transports shipments at weights below the company average, or takes longer on comparable trips.

Major competitive advantage accrues to the carrier who develops better back-haul or cross-haul balance, or is located closer to the market.

On Line 17, Table 9.5, we developed a rate per 100 pounds after taking into account stem miles and loaded to total miles. Also, it indicated a rate at the cost points based upon a profit margin of 7%. The next step in preparing the rate structure is to apply these rates at the cost points to a scale of mileage rates. To develop a line graph of rates, we plot each of these points on a line graph where the horizontal plane is distance, and the vertical plane is the rates. Graph 9.2 represents the rates at cost points developed in Table 9.6.

GRAPH 9.2

RATE PER 100 POUNDS

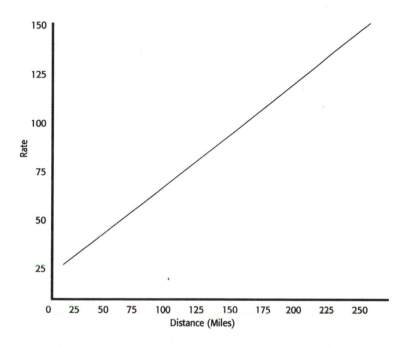

The relatively straight line drawn between the rates indicates the applicable rate at any point on the graph. By reading the line, we can procure a scale of distance rates, such as that shown in Table 9.7.

TABLE 9.7

SPECIALIZED CARRIER DISTANCE RATES (In cents per 100 pounds)

Miles	Rate	Miles	Rate
0-5	22	100-110	*75
5-10	*24	110-120	81
10-15	*27	120-130	86
15-20	30	130-140	91
20-25	*33 1/2	140-150	96
25-30	*36 1/2	150-160	102
30-35	38 1/2	160-170	108
35-40	40 3/4	170-180	114
40-45	42 1/4	180-190	120
45-50	*44	190-200	126
50-60	*46	200-220	132
60-70	51	220-240	*138
70-80	56	240-260	*145
80-90	62	260-280	152
90-100	*67 1/4	280-300	159

Rates in Table 9.7 are predicated on figures in line 17 of Table 9.6. The first step in preparation of the distance rates is to enter the rate at the cost points, indicated by the asterisks in Table 9.7. In this case, the cost points are between two mileage brackets in the rate scale. For example, the rate in Table 9.6 at 10 miles is $.252; however, at that point in Table 9.7, there is a break in the mileage brackets of 5-10 and 10-15 miles. When this occurs, the rate is split so that the rate in the 5-10 mileage bracket is slightly less than the cost point, and the next higher mileage bracket is slightly higher.

After the rates at the cost points are entered, the line in Graph 9.2 is used as a guide to enter rates at intermediate points. It is not necessary to enter the exact rate at each mileage point; it is more important to produce a flow of rates through all of the mileage brackets to prevent large increments of increase followed by little increase. As the mileage goes up, the incremental increase in the rate also rises. The rate scale begins with an increase of 2 cents, and ends, at 300 miles, with an increase of 7 cents in rate. The mileage brackets in the short haul are narrow, just 5 miles. At longer distances, the brackets increase to 20 miles. Accordingly, a single rate at a longer length of haul must cover a wide range of distance.

The primary criteria in designing distance rates is maintaining a consistent relationship with the cost points, and, as nearly as possible, entering the same rate as read from the line graph while maintaining a smooth progression through the mileage brackets. In the days of a regulated environment, rate scales such as those illustrated in this chapter were included in tariffs issued by tariff publishing bureaus or by the regulatory agency. In free-market pricing, the carrier must develop some strategy for replacing the published tariffs. Initially, there will be a tendency to quote rates from old tariffs, but it will not take long for carriers to realize that most of those tariffs are already outdated. Clinging to the old rate structures by continuing the discount practice is a short-term solution, if it is a solution at all.

Carriers are faced with decisions about how they will inform shippers of pricing policies. They must also make decisions in directing the sales force. Without a current tariff for reference, the sales staff will not have price guidelines with which to sell company services. To address those issues, sound management will want to develop a pricing schedule that will project a positive image for the company rather than continuing to use old tariffs that many found difficult to understand. There is now an opportunity to design a promotional piece that can set the price structure in attractive terms.

In Table 9.7, we have provided one method for the carrier to use in advising its sales staff of rates: "these are our published rates; prior approval must be obtained from the sales manager before any deviation from these rates can be quoted to our customers." The distance rates developed in-house also can be included in a public relations piece. Such a piece would project the image of a competent firm concerned with pricing strategies for the benefit of its customers.

The distance rate scale is not, in itself, sufficient to establish and maintain a solid pricing system. The transportation system has not changed just because rates are no longer regulated; carriers must still offer a full range of services. Many of the accessorial services will need to be priced and provided to the shipping public. The remainder of this chapter will be devoted to cost and rate design of such services.

Anyone who has read a tariff recognizes that carriers quote rates for a variety of services. Few, however, have been required to design accessorial rates because that work previously has been done by tariff bureaus, or others. Accessorial rates encompass all services usually associated with trucking, including minimum shipment weights, free-time allowance, stop-in-transit, extra helpers, standby or demurrage, reconsignment and diversion, and so on. After reading this discussion, the analyst will be able to design rates predicated upon individual cost circumstances. The concept of design is similar in all instances. If a particular service is not described, the analyst will learn how to design applicable rates from the examples shown.

Minimum Weight Per Shipment is an important rule. It precludes a shipper from tendering a low-weight shipment that may not cover the cost of transportation. Minimum truckload shipment weights are normally set 1,000 to 2,000 pounds below average weights transported. Most specialized products are loaded to capacity, which means that the average load weights are between 50,000 and 55,000 pounds, depending upon the equipment configuration and weight laws. When a maximum shipment weight is 54,000 pounds, and the shipment weights average 53,000 pounds, the minimum weight per shipment is pegged at 52,000. This allows shippers to roam between 52,000 and 54,000 pounds.

"Free time" is the average time in loading and the average time unloading before additional charges begin. Free time can be quoted with a time allowance for loading and a separate time for unloading, or it can be established with one time increment applying to both.

The object of free time is to provide the customer with time limits for loading or unloading before an additional charge for standby is accrued. In Table 9.6, average times of 45 minutes for loading and 1 hour for unloading are used. For the sake of discussion, it is assumed that all specialized commodities require these times, although they may be higher than actual times. Our example assumes that they were actual times determined from a field survey of company operations.

To prevent shippers or receivers from retaining equipment for inordinate periods of time, the carrier should allow a specified time in the rate structure, when shipments are rated on a basis other than per hour. Time over the specified time receives an additional charge for standby. A typical free time rule might read as follows:

> *The rates provided for transportation at distance rates include 1 hour free time for loading and 1.5 hours for unloading. Time in excess of the free time shall be assessed at an additional charge of $10 for each quarter hour, or fraction thereof.*

How can individual carriers determine the correct additional charge? By following the same procedures as outlined in all of our demonstrations, a rate may be determined as follows:

Driver cost per hour	$ 18.051
Vehicle fixed cost per hour	12.828
Direct cost per hour	$ 30.879
Direct and indirect cost per hour	$ 37.384
Rate at 93 operating ratio	$ 40.00

The cost per hour employs the same direct cost increments as those used in Table 9.6, which are also the same costs as those developed in earlier chapters. The same indirect ratio is employed. Accordingly, since every rate must return a profit or other rates would subsidize this service, the $40 per hour rate includes a 7% profit margin. The running cost is not included because the vehicle is not moving while on standby.

Another rate often employed is Accessorial Services, which is really a catchall rate. It is also referred to as an Extra Helper rate. The purpose of this rate is to provide a method for the carrier to assess the shipper a charge for incidental work performed by carrier employees.

A typical Accessorial Services rate might read like this:

> *In the event carrier employees perform work not otherwise included in the transportation rate, an additional charge shall be assessed. Such work shall include, but is not limited to, sorting, stacking, counting, marking products, or assisting customer employees in their work. Such additional charge shall be $5.85 per quarter hour, or fraction thereof.*

The additional charge is determined by expanding the employee hourly labor cost to include indirect cost and profit.

Driver labor cost per hour	$ 18.051
Direct and indirect cost per hour	$ 21.854
Rate at 93 operating ratio	$ 23.384
Rate for quarter-hour	$ 5.85

The vehicle cost is not included in this determination because the vehicle is not being used to provide the service. Its cost is recovered in either the transportation or standby rate.

Stop-in-transit has also been called "stop-off" or "split pickup and delivery" All of these interchangeable terms require the carrier to provide a stop to partially load or unload a shipment in addition to the original loading and final unloading operations. Such rules might read like this:

> *In the event the carrier is required to stop in transit to load or unload a portion of the shipment, transportation charges shall be assessed using the distance traveled from the first point of origin to the final destination via all points of partial loading or unloading. In addition to the transportation charges, an additional charge of $30 shall be assessed for each stop to partially load or unload.*

The charge for each stop is determined using the cost per hour for labor and the vehicle fixed cost converted to the period of time for stop-in-transit found in the trip reports. Our illustration assumes that each stop takes 45 minutes.

Driver labor cost per hour	$ 18.051
Vehicle fixed cost per hour	12.828
Direct cost per hour	$ 30.879
Direct and indirect cost per hour	$ 37.384
Rate per hour at 93 operating ratio	$ 40.00
Rate per three-quarters of an hour	$ 30.00

Stop-in-transit rules are written differently in general freight LTL service. The difference will be discussed in the chapter dealing with this service.

Diversion and reconsignment are changes in the point of destination after the shipper has conveyed instructions to the carrier. A diversion occurs after the carrier is en route with the shipment; a reconsignment occurs at, or before, the time carrier's equipment reaches the shipper's loading facilities. Reconsignment services are not a function of cost.

The carrier's price schedule should contain a rule to apply when a diversion occurs after a shipment is in transit on the carrier's equipment:

When, at the request of the shipper, a shipment is diverted to a destination other than the destination shown in the shipping instructions, the transportation charges to be assessed shall be determined from the original point of origin to the point of final destination via all points of diversion.

This rule would compensate the carrier for its incurred cost without a separate charge.

Since reconsigned shipments require no special handling or additional cost to the carrier, no additional charges should accrue to the shipper. If the carrier dispatched its equipment to perform a specific haul, and the reconsignment creates a problem for the carrier, it may wish to assess an additional charge. This might occur where a short-haul shipment could have been handled by the equipment available, but the reconsignment created a longer haul, which required the driver to go on overtime. In this instance, the carrier and shipper may agree that an additional charge is required since the added cost was incurred through no fault of the carrier.

Other transportation rules should also be included in the carrier's price schedule. These include payment terms, loss and damage, overcharge, collect-on-delivery, hazardous materials, and rules describing methods to obtain shipment weights and distance measurements. Though the regulated system of rates no longer exists, carriers must still continue to provide shippers with parameters of service.

Even in a regulated environment, carriers and shippers have disagreed as to the assessment of charges for accessorial services. In an unregulated industry, such differences can be expected to escalate. Well-managed carriers will publish a price schedule that includes the rules discussed in this chapter to inform its customers that good business practices dictate a sound pricing policy that is consistent with a quality service. These price schedules will assist the firm's sales staff in soliciting business within the employer's stated policy. Price schedules should be used to attract new accounts, create additional business from existing accounts, and recover lost business. Price schedules should include more than a scale of distance rates and rules governing their application. Carriers also can use these schedules to offer additional services that would improve equipment utilization. There are two ways to accomplish this objective. The rental and leasing of vehicles, discussed in Chapter 8, illustrates the advantages of dedicated vehicles. ("Dedicated" in this sense means that utilization is increased in the usual leasing arrangements by providing full-time vehicles to the lessee.) Another method for increasing utilization is called "Volume Incentive Service," which is often found in, but not limited to, transportation contracts. Volume Incentive Service refers to reducing rates to a buyer in return for a commitment to ship various volumes of freight via the carrier.

How can specialized carriers reduce rates when shippers commit to a predetermined number of shipments or level of revenue? Again, the answer is that virtually all cost incurred by motor carriers is variable. The following example illustrates this principle.

A tank truck carrier delivers gasoline to service stations for a petroleum company within a specified commercial area. The pricing for this service has been determined through published tariffs on a rate of 100 pounds per shipment. Each shipment was rated separately, and prices were built on cost, as described in Chapters 4 through 7. (Cost and productivity in these chapters were built upon average figures for the fleet.)

In both leasing arrangements and Volume Incentive Service, cost and productivity is changed because the buyer commits to provide a greater volume of business than the carrier earns in shipment-by-shipment transactions. Commitment to greater vehicle utilization is rewarded with lower rates in return for improved productivity.

In this example, a tank truck carrier who shares the shipping volume with two other carriers determines from its cost analysis that significant rate reductions could be offered if the petroleum company would commit all, or at least a large part, of its volume to the carrier. The cost analysis for this determination begins with a review of shipping documents to measure the pattern of traffic. From that tabulation, the carrier finds that the petroleum company tendered 7 shipments per week per unit of carrier's equipment averaging 75 miles in length of haul, one way, for the past 12 months. From driver time sheets, the carrier learned that each vehicle traveled 35 miles per hour in elapsed total time for each trip. This means that the calculation of miles per hour includes loading and unloading or total elapsed trip time. The carrier reasoned that was a fairly fast speed, and that, with bottom loading and quick unload, the equipment was operating at peak efficiency and was manned by excellent drivers.

Table 9.8 is the present cost and rate to perform the service on a shipment basis. Figures used in Table 9.8 for vehicle cost are for a three-axle tractor and a long semitrailer (see Tables 5.9 and 6.7). The indirect ratio is the same as that used in previous examples: 17.4 percent. In actual practice, a tank truck carrier would most often use a truck and trailer, and the indirect expense ratio would probably be less.

TABLE 9.8

DEVELOPMENT OF RATE FOR XYZ PETROLEUM

Line No.	Item	Amount
1.	Labor Cost Per Hour (Table 4.15, Local driver)	$ 17.141
2.	Vehicle Fixed Cost Per Hour (Table 5.9)	12.133
3.	Vehicle Running Cost Per Hour (Table 6.7, 35 MPH)	18.305
4.	Direct Cost Per Hour	$ 47.579
5.	Direct Cost Per Trip (150-mile round-trip, 35 mph = 4.29 hours per trip)	$ 204.114
6.	Indirect Cost Per Trip	42.997
7.	Total Cost at 100 O. R.	$ 247.111
8.	Revenue Per Trip at 93 O. R.	$ 264.409
9.	Average Load (pounds)	53,000
10.	Rate per 100 Pounds	$ .50
11.	Revenue Per Mile	$ 1.76

The carrier then prepared a new analysis based upon an incentive for volume, using truck and trailer combinations that have traveled almost 800,000 miles since they were manufactured in 1984.

In order to reduce the rate significantly, the theoretical carrier decided to factor in some new circumstances. First, it deemed that new vehicles would be necessary to continue the service required by the shipper. A new truck, with tank, would cost $85,000, and a new trailer would be $30,000. The carrier expects to get 800,000 miles from the truck and 1,200,000 miles from the trailer. The vehicles are expected to be operated for 75,000 miles annually, which results in an expected life of 10 years for the truck and 16 years for the trailer.

The carrier first must determine the cost per mile for vehicle fixed cost. Table 9.9 is set up for that purpose.

TABLE 9.9

VEHICLE FIXED COST — XYZ PETROLEUM ACCOUNT

Line No.	Item	Amount Truck	Trailer
1.	Investment Cost	$ 85,000	$ 30,000
2.	Salvage Value (15%)	12,750	4,500
3.	Net Economic Value	$ 72,250	$ 25,500
4.	Economic Life	10 years	16 years
5.	Annual Cost	$ 7,225	$ 1,594
6.	Annual Fees and Insurance:		
7.	License Fees	$ 2,250	$ 850
8.	Federal Highway Use Tax	550	-
9.	Insurance	4,500	1,200
10.	Total Annual Fees	$ 7,300	$ 2,050
11.	Annual Vehicle Fixed Cost	$ 14,525	$ 3,644
12.	Cost Per Mile (75,000 miles)	$ .194	$ .049
13.	Cost Per Mile (combined)	$ .243	

Next, the imaginary carrier decides to review the running cost that is imputed into the cost projection. The maintenance costs were $.214 for the truck and $.033 for the trailer (see Table 6.6). However, the tractor manufacturer offers a 3-year limited warranty covering the drive train, and the trailer producer offers a similar warranty. The carrier, therefore, calculates that the maintenance cost for the first 3 years of the vehicles' lives would be reduced to $.06 for the truck and $.013 for the trailer. At 75,000 miles per year, the maintenance cost for the 3-year period would be reduced by $16,425. For the remaining 7 years, the cost would revert back to the current cost of $.247 per mile for the combination. The 7-year total would be $129,675, and the 10-year maintenance cost would be $146,100 for 750,000 miles, or $.195 cents per mile. Fuel and tire costs were not changed in the projection even though newer vehicles lower fuel consumption rates.

TABLE 9.10

VEHICLE RUNNING COST — XYZ PETROLEUM ACCOUNT

Line No.	Item	Amount
1.	Fuel Cost Per Mile (Table 6.1)	$ .207
2.	Tire Cost Per Mile (Table 6.3)	.069
3.	Maintenance Cost Per Mile	.195
4.	Direct Running Cost Per Mile	$ .471

The hypothetical carrier then turned to the final portion of direct cost - labor. The labor cost is very simple to calculate because the cost per trip is $73.53 ($17.141 x 4.29 hours, per Table 9.8). As each trip is 150 miles, the cost per mile for labor is $.490. Including labor and vehicle costs, our illustration will incur a total direct cost per mile of $1.20.

Finally, the carrier must determine the indirect cost if the company used a volume-incentive rate to capture the XYZ account in total. The shipper would dispatch the vehicle, and only one bill per month would be necessary. With competent drivers, service should remain high with very little supervision. For these and other considerations, the carrier decides that the indirect cost should be one-half the company overall figure of 17.4 as a ratio to total expense. The profit factor of 7% cannot be reduced because of the substantial cost of the money to acquire the new vehicles. In fact, at current financial rates, the profit margin must be increased to 8% to recover the cost of the money, allow for income tax, and maintain the desired level of net, after tax, profit necessary.

With all the data collected and calculated, Mr. Hypothetical creates the summary in Table 9.11.

TABLE 9.11

DETERMINATION OF VOLUME INCENTIVE RATE FOR XYZ

Line No.	Item	Amount
1.	Vehicle Fixed Cost Per Mile	$ .243
2.	Vehicle Running Cost Per Mile	.471
3.	Labor Cost Per Mile	.490
4.	Direct Cost Per Mile	$ 1.204
5.	Total Cost at 100 O. R.	$ 1.319
6.	Rate Per Mile at 8% Profit	$ 1.42

The hypothetical carrier can offer a rate of $1.42 per mile for each truck and trailer combination XYZ Petroleum is willing to use. Terms would be for a 1-year period with monthly payments due by the 15th of the month following the service. The monthly elapsed miles will be read from the odometer on the last day of each month, and billed by the 5th of the month following service. Replacement vehicles would be provided at the same rate when the volume incentive vehicles are out of service for preventive maintenance and/or safety inspections.

What savings did the hypothetical carrier create in the cost determination supporting the lower rate? To be viable, the Volume Incentive Service must increase equipment utilization. The illustration does that. The annual vehicle use hours increase to 2,143 hours per year. The vehicle traveled 35 miles per hour on each trip, and is expected to travel 75,000 miles per year in Volume Incentive Service. By purchasing new equipment, the carrier avoids some maintenance cost because the manufacturers provide limited warranties that reduce the maintenance cost for the first three years of the vehicle's lives.

Finally, this theoretical Volume Incentive Service is much like vehicle leasing in that the shipper does the dispatching. Because the carrier avoids the dispatch cost, the billing cost for each shipment, some middle management cost, and some other indirect expenses, the carrier can pass the savings along to the buyer and still generate profit similar to that earned on a shipment-by-shipment basis. Though the rate per mile is reduced from $1.76 to $1.42, adequate profits are still generated.

The concept of Volume Incentive Service is present in all motor carrier pricing structures. It was present even in the days of the old tariff construction, where one rate was quoted for one shipment, a lesser rate for two shipments, and so on. It is most prevalent, however, in contract transportation, where shippers and carriers enter into long-term agreements for transportation service. Generally, a shipper enjoys rates lower than the old tariff rates in return for a commitment to provide an increased volume of traffic to a carrier.

As they search for stability in an unregulated market, specialized carriers will consider entering into more transportation contracts. Buyers of transportation service will also consider Volume Incentive Service as a method for lowering the distribution cost of their products.

Private Fleet Operations

Now that economic deregulation of the intrastate trucking industry is firmly in place, private fleet operators will need to reevaluate the cost of product distribution. For those who distribute products through the for-hire trucking industry, there are new challenges ahead because price competition to obtain new business will surely escalate. New and innovative marketing strategy and pricing concepts will be accessible from both leasing companies and for-hire carriers. Moreover, operators of private fleets will find it simpler, and perhaps less expensive, to enter the for-hire arena where new opportunities for return loads and improved equipment utilization may be acquired.

Some of this imaginative competition could result in serious difficulties for the unwary buyer. This is true simply because there is no longer a regulatory watchdog to make sure the servicing trucking company is legitimate. Historical benchmarks such as filed tariffs and contracts are no longer available as pricing guidelines. To replace documents filed with regulatory agencies, trucking service will become more cost-oriented in terms of pricing as carriers search for new productivity gains and cost reductions.

Private carriers are in an excellent position to grasp new opportunities for improved equipment utilization. Under old regulatory requirements, private carriers desirous of transporting the goods of others were prohibited from doing so because of entry criteria. Applications for operating authority from state regulatory agencies often required financial disclosures objectionable to private fleet operators. Today, there are no requirements for entry other than the safety and insurance standards already maintained by private fleets. Without regulatory requirements, private fleets can actively solicit new business in the form of back-haul or cross-haul traffic. The gains to be made in equipment utilization from this activity can be sizable.

As new and innovative pricing strategies are presented, it will be absolutely essential that buyers fully understand underlying transportation economics. With this knowledge, buyers of transportation service will be better prepared to reduce distribution cost while maintaining, or improving, the system. Throughout this book we stress the importance of cooperation between buyers and sellers of truck transportation service; the ultimate objective of both parties should be economical and efficient service.

Buyers of transportation service should understand a transportation service's cost structure and rate construction so that all proposals may be fully and correctly evaluated. Competitors offering service should provide buyers with underlying data that supports each proposal. With such information, buyers can independently evaluate the propositions of competing carriers to determine which are based upon factual conditions. If a carrier proposal seems unrealistic, it probably is!

Private fleet operators are directly affected by the most recent legislative change because future price competition can influence individual distribution decisions, particularly the decision to continue private operations. Furthermore, management will find it necessary to address the issue of whether the fleet should be expanded into a profit center.

Justification for the transportation department revolves around cost. Management wants to know the answers to the following questions: "Can we provide our own distribution system more efficiently and at a lower cost than that provided by for-hire carriers? How can we construct our distribution cost in a way that is comparable to the cost methodology of a for-hire carrier? What cost elements are included in the overall distribution system by truck? Are there methods available for us to avoid the high cost of labor and equipment acquisition and still efficiently distribute our products?"

Each of these questions, and many others, requires the proper measurement of operating cost for the private fleet as well as for the potential for-hire carriage. In many cases, the decision to go proprietary was made several years ago, and that decision has not been reevaluated in terms of modern conditions. Today, price competition injected into the market changes circumstances surrounding the trucking industry because new players can enter the market easily, new pricing structures are available, additional efficiency opportunities are released, and excess vehicle capacity will reduce prices, eventually.

A hurdle that many private fleet managers have to overcome is gaining access to internal accounting and cost-support systems that accurately reflect operating results. Product manufacturers tend to focus on the cost to run production facilities, ignoring distribution costs. Questions put to fleet management regarding distribution costs often go unanswered.

Cost measurement for private fleets is similar to that used by for-hire trucking. Because the private carrier's objectives are not the same as those of the for-hire carrier, however, there are striking differences in the methods used. The most glaring among these differences is that private carriage seeks operating cost figures for management purposes, while the for-hire carrier seeks to establish correct prices for its service.

There are also technical differences between the two types of carriage. Private fleet managers are saddled, at least in their view, with an inordinate level of overhead cost. Proper allocation of overhead can become a political issue when department heads clash over who incurs what cost. On the other hand, for-hire carriers are in the trucking industry as a business; all of their overhead cost is an incurred cost.

Manufacturing firms with private fleets must allocate a part of the total overhead cost to the transportation department. The question is, how much? And that question creates theoretical disagreements between the manufacturing and the transportation departments. Manufacturing argues that a part of its overhead should be allocated to transportation because manufacturing also prepares the product for shipment. Transportation argues that it is only responsible for overhead cost involved directly with the loading dock to the distribution point operations.

Passage of legislation in 1994 eliminated economic regulations of intrastate motor carrier service. This action, together with the present interstate regulatory system, triggers unparalleled opportunities for private carriers. To seize these opportunities, operators of private fleets will find that a new operating system evaluation is necessary. Such evaluation should begin by determining the cost to operate the existing fleet. The cost analysis should be constructed in the same manner as the methods illustrated throughout this book. These methods will provide information about each individual operation within the fleet, and the results will be expressed in terms that facilitate comparison with for-hire cost presented by outside vendors. For-hire carriers that solicit your business should be brought in with cost studies in hand.

While outside suppliers are preparing their solicitations, the private fleet operator should be preparing a similar analysis to determine the labor cost for drivers, the running cost for operating the fleet on an individual vehicle basis, the investment cost per vehicle for the fleet, and the operating productivity for both the fleet and the individual equipment and driver. This analysis may also suggest alternate methods for distributing the product. Finally, a thorough cost preparation will address the overhead distribution issue.

The person preparing an operating cost analysis for a private fleet has several advantages over his or her counterpart in the for-hire industry. Fewer types of vehicles are employed in the private fleet because it is constructed to serve a particular need; therefore, less study detail is needed. For example, if the fleet is to transport truckload shipments from the point of manufacture to distribution warehouses, the only vehicles required are tractors and trailers. Likewise, if the fleet consists of small bread or dairy route vehicles, the study would include only small bobtails or straight trucks.

In similar fashion, the private fleet can operate with fewer employee classifications because the type of vehicle operated is uniform. Finally, private fleets are limited by the type of service provided. Tractor-trailer combinations operate between relatively few points of origin and destination, making the operational analysis significantly less intricate than that of a for-hire counterpart.

An analysis of private fleet cost is constructed to determine both the direct and the indirect costs, which comprise the total cost. The direct cost consists of driver labor, vehicle fixed cost, and vehicle running cost. These elements may be constructed using any appropriate common denominator. Historically, most for-hire rates have been expressed in terms of cost or rate per 100-pounds. This unit of measure is not particularly meaningful for the private carrier because it has no relationship to other production costs within the company. However, for cost comparison with for-hire carriers, 100-pound units of measurement are significant.

For purposes of discussion, the first step in analyzing the overall cost to operate a private fleet is to determine the total annual cost for each component. In this sense, a component is an individual unit of equipment or a route. Our example involves a manufacturer with distribution warehouses in various locations away from the point of manufacture. The company employs three-axle tractors and two-axle semitrailers. The methods described will be useful in comparing cost with vendor quotes, obtaining new management information systems, and developing new operating modes to reduce distribution cost.

In this illustration, the company operates 6 units of equipment, and each unit has a particular work assignment for 5 days per week. All vehicles are owned by the company; none are leased. Except for washing and fueling, maintenance is accomplished by an outside vendor. Tables 10.1 and 10.2, setting forth the route assignments for each of the 6 units of equipment, indicate that all vehicles return empty.

TABLE 10.1

VEHICLE ROUTE ASSIGNMENTS – SHORT HAUL

Vehicle Number	Round-trip Miles	Trips Per Day	Number of Stops Per Trip	Hours Per Trip	Average Weight Per Load
1	100	2	2	4.00	52,000
2	300	1	1	8.67	52,000
3	350	1	1	10.00	52,000

The data used to construct this operational analysis originates with driver trip reports such as that shown in Appendix A, Form 5. These reports should be completed in sufficient quantity so that the results reflect all of the operating conditions normally encountered in fleet operations. This would include traffic congestion, geographic area, driver ability, and vehicle configuration. In operations that include long-haul routes, the sample period might extend for several months. Productivity for shorter routes can be accurately determined in two weeks.

Data accumulated from the forms must be recorded so that each operational function can be separately determined. A data processing spreadsheet in software such as Lotus or Excel will facilitate the process. The object of the analysis for each route is to determine the time for loading at each stop, the running time and distance between each stop, and the time for unloading at each stop.

Data from the reports is summarized for each route so that separate loading and unloading times for all stops during the route may be determined. Running time and distance are recorded in a way that will determine the running speed. The spreadsheet should also include the vehicle number, driver name or number, and date. These final items may be used to compare productivity among the various units of equipment and drivers. The spreadsheet is structured to capture all elapsed time for each function performed during the work period.

One word of caution: it is important that drivers be properly instructed in preparation of the forms so that the information accurately reflects the actual operation. Drivers should be instructed not to change their normal pattern of operation during the test period.

In Table 10.1, the vehicles operate over relatively short distances. Each of the routes is operated daily, 5 days per week. Table 10.2 illustrates the route assignments for the rest of the 6-vehicle fleet. To demonstrate performance differences, these vehicles operate over longer distances. Notice the trip time is changed from daily to weekly.

TABLE 10.2
VEHICLE ROUTE ASSIGNMENTS – LONG HAUL

Vehicle Number	Round-trip Miles	Trips Per Week	Number of Stops Per Trip	Hours Per Trip	Average Weight Per Load
4	1,000	2	3	26.25	52,000
5	2,500	1	5	57.50	52,000
6	1,000	1	8	36.20	52,000

Fleet management wants to reach three results from the cost analysis. To evaluate the proposals of vendors, management needs to know how its current cost compares with the cost of trucking companies. It also needs to know the annual cost of operating the distribution system in-house. Finally, it needs to know if in-house costs can be significantly reduced through operational modifications.

The actual cost analysis begins with the hourly cost of labor. In our example, the transportation department is responsible for the costs of the drivers and the warehouseman who loads the trucks from the staging area. Table 4.15 is an illustration of one method to determine these costs, and Chapter 4 explains how the underlying components necessary for the determinations in Table 10.3 are developed. For purposes of this illustration, we have selected the Line Driver and Platform Worker classifications from the earlier table.

TABLE 10.3

DEVELOPMENT OF TOTAL LABOR COST PER HOUR

Line No.	Item	Line Driver	Warehouseman
1.	Base Hourly Wage Rate	$ 10.380	$ 10.280
2.	Overtime	-	.585
3.	Subtotal	$ 10.380	$ 10.865
4.	Vacation, Holidays, Sick and Funeral Leave	.798	.637
5.	Subtotal	$ 11.178	$ 11.502
6.	Health, Welfare, and Pension	2.569	2.073
7.	FICA	.855	.880
8.	Federal Unemployment Fund	.032	.025
9.	State Payroll Tax	.138	.111
10.	Workers Compensation	1.509	1.474
11.	Hourly Labor Cost	$ 16.281	$ 16.065
12.	Nonproductive Time	1.018	1.004
13.	Total Hourly Labor Cost	$ 17.299	$ 17.069

Totals are not consistent between Tables 10.3 and 4.15 because it is assumed that drivers in the Table 10.3 illustration do not receive overtime. We also changed the title in the second employee classification from Platform Worker to Warehouseman to better reflect the classifications in private carriage. Other considerations may be necessary if employees are paid on a different basis, such as by the mile. Discussion in Chapter 4 explained the difference in approach necessary to prepare total employee cost on a mileage basis.

Other employee classifications that may be directly involved in transportation must also be considered. These include riding helpers or additional employees necessary to load vehicles. If the expense of other employee benefits are borne by the company, they should be factored into the labor cost study as well.

The second element of direct cost is vehicle fixed cost, the cost to acquire, license, and insure vehicles. Chapter 5 discussed the concepts and considerations necessary to correctly determine vehicle investment cost, salvage value, and economic life. A review of that chapter will show how that cost is developed.

Technically, developing the vehicle fixed cost in a private fleet utilizes different concepts than those used for developing a similar cost in for-hire carriage. The for-hire carrier wants to develop a cost to be used in connection with setting rates; the private carrier measures such a cost for the purpose of determining the overall cost to improve management information systems. The difference in these two approaches is illustrated in connection with economic value. Private carriers should impute into the study the actual cost of the fleet being operated; the for-hire carrier must consider current outside economic circumstances because future pricing depends upon the recovery of an adequate cost to replace the existing fleet.

The rate of inflation affects the level of cost to be provided for economic value in for-hire carriage. If the existing fleet of power units includes the average of purchases made over the previous eight years, for example, the carrier would understate the replacement cost, and rates would fall short of the intended target, which is continued revenue sufficient to maintain quality equipment. On the other hand, the private carrier needs to determine **actual cost** because it will compare that result with for-hire carrier rate quotations. If, however, the private fleet analyst is determining the operational cost for a small fleet, the **historical cost** can be used for each vehicle on each route.

To illustrate the difference, Table 10.4 provides information similar to that prepared in connection with vehicle fixed cost in Table 5.5. Table 10.4 compares vehicle fixed cost on a historical basis (no inflationary influence) and a current cost basis that considers economic indicators.

Preparation of tables similar to Table 10.4 requires some planning to assure that results are in the proper format. For example, when the private carrier compares its cost with that of outside vendors, the fixed vehicle cost schedule should be the average cost of all vehicles in similar classifications. All three-axle tractors should be averaged so that one figure represents fleet cost.

TABLE 10.4

COMPARATIVE VEHICLE FIXED COST

Line No.	Item	Historical Cost		Current Cost	
		3-Axle Tractor	2-Axle Semitrailer	3-Axle Tractor	2-Axle Semitrailer
1.	Economic Value	$ 45,000	$28,000	$ 65,000	$ 28,000
2.	Salvage Value	12%	12%	15%	15%
3.	Net Value	$ 39,600	$24,640	$ 55,250	$ 23,800
4.	Economic Life (Years)	10	15	6	10
5.	Cost Per Year	$ 3,960	$ 1,643	$ 9,210	$ 2,380
6.	License Fees:				
7.	Registration	$ 25	$ 25	$ 25	$ 25
8.	Weight	900	950	900	950
9.	Value	875	550	950	650
10.	Subtotal	$ 1,800	$ 1,525	$ 1,875	$ 1,625
11.	Federal Hwy Use Tax	550	-	550	-
12.	Total Annual Fees	$ 2,350	$ 1,525	$ 2,425	$ 1,625
13.	Insurance Cost	$ 4,400	$ 1,800	$ 4,400	$ 1,800
14.	Total Annual Vehicle Fixed Cost	$ 10,710	$ 4,968	$ 16,035	$ 5,805

There are significant cost differences when historical cost is compared with current cost adjusted for inflation. The figures in Table 10.4 are not actual, but they effectively demonstrate that the vehicle fixed cost prepared for rate-making is not the same as that used by the private operator to measure actual historical cost of fleet operations.

This does not mean that private fleet operators need not be concerned with fleet replacement. However, given the three-fold purpose of private fleet analysis, it is necessary to compare existing in-house cost with rates quoted by potential vendors. Another objective is to discover the actual annual fleet operating cost to determine if corrective action is needed. Among other things, the operational analysis will disclose whether particular routes or drivers are more or less effective than others. Further, the comparison of individual elements of cost with those of outside vendors will provide benchmarks. One good example is the maintenance cost per mile, a common element of cost incurred by all truck operators.

Salvage value and economic life are intertwined, and reflect, in large part, management's willingness to reinvest in rolling stock. When vehicles are retained for a longer period, salvage value is reduced accordingly. Here again, the private carrier's objective is different from that of the for-hire carrier's. Private carriers are interested in operating a unit of equipment as long as possible within justifiable economics. Retention of heavy power units beyond 800,000 miles generally is not economical because the cost of repairs may exceed the cost of replacement. This, of course, is dependent upon current economic conditions, vehicle condition, and the willingness of management to invest in motor vehicles.

Insurance cost for the private fleet operator is quoted as a total fleet cost, either for the company as a whole or for each unit of equipment. The cost analyst must determine the cost attributable to the fleet so that the actual cost can be imputed into the cost summaries. The internal insurance department or the company insurance broker will be helpful in this determination.

Annual license fees are available from vehicle registration documents.

The final element of direct cost is the running cost, which consists of fuel, oil, tires, and maintenance. (See Chapter 6.) In Table 6.7, it was determined that the cost of operating a three-axle tractor and long semitrailer was $.523 per mile. The considerations leading to these figures should be reviewed, and a similar analysis prepared to determine the actual cost of the individual items.

Driver labor cost, vehicle fixed cost, and vehicle running cost comprise the direct cost to provide a truck transportation service. A summary of the data in Tables 10.1 and 10.3 furnishes the basis for allocating the direct cost to the particular operating processes. The summarized data from these tables will provide loading and unloading times and running speed for each of the routes operated. The analyst then can determine the annual operating cost for each route as well as the overall fleet cost by multiplying the trip cost by the annual number of trips. Though many private carrier accounting systems provide an overall fleet cost, these systems may not contain sufficient data to determine individual route or vehicle operating cost.

In the described cost system, the direct cost must be annualized to determine a ratio of indirect, or overhead, to direct cost. Annualization of the direct cost is necessary because indirect cost components in accounting records are summarized on an annual basis. That ratio of cost is added to the direct cost for each transportation service or route. The following tables merge the productivity measurements determined from the field study with the individual direct cost elements to capture the operating cost for individual vehicles and routes.

TABLE 10.5

ANNUALIZED DIRECT COST OF FLEET OPERATIONS

Line No.	Item	Vehicle #1	Vehicle #2	Vehicle #3	Vehicle #4	Vehicle #5	Vehicle #6
1.	Round-trip Miles	100	300	350	1,000	2,500	1,000
2.	Load Time	1.75	1.75	1.75	1.75	1.75	1.75
3.	Unload Time	1.75	1.25	2.00	1.50	1.50	2.25
4.	En route Time	2.25	7.42	8.00	21.75	52.00	26.95
5.	Trip Time	5.75	10.42	11.75	25.00	55.25	30.95
6.	Trips Per Year	506	253	253	104	52	75
7.	Hours Per Year	2,910	2,636	2,973	2,600	2,873	2,321
8.	Cost Per Trip:						
9.	Load (Warehouse $17.069)	$ 29.871	$ 29.871	$ 29.871	$ 29.871	$ 29.871	$ 29.871
10.	Labor Cost (Driver $17.299)	69.196	149.982	172.999	402.202	925.497	505.131
11.	Driver Subsistence	-	-	-	90.000	180.000	90.000
12.	Vehicle Fixed Cost ($15,678)	30.981	61.978	61.958	150.750	301.499	209.067
13.	Vehicle Running Cost ($.523)	52.300	156.900	183.050	523.000	1,307.500	523.000
14.	Direct Cost Per Trip	$182.348	$ 398.731	$ 447.878	$1,195.823	$2,744.367	$ 1,357.069
15.	Direct Cost Per Year	$ 92,268	$ 100,879	$ 113,313	$ 124,366	$ 142,707	$ 101,780
16.	Miles Per Year	50,600	75,900	88,550	104,000	130,000	75,000

Except for the running cost, which is brought forward from Chapter 6, and the Warehouseman cost, which is determined from an observation of vehicle loading times from the staging area, the data in Table 10.5 comes from field study analysis or from the direct cost in Tables 10.3 and 10.4. The times and distances shown are retrieved from spreadsheets prepared from the field survey. Load, unload, and en route times make up the total trip time. The number of trips per year and the cost per trip convert each route to an annual cost.

The cost per trip embodies all of the direct cost components discussed earlier. The load cost is the warehouseman hourly labor cost multiplied by the time per trip for loading at the manufacturing plant. The example uses a time of 1.75 hours for each loading. This is an arbitrary figure based on our example of loading 2-axle semitrailers. The cost for unloading is the time incurred by the driver for unloading the trailer. The cost per hour for the driver is multiplied by the time increment.

The vehicle fixed cost is the annual cost determined in Table 10.5 for a 3-axle tractor of $10,710 plus the trailer cost of $4,968. The annual cost of $15,678 is divided by the annual hours shown in Table 10. 5 as Hours Per Year in line 7. The resulting cost per hour is multiplied by the trip time to procure the trip cost for vehicle fixed cost. Vehicle running cost is the round-trip miles multiplied by the cost per mile.

The total of the three elements that comprise the direct cost gives the direct cost per trip for each route. The trip cost is multiplied by the number of trips to capture the cost per year for each route. Similarly, trip miles are multiplied by the number of trips to get the number of annual miles.

Thus, the direct cost to operate this fleet of 6 units would be $675,313 per year. Some operational processes, such as using one warehouseman to load all vehicles, have been assumed. The total annual hours would be 2,175, based upon 1.75 hours per load and 1,243 loads. Whether or not actual scheduling would allow this depends upon individual circumstances. If several vehicles were loaded at the same time, and each vehicle required 1.75 hours to load, employees from other job classifications might be required. If the other employees earned different wages, it would be necessary to use a weighted wage in the cost summary. One method to determine a weighted hourly wage was discussed in Chapter 4.

Our illustration of vehicle fixed cost per hour is accomplished by including loading hours at the manufacturing point in the determination of annual vehicle use hours. This method assumes that, even though stationary at the company facility, a vehicle is considered to be in operation when it is being loaded. The purpose of using this method is to construct a vehicle use hourly cost similar to that used by for-hire carriers. Those carriers include all hours in annual vehicle use hours.

The example makes other suppositions regarding indirect cost to illustrate the procedure. The transportation fleet requires some supervision to maintain quality control and safe operations, but the supervisor has other responsibilities in addition to transportation. Half of the supervisor's total cost of $80,000 annually (including fringes and payroll taxes) is allocated to transportation. The supervisor is assigned a secretary whose annual payroll cost to the company is $40,000. This person also has other responsibilities. Accordingly, half of this cost is also charged to transportation. Other costs allocated by the accounting department, including supplies, utilities, rent, and other overhead items, amount to $43,000 annually.

The analyst must carefully consider each element of cost included in the maintenance category because auxiliary items such as washing vehicles may not be included. If these items are not in the maintenance cost, they must be included in indirect cost. With all of these considerations, the annual indirect cost of transportation in our example would be $103,000, which is 15.3% of the direct cost of $675,313.

The total cost to operate the fleet for distributing the company products would be $778,313 per year, the sum of the direct plus indirect costs. Some interesting comparisons with outside vendor prices are possible with this information. The private fleet operator might consider whether, and to what extent, the annual budget could be reduced by transporting back-haul or cross-haul traffic for other accounts. It might consider price quotations from for-hire carriers, and should consider new concepts in rental and leasing of vehicles as discussed in Chapter 8.

The private fleet operator is no longer inhibited by for-hire entry requirements because states can no longer enforce economic regulations. With this new opportunity, private fleet operators should investigate whether return shipments are available. After deciding that scheduling such shipments will not interfere with company distribution policy, the analyst must calculate how that business will impact the transportation budget.

The demonstrations in Chapter 9, particularly the discussion of the ratio of loaded to total miles, will furnish an overview of the methods we used to calculate the impact of return shipments. Briefly, that ratio is used to allocate the operating cost among each participant in a particular transportation operation.

Addition of return loads in the transportation equation changes the trip productivity in terms of loading, running time, and unloading. Such shipments mean adding at least one more loading function, additional running time, and at least one additional unloading operation. When these operating conditions are added, the equipment availability also changes. The earlier example utilized the fleet to capacity in terms of elapsed route times.

The demonstration also requires the addition of two units of equipment to keep the company distribution from being disrupted, and to assure that the return shipments can be properly serviced. The vehicle route structure is also altered.

One important ingredient must be determined before the analysis of the return load impact is begun. The private carrier must determine its cost per mile, which becomes the basis of rate assessment to the customers in the illustration. The demonstration in Table 10.5 produced annual miles of 524,050 and a total annual cost of $778,313, or a cost per mile of $1.49.

The configuration of private fleet trips is changed in accordance with the data in Tables 10.6 through 10.11 to measure the impact of return loads. Our example assumes that all outbound routes will obtain return loads, though in actual practice this is not likely. Modifying the totals after completing the analysis will reflect actual circumstances.

TABLE 10.6

PROJECTED ANNUALIZED COST OF FLEET OPERATIONS WITH RETURN LOADS

Line No.	Item	Vehicle #1	Vehicle #2	Vehicle #3	Vehicle #4	Vehicle #5	Vehicle $6
1.	Round-trip Miles	130	400	425	1,300	2,550	1,250
2.	Load Time	1.75	1.75	1.75	1.75	1.75	1.75
3.	Load Time - En route	1.33	2.00	.83	2.50	3.25	1.33
4.	Unload Time - En route	3.00	2.00	4.00	1.67	2.25	3.25
5.	En route Time	2.93	9.90	9.70	28.26	53.13	33.69
6.	Trip Time	9.01	15.65	16.28	34.18	60.38	40.02
7.	Trips Per Year	350	190	190	60	52	52
8.	Hours Per Year	3,154	2,974	3,093	3,555	3,140	3,001
9.	Cost Per Trip:						
10.	Load						
	(Warehouse $17.069)	$ 29.871	$ 29.871	$ 29.871	$ 29.871	$ 29.871	$ 29.871
11.	Labor - En route						
	($17.299)	125.591	240.456	251.354	561.007	1,014.240	662.033
12.	Subsistence	-	-	-	90.000	180.000	90.000
13.	Vehicle Fixed Cost						
	($15,678)	44.789	82.507	82.523	150.734	301.477	209.064
14.	Vehicle Running Cost						
	($.523)	67.990	209.200	222.275	679.900	1,333.650	653.750
15.	Direct Cost Per Trip	$ 268.241	$ 562.034	$ 586.016	$1,511.512	$2,859.238	$ 1,644.71
16.	Direct Cost Per Year	$ 93,884	$ 106,786	$ 111,343	$ 90,691	$ 148,680	$ 85,525
17.	Miles Per Year	45,500	76,000	80,750	78,000	32,600	65,000

Table 10.6A picks up the balance of the annual trips that cannot be handled by the original equipment because of additional miles traveled and new loading and unloading operations. For example, in Table 10.5, Vehicle #1 made 506 trips annually. In Table 10.6, it produces only 350 trips. The remaining 156 trips are handled by Vehicle #7, included in Table 10.6A.

TABLE 10.6A

PROJECTED ANNUALIZED COST OF FLEET OPERATIONS WITH RETURN LOADS

Line No.	Item	Route #1	Vehicle #7 Route #2	Route #3
1.	Round-trip Miles	130	400	425
2.	Load Time	1.75	1.75	1.75
3.	Load Time - En route	1.33	2.00	.83
4.	Unload Time - En route	3.00	2.00	4.00
5.	En route Time	2.93	9.90	9.70
6.	Trip Time	9.01	15.65	16.28
7.	Trips Per Year	156	43	43
8.	Hours Per Year	3,154	2,974	3,093
9.	Cost Per Trip:			
10.	Load			
	(Warehouse $17.069)	$ 29.871	$ 29.871	$ 29.871
11.	Labor Cost			
	(Driver $17.299)	125.591	240.456	251.354
12.	Vehicle Fixed Cost			
	($15,678)	44.789	82.507	82.523
13.	Vehicle Running Cost			
	($.523)	67.990	209.200	222.275
14.	Direct Cost Per Trip	$ 268.241	$ 562.034	$ 586.023
15.	Direct Cost Per Year	$ 41,846	$ 24,167	$ 25,199
16.	Miles Per Year	20,280	17,200	18,275

Table 10.6B shows trips transported by new Vehicle #8.

TABLE 10.6B

PROJECTED ANNUALIZED COST OF FLEET OPERATIONS WITH RETURN LOADS

Line No.	Item	Vehicle #8			
		Route #2	Route #3	Route #6	Route #4
1.	Round Trip Miles	400	425	1,250	1,300
2.	Load Time	1.75	1.75	1.75	1.75
3.	Load Time - En route	2.00	.83	1.33	2.50
4.	Unload Time - En route	2.00	4.00	3.25	1.67
5.	En route Time	9.90	9.70	33.69	28.26
6.	Trip Time	15.65	16.28	40.02	34.18
7.	Trips Per Year	20	20	23	44
8.	Hours Per Year	2,974	3,093	3,001	3,555
9.	Cost Per Trip:				
10.	Load ($17.069)	$ 29.871	$ 29.871	$ 29.871	$ 29.871
11.	Labor ($17.299)	240.456	251.354	662.033	561.007
12.	Subsistence ($45)	-	-	90.000	90.000
13.	Vehicle Fixed Cost ($15,678)	82.507	82.523	209.064	150.734
14.	Vehicle Running Cost ($.523)	209.200	222.275	653.750	679.900
15.	Direct Cost Per Trip	$ 562.034	$ 586.016	$1,644.718	$ 1,511.512
16.	Direct Cost Per Year	$ 11,241	$ 11,720	$ 37,829	$ 66,507
	Miles Per Year	8,000	8,500	28,750	57,200

In Tables 10.6 through 10.6B, the routes are reconstructed to distribute the system over eight units of equipment instead of the original six, and to reflect additional loading and unloading. There are, clearly, a myriad of route combinations that will accomplish the objective. The first consideration is to be certain that all of the stops on the original routes are covered in the new structure. In the illustration, there were 1,243 shipments during the annual period. Since the primary objective is to serve company distribution needs, the new route structure must cover the same delivery point frequency. Other considerations are distribution of work so that all of the vehicles are utilized to the fullest extent possible. In the demonstration, vehicles 7 and 8 pick up the overflow from the original fleet of six units.

The columns in Tables 10.6A and 10.6B represent the routes to be serviced by the two additional vehicles. To obtain the annual miles or the annual cost for each of these units, the columns must be added horizontally. Selecting routes to be operated by the additional vehicles was accomplished by reviewing the number of trips to be made and the elapsed trip times. In Table 10.6, the round-trip miles are increased over the round-trip miles in Table 10.5, which used only outbound shipments with empty returns. Table 10.6 depicts the same routes, but adds the miles traveled to pick up return loads. Accordingly, routes for the new vehicles were selected to evenly distribute the overall fleet workload.

Vehicle annual hours worked are, in some cases, beyond hours that a single driver could work in terms of the employee annual hours worked calculated in Chapter 4. The analyst may project new annual employee hours to regain the proper relationship to the annual vehicle hours.

Tables 10.6 through 10.6B also add load and unload time en route. The time indicated for loading is incurred to pick up shipments for customers of the private fleet (in this instance, now a for-hire carrier). Unloading en route includes unloading for both the company and customer shipments. These additional operations increase the annual cost to operate the private fleet.

To demonstrate the full concept, it is necessary to determine the total annual cost after infusion of the added cost of customer shipments. The annual cost is simply the total cost determined in Tables 10.6 through 10.6B. Adding the cost incurred by all routes produces an annual direct cost of $855,418. Addition of two units of equipment for the purpose of servicing the new accounts increases the overhead cost as well as the direct cost. Supervisorial and secretarial costs assigned to the transportation department increase by one-third, and additions must be made to the sales force to create new business.

Finally, other indirect costs, such as telephone solicitation, will increase also.

Supervisory and secretarial labor are increased to $80,400 in our example, and the addition of a salesperson adds another $50,000 to overhead labor. Other indirect cost necessary to support the additional volume increases from $43,000 to $65,000. Accordingly, the indirect cost will be $195,400, or 22.8% of direct expense. The total cost to operate the fleet then becomes $1,050,818. The increase in annual miles to 636,055 increases the cost per mile to $1.65 from $1.48. This increase is attributable to the additional time necessary to load and unload customer shipments.

The purpose of increasing the fleet is to generate new business that will more than offset the additional cost. To determine whether this can be accomplished, it is necessary to allocate the cost among the parties involved in the transactions. Private fleet management should try to achieve a low cost by determining how much it will cost to load each company shipment at the point of manufacture and transport it one way to distribution warehouses. If this can be accomplished, the transportation cost to distribute company products will be minimized because outside revenue will support the return of equipment to its point of domicile.

Accordingly, customer shipments should be rated in a fashion that will cover the cost of all additional miles, the loading and unloading of outside shipments, the return to the point of domicile, plus the increased overhead cost. One way to do this is to reconstruct Tables 10.6 through 6B, utilizing only the cost elements directly attributable to company distribution. These costs would include the costs of loading and unloading company shipments and the one-way miles to transport them before any vehicle acquisition.

TABLE 10.7

ANNUALIZED COST OF FLEET OPERATIONS — NET OF CUSTOMER SHIPMENTS

Line No.	Item	Vehicle #1	Vehicle #2	Vehicle #3	Vehicle #4	Vehicle #5	Vehicle #6
1.	One-way Miles	50	150	175	500	1,250	500
2.	Load Time	1.75	1.75	1.75	1.75	1.75	1.75
3.	Unload Time	1.75	1.25	2.00	1.50	1.50	2.25
4.	En route Time	1.13	3.71	4.00	10.87	26.04	13.48
5.	Trip Time	4.63	6.71	7.75	14.12	29.29	17.48
6.	Trips Per Year	506	253	253	104	52	75
7.	Hours Per Year	2,910	2,636	2,973	2,600	2,873	2,321
8.	Cost Per Trip:						
9.	Load (Warehouse $17.069)	$ 29.871	$ 29.871	$ 29.871	$ 29.871	$ 29.871	$ 29.871
10.	Labor (Driver $17.299)	49.821	85.803	103.794	213.989	476.414	272.113
11.	Subsistence	-	-	-	-	45.000	-
12.	Vehicle Fixed Cost ($15,678)	24.946	39.911	40.866	85.144	159.836	118.077
13.	Vehicle Running Cost ($.523)	26.150	78.450	91.525	261.500	653.750	261.500
14.	Direct Cost Per Trip	$ 130.788	$ 234.035	$ 266.056	$ 590.504	$ 1,364.871	$ 681.561
15.	Direct Cost Per Year	$ 66,179	$ 59,211	$ 67,312	$ 61,412	$ 70,973	$ 51,117
16.	Miles Per Year	25,300	37,950	44,275	52,000	65,000	37,500

The annual direct cost on this basis is $376,204. Because the operational change does not affect the indirect annual dollar cost of $103,000, the total cost on an annual basis is $479,204. A savings of $299,109 can be obtained when measured against the original fleet cost of $778,313 to provide the entire round-trip operations. This comparison, however, is not conclusive because there is additional cost incurred to service outside accounts. The final analysis is to determine whether other shipper rates would pay for these cost savings plus the additional cost of servicing new business.

For this analysis, the total cost for each of the vehicles and routes will consider only the cost to load shipments, transport them distances not covered by private fleet cost, and unload them. Customer rates must also cover the added indirect cost. Accordingly, Tables 10.6 through 10.6B should be reconstructed using only the added miles created by the return shipment. The mileage would include miles created in addition to the one-way figures in Table 10.7. For example, in the Vehicle #1 column of Table 10.7 the one-way miles are 50, but in Table 10.6 the round-trip miles are 130. This example demonstrates that the cost for 80 miles must be recouped from the customer if the private carrier is to support only the outbound cost. In similar fashion, the customer must also pay for the cost of loading and unloading its shipments.

Tables 10.8 through 10.10 isolate the cost to be borne in a rate structure assessed to a customer.

TABLE 10.8

CUSTOMER-BORNE FLEET OPERATIONS — ANNUALIZED COST

Line No.	Item	Vehicle #1	Vehicle #2	Vehicle #3	Vehicle #4	Vehicle #5	Vehicle #6
1.	One-way Miles	80	250	250	800	1,300	750
2.	Load Time	1.33	2.00	.83	2.50	3.25	1.33
3.	Unload Time	1.25	.75	2.00	.17	.75	1.00
4.	En route Time	1.80	6.19	5.70	17.39	27.09	20.21
5.	Trip Time	4.38	8.94	8.53	20.06	31.09	22.54
6.	Trips Per Year	350	190	190	60	52	52
7.	Hours Per Year	3,154	2,974	3,093	3,155	3,140	3,001
8.	Cost Per Trip:						
9.	Load (Warehouse $17.069)	$ -	$ -	$ -	$ -	$ -	$ -
10.	Labor Cost (Driver $17.299)	75.770	154.653	147.560	347.018	537.826	389.919
11.	Subsistence	-	-	-	90.000	135.000	90.000
12.	Vehicle Fixed Cost ($15,678)	21.773	47.132	43.239	88.465	155.232	117.749
13.	Vehicle Running Cost ($.523)	41.840	130.750	130.750	418.400	679.900	392.250
14.	Direct Cost Per Trip	$ 139.383	$ 332.535	$ 321.549	$ 943.883	$1,507.958	$ 989.918
15.	Direct Cost Per Year	$ 48,784	$ 63,182	$ 61,094	$ 56,633	$ 78,414	$ 51,476
16.	Miles Per Year	28,000	47,500	47,500	48,000	67,600	39,000

TABLE 10.9

CUSTOMER-BORNE FLEET OPERATIONS — ANNUALIZED COST

Line No.	Item	Routes-Vehicle #7 1	2	3
1.	One-way Miles	80	250	250
2.	Load Time	1.33	2.00	.83
3.	Unload Time	1.25	.75	2.00
4.	En route Time	1.80	6.19	5.70
5.	Trip Time	4.38	8.94	8.53
6.	Trips Per Year	156	43	43
7.	Hours Per Year	3,154	2,974	3,093
8.	Cost Per Trip:			
9.	Load (Warehouse $17.069)	$ -	$ -	$ -
10.	Labor Cost (Driver $17.299)	75.770	154.653	147.560
11.	Vehicle Fixed Cost ($15,678)	21.773	47.132	43.239
12.	Vehicle Running Cost ($.523)	41.840	130.750	130.750
13.	Direct Cost Per Trip	$ 139.383	$ 332.535	$ 321.549
14.	Direct Cost Per Year	$ 21,744	$ 14,299	$ 13,827
15.	Miles Per Year	12,480	10,750	10,750

TABLE 10.10

CUSTOMER-BORNE FLEET OPERATIONS — ANNUALIZED COST

Line No.	Item	6	Routes-Vehicle #8 2	3	4
1.	One-way Miles	750	250	250	800
2.	Load Time	1.33	2.00	.83	2.50
3.	Unload Time	1.00	.75	2.00	.17
4.	En route Time	20.21	6.19	5.70	17.39
5.	Trip Time	22.54	8.94	8.53	20.06
6.	Trips Per Year	23	20	20	44
7.	Hours Per Trip	3,001	2,974	3,093	3,555
8.	Cost Per Trip:				
9.	Load (Warehouse $17.069)	$ -	$ -	$ -	$ -
10.	Labor Cost (Driver $17.299)	389.919	154.653	147.560	347.018
11.	Subsistence	90.000	-	-	90.000
12.	Vehicle Fixed Cost ($15,678)	117.749	47.132	43.239	88.465
13.	Vehicle Running Cost ($.523)	392.250	130.750	130.750	418.400
14.	Direct Cost Per Trip	$ 989.918	$ 332.531	$ 321.549	$ 943.883
15.	Direct Cost Per Year	$ 22,768	$ 6,651	$ 6,431	$ 41,531
16.	Miles Per Year	17,250	5,000	5,000	35,200

In our example, a rate structure assessed to outside customers sufficient to recapture a cost of $579,234 would be necessary for the private carrier to recoup its return empty miles. This dollar amount is determined by adding the totals in Tables 10.8 through 10.10 for a direct cost of $486,834. The new operation would also incur an increased indirect cost of $92,400, which would bring the total to $579,234. The ratio of indirect to direct cost would be 18.98%.

The following chart provides a simple rate structure to recapture this cost:

Vehicle #	Direct Cost	Indirect Cost	Total Cost	Miles	Cost Per Mile
1	$ 70,528	$ 13,386	$ 83,914	40,480	$ 2.07
2	84,132	15,968	100,100	63,250	1.58
3	81,352	15,441	96,793	63,250	1.53
4	98,164	18,632	116,796	83,200	1.40
5	78,414	14,883	93,297	67,600	1.38
6	74,244	14,092	88,336	56,250	1.57
	$486,834	$ 92,402	$ 579,236	374,030	$ 1.55

This analysis of a simple mileage rate structure indicates that customers of the private fleet would be pleased to accept transportation of their products at a rate of $1.55 per mile. Clearly, the rate would reduce their shipping cost significantly as they would not pay for empty return miles. Obviously, neither party would incur cost for empty miles, and productivity would be significantly increased.

Aggressive private fleet operators can readily reduce their shipping cost by the expansion of fleet and sales opportunities. Though the examples selected are best-case scenarios because it is highly unlikely that all outbound shipments would receive return shipments, all of them created a large number of extra miles by adding return loads. If only half of the outbound shipments received return loading, the result would still be a substantial savings to both parties.

Unquestionably, this form of competition will rearrange market forces in some sectors. Producers of products transported in regular van trucks, trailers, and flatbed equipment are most likely to investigate the possibilities of for-hire entry. Shippers and receivers of specialized commodities like bulk cement are less likely to venture into this type of for-hire carriage because opportunities for back-haul are limited, and equipment is specially designed to transport a limited number of commodities.

Technically, the illustrated routes included one for short-haul that displayed proportionally higher loading and unloading times. Route #1 was a 100-mile round-trip before adding new customer shipments. When customers were added, mileage increased to 130, but additional loading and unloading functions increased the cost per mile. This illustrates that a cost and/or rate per mile is not always the proper unit of measure. This is particularly true in connection with short-haul traffic where a number of loadings and unloadings occur.

Short-haul transportation creates a relatively higher cost per mile than longer haul. This is because the loading and unloading cost is a larger portion of the total cost on short-haul shipments, and no miles are operated during those functions. This is one significant reason why trucking rates are often quoted in cents per 100 pounds or some other unit of measure. Since rates per 100 pounds consider weight and distance in underlying cost construction, they more nearly reflect actual transportation conditions.

The data created in this chapter is readily adaptable to a cost or rate per 100 pounds because the trip report summary in Tables 10.1 and 10.2 recorded shipment weights. Weights for all trips in the field survey are recorded for each route and averaged. A schedule similar to that in Table 10.11 describes a typical hundredweight scale of rates based on an average load weight of 52,000 pounds. Employing the cost figures in Tables 10.8 through 10.10, the private carrier (now for-hire) could assess the hundredweight rates in Table 10.11.

TABLE 10.11

RATE PER 100 POUNDS

Line No.	Item	Direct Cost	Indirect Cost	Sub Total	Rate Including 7% Profit	Average Weight Pounds	Rate Per 100
1.	Route #1	$ 139.38	$ 26.55	$ 165.93	$ 177.55	52,000	$ .340
2.	Route #2	332.54	63.34	395.88	423.59	52,000	.815
3.	Route #3	321.55	61.25	382.80	409.60	52,000	.790
4.	Route #4	943.88	179.79	1,123.67	1,202.33	52,000	2.310
5.	Route #5	1,507.96	287.23	1,795.19	1,920.85	52,000	3.690
6.	Route #6	989.92	188.56	1,178.48	1,260.97	52,000	2.420

Private carriers will find that hundredweight rates are the preferable method of rate quotation to transportation service buyers. This is because these rates reflect the cost circumstances of each transportation service, are universally accepted, make comparisons easier, and let the carrier collect for all freight transported. When the shipper tenders a greater weight than the average load in the example, a comparable rate assessment is made on actual weight. On the other hand, when hundredweight rates are used, the carrier must include a minimum weight to prevent shipments being tendered at lower weights. For example, if the average weight per shipment in the field study was 52,000 pounds, a minimum weight of 50,000 would be appropriate. Shipments tendered at weights higher than 52,000 will receive a higher shipment charge. If properly constructed, the rate structure will be fair to both parties.

Summary

Illustrations in this chapter have been limited to the operation of a truckload private carrier fleet. The principles of cost development apply equally to the operation of routes with several stops for loading or unloading less-than-truckload shipments. LTL route operations, in many instances, can improve productivity by transporting shipments for other suppliers where pickups or deliveries are to the same, or nearby, customers. Instead of emphasis on return loads, the effort is to reduce cost by adding shipments where the load factor is presently less than 100%. (Chapter 12 analyzes cost considerations in determining prices for LTL service.)

Some private carriers also have new opportunities to lease equipment in a variety of ways. For-hire carriers will enter into agreements to provide transportation where it supplies both drivers and vehicles. Where rates are properly constructed and carriers can supply expert employees, such agreements can be lucrative for both parties. Under these arrangements, the private carrier controls the operations, but does not incur some labor relations obstacles of driver employees. Other arrangements with for-hire carriers might involve leasing of equipment only, with company employees operating the equipment and the for-hire carrier providing full-service equipment leases.

For-hire carrier leasing arrangements, as well as agreements with leasing companies, are discussed in Chapter 9. A review of that chapter will disclose combinations of cost-reduction activities to fit almost every private carrier need. Leasing of vehicles combined with the provision of for-hire service could both improve productivity and reduce operating cost. Relaxation of regulatory restraints affords the opportunity to rethink private carriage objectives.

Private carriers can determine their own cost per hundredweight for transporting shipments in-house with technology similar to that used for for-hire carriers. Such cost may be compiled for comparison with for-hire carrier rates to assist in the proprietary versus for-hire decision. Private carriers can also determine cost reduction features when outside customers are introduced into the system.

Finally, analyses such as those described in this chapter offer private carriers an opportunity to determine a transportation department operating cost predicated upon actual operations.

Transportation of Household Goods

Even though household goods transportation was excluded from federal pre-emption of state regulation in the 1994 legislation, pricing issues have been an industry concern for some time. Several states have deregulated the entire trucking industry in recent years, including the household goods sector. Because the household goods moving industry is highly fragmented and very competitive, it is an appropriate subindustry for discussion.

At the interstate level, van lines are authorized by the Interstate Commerce Commission. Van lines operating in interstate commerce issue shipping documents and take responsibility for shipments but do not, generally, own vehicles. The actual transportation is provided by owner-operators who supply the power units and much of the loading and unloading services. Van lines enter into agency agreements with local entities to provide shipment-handling services in connection with interstate transportation. The agents own most of the trailing equipment and lease them to the van lines. Local services provided by agents include storage, packing, loading, unloading, and unpacking of shipments. For these services, agents receive a portion of the shipment revenue.

Local agents are also carriers. Most are authorized by state agencies to provide intrastate service. As carriers, they are structured in somewhat the same fashion as van lines. Although agreements do not exist between agencies, there is a high level of cooperation in servicing shipments at the points of origin and destination. This is particularly true where an agent books a shipment with a destination over 200 miles from its point of domicile. It is more efficient to hire a local agent at the destination to assist with destination services than it is to pay a riding helper. Also, it is more efficient to store shipments at the destination as a convenience to the customer.

Local agents, or carriers, also use independent contractors for moving services to control cost. The contractors are paid a percentage of revenue in much the same fashion as the interstate owner-operators. The industry is split, however, as to whether the independent contractor system is appropriate in local service. If an independent contractor is truly independent, the overlying carrier cannot instruct it as to how the work is to be performed, and instructions are limited as to when and where the work will be accomplished. Accordingly, when the contractor does not perform to overlying carrier standards, the system breaks down.

As the industry has become increasingly fragmented, the three competitive strategies described earlier in the book become more visible.

Differentiation

Differentiation is apparent in the van line agency family. Van lines with a high level of name recognition experience little difficulty in attracting good agents. Smaller van lines experience greater difficulty, not only because of name recognition but also because local agents believe larger van lines can provide a greater volume of shipments and return revenues. Consequently, differentiation tends to consolidate the industry, with better agents gravitating toward better van lines.

Another reason that consolidation of van lines is likely in the near future is because aggressive carriers hope to capture a larger share of a shrinking market. Growth in the interstate level of household goods transportation has been slow in recent years. To increase their market share, aggressive interstate carriers must acquire weaker carriers. This is illustrated in the acquisition of Mayflower Transit, Inc. by United Van Lines, a merger that can be expected to trigger further consolidation at the interstate level. However, similar consolidation is not expected at the intrastate level because fragmentation is too great.

Aggressive local carriers gain very little through a merger because too many carriers exist for the merger to make a significant increase in the market share.

Differentiation also appears in connection with warehouse location. Several years ago The Bekins Company seemed to have a storage facility near every highway interchange. It was differentiation at its finest. Today, some local agents attempt to differentiate by requiring employees to wear clean uniforms; others concentrate on clean and colorful vehicles; and still others advertise on local radio and television. The watch word in household goods moving is "professional." Industry participants try to stand out from the rest of the industry by being "professional." All of these characteristics invoke the differentiation competitive strategy, and those who use them are generally more successful than their counterparts.

Focus

Household goods moving is no longer simply household goods moving. Local agents and, to some extent, van lines have been highly successful in developing new business by concentrating on particular markets. In terms of strategy, this is referred to as focus. Many of them focus on high-value products, such as electronic data processing equipment, in areas where sufficient business is available. Transportation of displays and exhibits for conventions and trade shows has become a big business for the industry, with household goods carriers positioning themselves to move almost all of these products.

Local agents have also injected themselves into the fabrication of exhibits for these shows. When properly positioned, these local movers can create transportation business while generating profits in an accessorial operation. In most cases, these operations achieve higher transportation rates because carriers are viewed as indispensable by their customers.

Other local movers focus on office and industrial moving. In fact, office moving in metropolitan areas is a significant contributor to industry revenue. Movers who concentrate on this activity experience different operating conditions. Most office moving is accomplished at night and on weekends to minimize business disruption. So the challenge for the mover is to locate and maintain sufficient numbers of quality employees as these moves can require many workers for a concentrated period of time. Office movers also provide accessorial equipment such as dollies for transferring larger pieces of office equipment. Employee training and supervision are the keys to success in this activity.

Even within the household goods transportation system there are opportunities for the focus strategy. Both van lines and local agents actively solicit what the industry refers to as "national accounts." These are shippers who transfer employees between company facilities. It is a large market for many movers who concentrate upon it. As with other focus strategies, participants must be highly motivated to produce a quality product. Focus strategy is a hands-on operation because a high level of quality service is mandatory for success.

Others who transport only household goods concentrate on the COD shipper, the householder who is moving on his or her own accord. The focus here is quite different from other activities, primarily because of government intervention. Competitors in this market must comply with stringent "consumer protection" rules. Accordingly, employees must be highly trained to understand how the rules are constructed and how to apply them.

Low-cost Operators

Low-cost participants in the household goods transportation industry are the one- or two-truck operators who are not classified as full-service movers.

They are generally people who do not conform with government regulation, comply with vehicle maintenance and safety standards, utilize trained employees, or maintain storage facilities. Also, they are not agents for recognized van lines.

The low-cost mover does not stay in the industry over the long term for a variety of reasons. There is significant risk in operating at the lowest cost. Such competitors are generally undercapitalized and unable to adjust to changing economic conditions. If a cost element such as fuel suddenly increases, or available business is reduced, the low-cost competitor cannot adjust. Another hazard for this competitor is the increasing activity by state regulatory agencies against unauthorized carriers. Because untrained employees are a greater risk on the highway, they create a high number of loss or damage claims for the low-cost carrier.

This form of competition is not expected to subside. There are always others to fill the void when one competitor exits the market. Entry into the business at this level is very inexpensive, and does not require a high degree of training.

Full-service movers cannot compete on a lowest-cost basis as virtually all production cost is variable, and must be paid from current income. Variable cost for the full-service mover includes quality workmanship and safe and dependable equipment. To provide such service, the full-service mover must recover sufficient revenue in its rate structure to cover these costs on a pay-as-you-go basis. Once the operation has reached reasonable efficiency, and cost is under control, there is little room for price reduction.

Industries with high fixed cost can apply a broader range of prices to the market because they can spread the fixed cost over their entire book of business. In the household goods industry as much as 90% of cost is variable and must be paid in the short term. This scenario helps explain why, after a brief shake-out period, carriers in deregulated states found relatively few severe price-discounting situations in household goods transportation. Once industry participants understand the incurred cost of quality business, the likelihood of price instability decreases.

The other side of the competitive spectrum is competition at higher prices. Household goods carriers find it difficult to increase prices above going rates. A large number of competitors in a fragmented industry preclude such price increases. Differentiation and focus strategies tend to alleviate this condition but, overall, assessment of rates above the market is extremely difficult in this industry.

All of these circumstances contribute to industry fragmentation and high competitive levels. The industry is so competitive that a few unscrupulous operators have created a need for inordinately high levels of government interference. The Interstate Commerce Commission and most states prescribe rules of conduct for household goods carriers that include estimating practices, content of shipping documentation, loss or damage claims administration, and carrier performance reports. This government regulation of household goods services is costly. Lengthy estimating forms, detailed shipment inventories, and complex shipping documents and performance reports all contribute to indirect, or overhead, ratios that are nearly twice that of most other carrier types. Industry studies indicate that the indirect ratio hovers near 35% of the total expenses so it follows that household goods rates must be high enough to recover this added cost.

Some of the indirect cost is unavoidable because of the high sales cost required to properly quote prices. Estimating rules require the completion of several pages of complicated forms. Accounting costs are also relatively high for much the same reason. Household goods forms are difficult to prepare by data processing techniques because of the variety of services provided and the descriptive information required.

Studies have shown that the labor cost for local moving companies is about 80% of the total cost. Labor cost together with vehicle cost account for 90% of total cost. Vehicle cost as a percentage of the total cost is lower than that of other carrier groups because local household goods equipment travels relatively fewer miles. Most of the local moving process involves loading and unloading of the vehicle while it is stationary, which creates no fuel expense and very little maintenance cost. Accordingly, the life of the vehicle is longer.

Household goods carriers tend to be price-takers in the market. Rather than prepare and understand a full-cost analysis of their business, they tend to determine and follow going rates in the market. A common practice is to anonymously telephone competitors to seek out their price structure. Once the competitive price is known, all industry prices tend to equalize.

The difficulty with this practice is that it assumes that all competitor cost is the same. This is, of course, not true. In a fragmented industry, every competitor in every market incurs different cost. Labor rates, workers compensation rates, insurance premiums, and warehouse leases are not the same. Management is not paid the same amount, and maintenance cost is not the same. Because no competitor incurs the same costs, it is a competitive error to blindly follow the pricing strategy of any rival. There is no substitute for analyzing operating cost, constructing prices based upon this cost, instructing sales people on cost-based pricing, and adhering to such cost-based prices whenever possible. This does not mean that each rate and each shipment must generate the same return; competition makes this impossible. In this chapter all pricing situations of local household goods carriers are discussed in the context of cost/price relationships that will provide profit.

Local Rates

Transportation rates for household goods carriers are expressed per hour in local moving. The definition of "local moving" for pricing purposes varies for distances up to 100 miles. Some carriers prefer to quote rates on an hourly basis for shipments over 75 miles, while others prefer hourly rates for shipments up to just 25 miles.

In this chapter hourly rates are applied on shipments moving 50 miles and less. Rates for shipments transported over 50 miles vary by distance and weight in our example. These rates will be expressed per 100 pounds. Packing and unpacking rates will be expressed both per hour and per carton to allow carriers a choice.

Other accessorial services rates such as stop-in-transit, long carry, and warehouse handling will also be illustrated. From time to time, other rate-making philosophies also have been considered by the household goods moving industry. These include rates per cubic foot, guaranteed price rates, and single factor rates. Because none of these special rates have been successfully implemented by the industry, they need no discussion.

Hourly rate development for household goods carriers is similar to the hourly rate examples shown for other carriers. In earlier discussions of various rate developments, we referred readers back to previous tables. Because several rate structures will be illustrated in this chapter, we include all of the tables necessary for total cost analysis, making it easier for readers to follow the various preparations.

Labor Cost

Household goods carriers classify direct labor differently from other carriers because several functions are performed in connection with transportation. These functions include packers who prepare shipments for transport, regular helpers who ride with the vehicle to assist in loading and unloading, and extra helpers who generally work part-time and fill in to assist with particular shipments. Table 11.1 demonstrates a method to determine total hourly labor cost for direct labor in local moving.

TABLE 11.1

DEVELOPMENT OF LABOR COST PER REVENUE HOUR

Line No.	Item	Drivers and Packers	Helpers	Extra Helpers
1.	Base Rate Per Hour	$ 11.763	$ 9.910	$ 8.424
2.	Vacation, Holidays, and Sick Leave	981	1.125	.956
3.	Subtotal	$ 12.744	$ 11.035	$ 9.380
4.	Workers Compensation Insurance	3.205	2.775	2.359
5.	Payroll Taxes	1.114	1.042	.917
6.	Health, Welfare, and Pension	1.416	1.926	1.926
7.	Subtotal	$ 18.479	$ 16.778	$ 14.582
8.	Non-revenue Time	2.402	2.181	1.896
9.	Total Labor Cost Per Hour	$ 20.881	$ 18.959	$ 16.478
10.	Annual Hours Worked	1,563	1,149	1.149

11.	Vacation	7.6	days
	Holidays	6.0	
	Sick leave	2.7	
	Total	16.3	days, or 130.4 hours

12.	Line 5 is 7.65% for FICA; 2.7% for SUI, and .8% of FUF, each unemployment insurance based upon $7,000 annual earnings.			
13.	Line 6 is $184.40 per month x 12			
14.	Line 2 as a % of line 1	8.34	11.35	11.35
15.	Line 4 as a % of line 3	25.15	25.15	25.15
16.	Line 5 as a % of line 3	8.74	9.44	9.78
17.	Line 8 as a 5 of line 7	13.00	13.00	13.00

Base rates per hour are determined from payroll records of various employee work classifications. In the example, local drivers and packers receive the same pay rate. Helpers are generally newer employees who receive lower pay rates as they have less training in the industry. Extra helpers are trainees who begin employment on a part-time status at even lower rates of pay. If the firm uses different pay rates for these two classifications, separate constructions would be needed. Employees within the same work classification may receive different pay rates, depending upon the time they have been employed by the firm. A weighted pay rate may be determined by weighting the various pay rates by the number of employees receiving the rate. Table 4.2 illustrates this method.

Vacation, holiday, and sick leave cost represents company policy within the employee benefit package. The costs represent actual historical benefits taken by employees, not the available amount. For example, a sick leave policy may provide for 6 days per year, but employees only take, on the average, 2.7 days. The incurred cost to the firm would be 2.7 days, not the full 6 days. Vacation pay normally depends on the length of time the employee has been with the firm. Table 4.6 provides a method for determining the actual vacation benefits taken by employees within each work classification.

Holidays are somewhat different from vacation or sick leave pay in that all employees receive the same number of holidays. Accordingly, no weighting of cost or other calculation is necessary. If the firm provides 6 holidays per year, the cost calculations should also be based upon 6 holidays.

To convert vacation, holiday, and sick leave benefits to a cost per hour, the analyst must determine, from payroll records, the average number of hours worked annually by each employee in each work classification. In the example shown, local drivers and packers work an average of 1,563 hours per year, and do not receive overtime compensation. In the event a firm pays overtime, it should review the discussion in Chapter 4 for proper handling of overtime pay.

Too many carriers and excess capacity in a particular market reduces productivity. Also, the industry is susceptible to seasonal volume fluctuations. Employers lay off employees during the winter months, or at least cut back on the number of hours worked. The example of hours worked in Table 11.1 is intentionally kept low to illustrate the point that the industry is highly fragmented for these reasons. Firms who prepare rate-making studies similar to those illustrated will obviously achieve different results.

Workers compensation rates for the household goods moving industry are substantially higher than for other carrier groups because of the work hazards involved. Back troubles and other injuries occur more often because employees handle goods shipped more frequently, and such goods can be heavy and awkward. The effective workers compensation rate is measured against the total payroll because the illustration does not include a provision for overtime pay. If overtime is paid, the workers compensation rate in most states is only applied to the straight time portion of overtime pay.

The payroll tax rates are based upon 7.65% of earnings for FICA. Because none of the employees shown earn more than the maximum taxable wage, the statutory rate is applied to all wages. The state payroll tax rate shown is 2.3% of the first $7,000 of annual earnings, which produces an annual cost of $161. Federal Unemployment Fund contributions are based upon .8% of the first $7,000 of annual earnings. State and federal unemployment taxes result in an annual cost of $217, or $.139 per hour for drivers. The addition of $.975 for FICA produces a cost per hour of $1.114 for all payroll taxes.

The illustrated cost for health, welfare, and pension employer contributions uses a monthly cost per employee of $184.40, which is then multiplied by 12 months and divided by the annual hours worked in each work classification.

Non-revenue time is more of a problem for household goods carriers than for other carrier groups because daily vehicle inspection and preparation takes more time. Drivers and packers must arrange packing materials, blanket wraps, and other accessorial equipment necessary to provide this specialized service. This work is in addition to regular safety and maintenance inspections.

In the illustrations in Table 11.1 slightly more than 1 hour per day is imputed for non-revenue time. This time is incurred by the carrier because the employee is on duty, but it is not collectible on an individual shipment basis because most of the time cannot be identified with particular movements. The carrier recovers the cost by adding a portion of this time to each hour charged to shipments. In Table 11.1 the labor cost per hour is increased by 13% to recover the cost of this time in the rate charged to the customer.

Vehicle Fixed Cost

The second portion of direct cost is the vehicle fixed cost, which is the acquisition cost plus the costs of licensing and insurance. A full discussion of this cost increment may be reviewed in Chapter 5. Discussion in this chapter is in connection with the considerations necessary for the proper determination of this cost in relation to the moving industry.

Local household goods moving involves relatively few vehicle types; typically, service is provided by bobtails and two-axle tractors with short semitrailers. Variations in vehicle types are involved in transporting storage vaults on flatbed trailers to be loaded at the shipper's premises, straight trucks with lift gates to handle high-value products, and tractors with long trailer combinations. Discussion and illustration of the vehicle fixed cost is limited to the major units of equipment described in earlier chapters. Other types may be substituted as needed.

TABLE 11.2

DEVELOPMENT OF VEHICLE FIXED COST

Line No.	Item	2-Axle Truck	2-Axle Tractor	Semitrailer
1.	Historical Cost	$ 28,950	$ 40,850	$ 19,850
2.	Salvage Value	4,343	6,128	2,978
3.	Service Value	$ 24,607	$ 34,722	$ 16,872
4.	Service Life	12	12	15
5.	Annual Vehicle Fixed Cost	$ 2,051	$ 2,894	$ 1,125
6.	Taxes And Licenses:			
7.	Registration Fee	$ 23	$ 23	$ 23
8.	Weight Fee	300	300	450
9.	License Fee	185	261	104
10.	Federal Highway Use Tax	550	550	-
11.	Total Tax and License	$ 1,058	$ 1,134	$ 577
12.	Other Fixed Cost:			
13.	Van Equipment	$ 480	-	$ 660
14.	Insurance (except cargo)	2,411	4,750	701
15.	Total Other Fixed Cost	$ 2,891	$ 4,750	$ 1,361
16.	Annual Vehicle Fixed Cost	$ 6,000	$ 8,778	$ 3,063
17.	Annual Use Hours	1,250	1,400	1,400
18.	Vehicle Fixed Cost Per Hour	$ 4.800	$ 6.270	$ 2.188

Historical Cost is simply the cost of each vehicle within the classification at the point of acquisition. The cost of vehicles purchased in each year over the life indicated is averaged to obtain a cost per year. The total for each year is added, and the result divided by the number of years. The result reflects the increased price during the equipment life resulting from historical inflation rates, equipment design improvements, and changes in vehicle configuration. The cost calculated in this manner produces an average fleet cost predicated upon historical purchases. This figure does not take into account the predicted inflation to be incurred for future rates. If the carrier anticipates acquisition of vehicles during the term the developed rates are to be in effect, it may be necessary to impute an increment of cost for inflation. When the industry is experiencing cost increases, the historical cost built into rates will not recover sufficient cost to replenish the fleet. An exception to this statement is made if used vehicle prices increase at, or near, the same rate as new vehicles. In this instance, Salvage Value received for traded vehicles may equal the increase in new vehicle cost.

The Salvage Value in Table 11.2 is taken as 15% of the acquisition cost. This value is dependent upon several variables, not the least of which is the market availability of this type of used equipment. While supply and demand has a significant effect on used vehicle prices, the geographic area also impacts the used truck and trailer market.

Service Value is the residual cost to be recovered in the rate structure over the life of the fleet. It is the difference between the acquisition cost and the amount expected at the trade-in time. This difference is the net cost of owner-ship that must be recovered in the rate structure. The calculation of Service Value is shown on line 3 of Table 11.2.

As vehicles used in household goods transportation tend to last longer because they travel less miles, their lives are extended accordingly. A 12-year vehicle life is virtually unknown in other parts of the industry. Service Life is the divisor used to convert Service Value to the cost per year shown on line 5. Figures on line 5 are the amounts that must be recovered by the carrier each year to maintain a productive fleet.

Vehicle license fees include a flat annual fee for registering the vehicles plus an incremental fee based upon the weight and value of the unit. The illustrat-ed fees take into account these licensing characteristics. Such costs are obtained from registration records and Federal Highway Use Tax information.

Other fixed cost includes on-board equipment such as tie-downs, ropes, straps, ladders, and other equipment that remains with the vehicle. It also includes insurance expense, as indicated on lines 13 and 14 in Table 11.2. As insurance costs vary widely throughout the country, the figures may not be realistic in all areas.

Annual vehicle hours may be considered lower than those a found in other segments of the industry. The demonstration takes into account the fact that many carriers support vehicles that are not necessarily used in daily operations. Household goods carriers tend to maintain a larger fleet than pure economics would dictate. The logic used by such carriers is that additional equipment is necessary to support the seasonal high-volume variations. Whether logic supports this decision is dependent upon the particular circumstances; in some instances, it may be less costly to rent vehicles on an as-needed basis. A review of Chapter 8 will provide some insight into the economics of vehicle rental. At any rate, lower-than-anticipated vehicle use hours means higher per-hour cost and overcapacity.

....

Vehicle Running Cost

The final element of direct cost is the running cost, which consists of fuel, oil, tires, and maintenance. Table 11.3 illustrates a method for determining such cost.

TABLE 11.3

DEVELOPMENT OF VEHICLE RUNNING COST

Line No.	Item	2-Axle Truck	2-Axle Tractor	Semitrailer
1.	Fuel Cost:			
2.	Per Gallon	$ 1.240	$ 1.240	-
3.	Miles Per Gallon	6.2	5.4	-
4.	Cost Per Mile	$ .200	$ .230	-
5.	Oil Cost Per Mile	.002	.002	-
6.	Tire Cost Per Mile	.021	.023	.015
7.	Repair Cost Per Mile	.180	.208	.044
8.	Running Cost Per Mile	$ .403	$ .463	$ .059
9.	Miles Per Use Hour	6.4	8.4	8.4
10.	Running Cost Per Hour	$ 2.579	$ 3.889	$ .496

Fuel cost per gallon is a straightforward expense and should reflect current fuel prices from bulk purchases or retail invoices. If retail fuel is purchased, sufficient invoices should be included in the calculations to produce a reliable current average cost. Fuel consumption rates can be obtained from a one-week period or from another reliable sampling of operations.

Vehicles should begin and end the test period with full tanks. Fuel added during the test period should be added to the gallons put in at the end of the period to determine the total fuel consumption. Odometer readings should be recorded at the beginning and end of the test period to determine the elapsed miles. As noted, both the fuel consumption and the mileage traveled during the work period can be measured. Miles per gallon divided into cost per gallon produces cost per mile for fuel, which is shown on line 4 of Table 11.3.

Few household goods carriers maintain their own vehicle repair shops, so most repairs are accomplished outside. If the same shop is used for all repairs, preparation of the repair cost per mile is not difficult. Outside repair shops prepare invoices that include a description of the work plus the vehicle number, date, and odometer reading. By simply sorting invoices into vehicle numbers over at least a two-year period, the analyst can determine the repair cost per mile. Vehicle repair costs are then sorted by vehicle type to comply with a table similar to 11.3.

If repairs are done in-house, mechanic time sheets will provide descriptions of work. Work orders should show both parts and vehicle fleet numbers. From this data, the analyst can obtain the repair cost per mile. If record-keeping is lax, however, additional clerical effort will be required. The objective is to determine the correct figure for maintenance cost.

A review of Chapter 6, which discussed the development of tire cost per mile, will show how household goods carriers can prepare this cost. Since household goods vehicles travel few miles in local service, a longer period of time for observation is necessary to capture all of the tire cost involved with recapping and repair. Dealers maintain accurate records when all tire purchases and repairs are made at the same point of purchase. These records may be used for source information if in-house records are not adequate.

Running cost per mile will be converted to a cost per hour so it can be included in total cost per hour to construct an hourly rate. The method used is to find the number of miles traveled during the number of hours the vehicles are away from the point of domicile. For example, if the vehicles are away from the point of domicile for 8 hours, and travel 50 miles during the same period, the miles-per-use-hour on line 9 of Table 11.3 would be 6.25. The result obtained from this data converts the vehicle running cost per mile to the running cost per hour, making it possible to measure all direct cost in terms of the same unit. Increments of vehicle running cost are not converted from cost per mile to cost per hour because the total conversion may be done in one calculation using total vehicle running cost per mile.

Hourly Cost Summary

The data assembled in Tables 11.1 through 11.3 will help the analyst consolidate various direct cost items into total cost measurements.

TABLE 11.4

DEVELOPMENT OF TOTAL COST PER HOUR

Line No.	Item	2-Axle Truck	Tractor Semitrailer
1.	Vehicle With Driver and Helper:		
2.	Vehicle Fixed Cost	$ 4.800	$ 8.466
3.	Vehicle Running Cost	2.579	4.385
4.	Driver Cost	20.881	20.881
5.	Helper Cost	18.959	18.959
6.	Direct Cost Per Hour	$ 47.219	$ 52.691
7.	Indirect Cost	26.561	29.639
8.	Total Cost at 100 Operating Ratio	$ 73.780	$ 82.330
9.	Vehicle With Driver:		
10.	Vehicle Fixed Cost	$ 4.800	$ 8.466
11.	Vehicle Running Cost	2.579	4.385
12.	Driver Cost	20.881	20.881
13.	Direct Cost	$ 28.260	$ 33.732
14.	Indirect Cost	15.896	18.974
15.	Total Cost at 100 Operating Ratio	$ 44.156	$ 52.706
16.	Extra Helper:		
17.	Direct Cost	$ 16.478	
18.	Indirect Cost	9.269	
19.	Total Cost at 100 Operating Ratio	$ 25.747	
20.	Packing And Unpacking Labor:		
21.	Direct Cost	$ 20.881	
22.	Indirect Cost	11.746	
23.	Total Cost at 100 Operating Ratio	$ 32.627	

Table 11.4 brings forward each of the direct cost categories prepared in Tables 11.1 through 11.3 and summarizes them to produce a total cost for the vehicles operated in local service. The determination of indirect cost will be discussed in detail in connection with distance rates. Here it is sufficient to indicate the ratio employed is 36% of the total cost, or 56.25% of the direct cost. When direct and indirect cost are combined, as shown in Table 11.4, the result is the total cost at 100 operating ratio, or the break-even point.

The construction of cost in Table 11.4 is not, however, the unit of measure in which hourly rates are normally expressed in household goods transportation. In other words, these carriers usually do not use one rate for a bobtail and another for tractor-trailer combinations.

The basis to blend the cost for a straight truck with that of a tractor-trailer combination is data contained in the field study. This data includes a record of the type of equipment used in various services. From the determination of overall usage of each vehicle type, the individual total costs can be weighted to achieve a single cost for the fleet used in hourly rated transportation. The field study for household goods transportation will also be discussed in relation to distance rate construction.

The illustration in Table 11.5 employs a ratio of 70% for bobtail usage and 30% for tractor-trailer usage in construction of the Van With Driver and Helper rate, while the Van With Single Driver rate uses ratios of 80% for the bobtail and 20% for the combinations. The reason for the difference is that bobtails tend to transport smaller shipments that require only one person to provide the service. On the other hand, tractor-trailer combinations tend to transport larger shipments requiring two or more employees.

The other consideration used in preparing Table 11.5 is profit margin. The figures in Table 11.4 must be enlarged to include profit. An operating ratio of 93% is used in this book only because that is the ratio most frequently used in constructing rates in a regulated environment. The increment of profit added to cost at the break-even point depends upon competition, cost of borrowed funds, income tax consideration, and individual firm requirements. The 7% net profit figure includes the cost of money, income tax, and return on equity.

TABLE 11.5

DEVELOPMENT OF HOURLY RATES IN HOUSEHOLD GOODS TRANSPORTATION

Line No.	Item		2-Axle Truck	Tractor Semitrailer
1.	Vehicle With Driver and Helper:			
2.	Cost at 100 Operating Ratio		$ 73.780	$ 82.330
3.	Weighting		70%	30%
4.	Weighted Cost		$ 51.646	$ 24.699
5.	Single Factor Cost		$ 76.345	
6.	Van And Two Person Rate (93 O. R.)		$ 81.70	
7.	Vehicle With Driver:			
8.	Cost at 100 Operating Ratio		$ 44.156	$ 52.706
9.	Weighting		80%	20%
10.	Weighted Cost		$ 35.325	$ 10.541
11.	Single Factor Cost		$ 45.866	
12.	Van With Driver Rate (93 O. R.)		$ 49.10	
13.	Extra Helper:			
14.	Cost at 100 Operating Ratio	$ 25.747		
15.	Extra Helper Rate (93 O. R.)	$ 27.55		
16.	Packing And Unpacking Labor:			
17.	Cost at 100 Operating Ratio	$ 32.627		
18.	Packing Rate Per Hour (93 O. R)	$ 34.90		

Table 11.5 is an illustration of hourly rate construction for household goods local transportation. As with all examples, this construction has no specific reference to a particular transportation circumstance or carrier. Obviously, all of the cost increments vary geographically and even from carrier to carrier. The illustration is for the sole purpose of providing the methods to determine the rates.

The purpose of the table is to combine vehicle configurations so that the rate will express the cost for all vehicle types used in each service. According to the cost summarized in Table 11.5, the rate for a van and two men, based upon the operating cost, would be $81.70 per hour; the van and one man would be $49.10. Extra helpers would be charged at a rate of $27.55 per hour; the packing and unpacking hourly rate would be $34.90.

Per-carton Packing Rates

Many local movers have developed a lucrative packing and unpacking business as an outgrowth of the moving business. Selling cartons and packing materials over the counter at mover facilities is also a profit center for many movers. Most local movers prefer to assess packing and unpacking rates on a per-carton basis. These rates are normally quoted in three increments: a price for the carton, the packing labor, and the unpacking labor. The reason for this construction is to provide a rate for cartons sold separately from the actual packing and unpacking service.

The reason for splitting labor into two separate rates is simply productivity. It takes longer to pack than to unpack, and many shippers prefer that the carrier pack the goods only as they would rather unpack themselves. Separate rates provide charges to satisfy all customers.

TABLE 11.6

DEVELOPMENT OF PACKING CONTAINER RATES

Line No.	Item	Container Cost	Material Percent	Material Cost	Direct Cost	Total Cost	Rate
1.	Dish pack	$3.740	59	$ 2.207	$ 5.947	$ 9.292	$ 9.94
2.	Less than 3 cubic ft	.949	42	.399	1.348	2.106	2.25
3.	3 cubic feet	1.105	42	.464	1.569	2.452	2.62
4.	4 1/2 cubic ft	1.547	34	.526	2.073	3.239	3.47
5.	6 cubic ft	1.742	36	.627	2.369	3.702	3.96
6.	6 1/2 cubic ft	1.742	28	.488	2.230	3.484	3.73
7.	Wardrobe	5.681	8	.454	6.135	9.586	10.26
8.	Mattress, crib	4.134	7	.289	4.423	6.911	7.39
9.	Mattress - Not over 39 x 75	6.890	5	.345	7.235	11.305	12.10
10.	Mattress - Not over 54 x 75	8.983	5	.449	9.432	14.738	15.77
11.	Mattress - 39 x 80	9.460	4	.378	9.838	15.372	16.45
12.	Mattress - Over 54 x 75	9.660	6	.580	10.240	16.000	17.12
13.	Corrugated containers	4.563	31	1.415	5.978	9.341	9.99

The container cost is the invoice cost of the containers purchased from suppliers plus sales tax. The Material Percent column produces the amount of packing material (bubble pack, newsprint, tape, etc.) necessary to protect the packed goods in each carton. The percentages in this analysis for packing material were produced in a study done by the California Department of General Services. While they are the specific results of an industry study of 219 movers, the numbers will vary from mover to mover. The column headed Direct Cost is the sum of the container and material cost for each carton size.

Discussion of carton cost and pricing is particularly timely in various parts of the country. Increases in container cost on the West Coast are expected to reach 50% in 1995. The methods described relative to packing rates provide movers with a method to construct rates to keep pace with cost increases.

The illustration adds an indirect cost of 36% to the cost of cartons. There are two reasons for this added cost beyond the usual overhead considerations. The philosophy of this book is that no rate subsidizes another one. That is, in relation to cost construction, every rate must generate an increment of profit. Because of the competitive forces, actual practice may produce a different result.

The second reason for the addition of indirect cost is because such cost is actually incurred. Upon arrival at a mover's premises, the material is moved to a storage area. While stored, it occupies space that would otherwise generate household goods storage revenue, and requires the maintenance of material inventories by clerical personnel. These are overhead, or indirect, costs that must be recovered in the rate structure.

The method used in the illustration in Table 11.5 for the inclusion of indirect cost is to divide the direct cost by the complement of the indirect percentage. For example, in the illustration, the indirect cost is 36% of the total cost. To find the total cost when the direct cost is known, divide the direct cost by 64%, which is the direct percentage complement.

In addition to carton rates, movers need to assess charges for packing and unpacking labor in connection with both local- and long-distance moving. These rates and charges are a function of hourly labor cost, production per carton, and cartons packed per shipment. Table 11.7 illustrates the cost construction and rate development for these mover services.

TABLE 11.7

DEVELOPMENT OF PACKING RATES PER CONTAINER

Line No.	Item	Hours Per Container	Packing Labor Cost*	Direct and Indirect	Rate Per Container
1.	Dish pack	53.95%	$11.265	$17.602	$18.83
2.	Less than 3 cubic ft	12.58	2.627	4.105	4.39
3.	3 cubic feet	16.77	3.502	5.472	5.86
4.	4 1/2 cubic feet	19.30	4.030	6.297	6.74
5.	6 cubic feet	21.65	4.521	7.064	7.56
6.	6 1/2 cubic feet	23.17	4.838	7.559	8.09
7	Wardrobe	19.37	4.045	6.320	6.76
8.	Mattress, crib	2.60	.543	.848	.91
9.	Mattress - Not over 39 x 75"	3.37	.704	1.100	1.18
10.	Mattress - Not over 54 x 75"	5.47	1.142	1.784	1.91
11.	Mattress - 39 x 80"	4.65	.971	1.517	1.62
12.	Mattress - 54 x 75"	11.12	2.322	3.628	3.88
13.	Corrugated containers	19.75	4.124	6.444	6.90

* Labor cost per hour $20.881, Table 11.1, Packer Wage.

Table 11.7 utilizes the Packer Total Hourly Labor Cost in Table 11.1. The hourly breakdowns for each carton were originally developed in a study conducted by Allied Van Lines. Carriers who prepare their own study analysis using procedures set forth in the packing rate table should determine independent packing times for their particular operation. Such analysis is not difficult, and results will prove helpful in constructing an appropriate pricing structure.

Unpacking cost per carton follows the methods outlined in connection with packing. Table 11.8 depicts a proven method to determine unpacking rates per carton.

TABLE 11.8

DEVELOPMENT OF UNPACKING RATES PER CONTAINER

Line No.	Item	Hours Per Container	Unpacking Labor Cost*	Direct and Indirect	Rate Per Container
1.	Dish pack	11.92%	$2.489	$3.889	$4.16
2.	Less than 3 cubic feet	2.68	.560	.875	.94
3.	3 cubic feet	4.78	.998	1.559	1.67
4.	4 1/2 cubic feet	4.52	.944	1.475	1.58
5.	6 cubic feet	4.73	.988	1.544	1.65
6.	6 1/2 cubic feet	4.70	.981	1.533	1.64
7.	Wardrobe	3.02	.631	.986	1.06
8.	Mattress, crib	.62	.129	.202	.22
9.	Mattress - not over 39 x 75"	1.07	.223	.348	.37
10.	Mattress - not over 54 x 75"	1.73	.361	.564	.60
11.	Mattress - 39 x 80"	1.47	.307	.480	.51
12.	Mattress - 54 x 75	3.23	.674	1.053	1.13
13.	Corrugated containers	4.25	.887	1.386	1.48

* Labor cost per hour $20.881, Table 11.1, Packer wage.

Figures in the column headed Hours Per Container came from the Allied Van Lines study referred to in the packing rates discussion. The same hourly wage rate was used.

Properly constructed, these procedures produce a reliable rate structure that carrier management can use to assess local rates. Additionally, the procedures are helpful in determining whether the revenue splits received for servicing interstate shipments are appropriate. Finally, carriers who employ a sales staff can use these rates to furnish guidelines for soliciting business.

Distance-rated Moving

Industry fragmentation exists in the distance-rated sector just as it does in other segments of household goods transportation. Van line agency agreements usually contain a clause that restricts the hauling radius of local carriers or agents. While these conditions vary among van lines, many of them restrict the agent to transportation within a 250-mile radius from the point of domicile. Thus, van lines try to transport all shipments over 250 miles, allowing the local industry to transport shipments only within 250 miles.

In actual practice, there are variations in this orderly distribution of revenue, as well. Local movers who book, or sell, small shipments weighing less than 2,000 pounds prefer to turn them over to the van line because the revenue generated from shipments of this size is not sufficient to return the vehicle to the point of origin. Local movers prefer to transport large shipments on their own equipment because the revenue is significant in terms of cash flow. The customer pays its freight bill at the conclusion of the transaction, and these funds offset labor, fuel, and other direct costs incurred by the mover.

Van lines, on the other hand, also prefer the larger shipments for much the same reason. As common carriers, they must accept the smaller shipments, but, for reasons of economics, they make every effort to obtain the larger ones. Consequently, small shipments are often not serviced as well as they might be.

Another type of carrier has emerged to service the smaller shipments moving under distance rates. Industry terms this mover the "hauling carrier." The concept of the hauling carrier is that it will transport small shipments, particularly if a heavy traffic lane is involved. Examples of heavy traffic lanes are Los Angeles-San Francisco, Washington-New York, Kansas City-St. Louis, and others. There is a sufficient number of small shipments available in the system to make it profitable for hauling carriers. The hauling carrier, in most cases, is a local mover-agent that elects to fill the niche left by local agents and van lines. In some cases, van lines even support these activities. Because these situations exist, they must be factored into industry economics.

In all of these arrangements, handling of small shipments varies widely. In some cases, the origin agent picks up the shipment and brings it to the storage facility for loading on the hauling carrier's equipment. In others, the van line or hauling carrier picks up the shipment and transports it directly. Some shipments are delivered to storage facilities at the destination, for carrier convenience; some are transported directly to the point of destination. The purpose of this discussion is to illustrate why distance rates are constructed to include several operating processes.

Distance rates include not only the actual cost of transportation between two points, but also an element of cost for shipments taken to or from storage facilities prior to or after line-haul transportation. This is not the same as storage-in-transit where the customer orders such storage. In the instances described here, it is done for carrier convenience and shipment efficiency. Small shipments are brought to terminal facilities to await loading on line-haul vehicles. Such shipments are combined with others to spread line-haul cost among the various shipments. To recover the cost of these operations, cost studies supporting distance rates include pickup and delivery and platform handling costs.

Inclusion of these costs is similar to the concept of the ratio of loaded to total miles discussed in Chapter 9. The Household Goods Carrier's Bureau Mileage Guide provides actual distances between two named points. It is important to note that distances provided in the guide include only actual miles between two named points; they do not include additional miles traveled by the carriers to service the shipment. If the servicing carriers at either origin or destination, or both, are required to incur additional miles and cost to service shipments, they must recover that cost in the rate. The methods to accomplish this objective are by pickup and delivery and platform studies. The pickup and delivery portion of the study covers the travel time and distance to the pickup or delivery point; the platform portion covers the transfer of small shipments at the mover's premises. Another purpose for the pickup and delivery study is to record loading and unloading time.

Not all local movers are interested in distance rates because they are not involved in this particular type of transportation. These movers choose to turn over all shipments in excess of the radius of local moves to van lines or hauling carriers. However, those movers who are either hauling carriers or local movers involved with this system should be particularly interested.

With the advent of rate discounting and deregulation in many sectors, prior benchmarks in published tariffs no longer exist. Consequently, rate and revenue splits are not always acceptable to the players in a particular shipment transaction. A distance rate structure, based upon the operating cost of the hauling carrier with a typical pickup and delivery cost included, is an invaluable tool in solving this problem. The hauler can issue its rates to local movers, and specify that, when the hauler transports shipments for them, revenue splits will be based upon the rate construction provided. If the hauling carrier has developed its rates properly, the rates will reflect high average loads, which will reduce the rates per 100 pounds. Accordingly, the hauling carrier should be very competitive in terms of revenue splits with local agents.

It is important to note that the hauling carrier can issue the rates it will charge another carrier to transport its shipments, if these rates are independently determined. It is not appropriate for local agents and hauling carriers to collectively determine rates to be assessed to customers. Without immunity from anti-trust law, local carriers and hauling carriers cannot jointly establish rates to be assessed to the public. However, at the present time, interstate van lines authorized by the Interstate Commerce Commission can collectively set rates.

There are also other applications of the distance-rated construction. Historically, not all carriers have participated in collective rate-making through tariff bureaus. Those who do not can use the procedures in this book to establish and maintain an independent rate structure. Others who can use the methodology effectively are local carriers that negotiate with van lines on issues of authorized shipment radius and revenue splits for trailer rental fees or other services rendered on interstate shipments. Finally, models can be developed from the format to determine the impact of changes in owner-operator percentages upon the rate structure.

Discussion of rate-making for shipments moving on a distance basis begins in a similar fashion to discussions for other trucking systems. Cost is based upon the concept of direct and indirect costs. Direct cost includes labor, the vehicle fixed cost, and the vehicle running cost. These costs are often referred to as out-of-pocket cost. Indirect cost, while variable in nature, does not vary with individual shipments. Such cost varies with the overall business volume, and must be recovered in rate structures predicated upon fully allocated cost.

All tables necessary for distance rate construction are included in this chapter to facilitate reader reference. The numbers used are for demonstration purposes only; they do not reflect a particular household goods operation. It is believed, however, that the correlation of the numbers in the demonstrations are sufficient to provide typical rate relationship results.

In addition to study design issues presented in Chapter 3, the analyst must determine the weight brackets in which rates will be expressed and the cost points at which the cost by length of haul will be determined. In the first instance, weight brackets are necessary to reflect reductions in the hundred-weight rate as shipment weights increase. Bracket width determines the range of application of each rate at a single distance. If the brackets are too wide, the relationship of cost to rate will be impaired. For example, if a weight bracket of 5,000 to 15,000 pounds is selected, rates at either side of the bracket are too low in relation to the cost points to be compensatory, on the one hand, or are unreasonably high, on the other. In this example, shipments weighing between 5,001 and 14,999 pounds would take the same rate.

Cost is determined at the average weight per shipment within the bracket. If the average weight per shipment was 10,000 pounds, the carrier would be undercompensated on shipments weighing less than average and overcompensated on shipments above the average. Accordingly, the weight brackets selected should be as narrow as possible. If the brackets selected are too narrow, however, they will jeopardize the break-back provision that accompanies distance rates. The break-back point is defined as the weight at which a shipment rated on actual weight will produce the same revenue as that of a shipment rated at the next higher minimum weight using the next lower rate. The purpose of this rule is to provide the shipper with the lower of the two rate applications, and to prevent the carrier from assessing a higher charge for a lesser weight than for greater weight.

For example, a 5,000 to 15,000 bracket might produce a break-back point at 12,000 pounds. In that case, the carrier would be compensated at the bracket rate up to 12,000 pounds or at the next higher minimum weight of 15,000 pounds at a lower rate. All shipments weighing in excess of 12,000 pounds would be rated at the next minimum weight and lower rate. All shipments weighing less than 12,000 pounds would be rated at actual weight.

If weight brackets are too narrow, the break-back points will overlap, creating inequities in the structure. This point is illustrated in Table 11.23A. The 1,000 pound to 2,000 pound weight bracket for shipments moving between 50 and 60 miles shows a rate of $25.15 per 100 pounds. The break-back weight is $1,491. In Table 11.16, it was determined that the average weight per shipment for this weight bracket was 1,500 pounds. At the average weight per shipment of 1,500 pounds, and with a rate of $25.15 per 100 pounds, the revenue needed to cover the fully allocated cost was $377.25.

At the break-back point of 1,491 pounds, the revenue generated was only $374.99, less than that required to recover the cost. At the minimum weight of 2,000 pounds, the next higher minimum weight, the rate was $18.75 per 100 pounds. At the minimum weight, this rate produces only $375.00. Again, this is less than the revenue necessary to cover the cost.

In this example, all shipments weighing less than 1,500 pounds produce less revenue than would be produced at the average shipment weight. All shipments weighing more than 1,491 pounds take the 2,000 pound minimum weight, which also produces less revenue than required. Therefore the selected weight bracket is not sufficient to provide cost recovery at the average weight per shipment. Accordingly, selection of weight brackets consistent with the field study average shipment weights is a major consideration in a study design.

Selection of cost points by lengths of haul is equally critical. That selection will ultimately determine the flow of rates through all of the distances. Obviously, no study can be made of the cost at each increment of distance— the mile. Nor is such a study necessary. If the cost is known at a significant number of distances, a curve can be plotted that will express the cost and the rate at any distance. To plot the costs at the selected distances, draw a line through the points in a graph, and read from the graph at any point desired. This method not only produces a smooth progression of cost but it also provides a well-constructed rate structure.

In the illustrations of the costs and the rates in this chapter, the following weight brackets were selected: less than 1,000 pounds, 1,000 to 1,999, 2,000 to 4,999, 5,000 to 7,999, 8,000 to 11,999, 12,000 to 15,999, and over 16,000 pounds. Cost points on a distance basis are 50, 100, 250, 400, and 600 miles. The total cost per 100 pounds and ensuing rates will be developed within these brackets and at each mileage point.

All of the information and data in the study will be compiled and categorized within these weight brackets and at these mileage points. Field observations of these functions must be conducted to obtain factual information about long distance household goods transportation. This data, together with the cost developments set forth in the following cost tables, will provide an orderly construction of rates that ultimately will reflect all of the cost incurred in each transportation service.

Productivity Study - Distance Moving

The purpose of this field study is to collect performance and productivity data for all services. This data includes loading and unloading hours for various shipment weights in pickup and delivery service, running time and distance in pickup and delivery service, average load weight in various lengths of line haul, average weight per shipment for various weight brackets, types of vehicles employed by length of line haul, and running speed by length of line haul.

Collection of the data must be uniform in terms of format and technique. The same type of form should be used to achieve reliable and accurate information. To assure reliable results, drivers must be thoroughly informed on the proper methods to complete the forms. Observers or supervisors should collect the forms daily, review them with the driver, and make sure that all data is entered and accurate.

Samples of the forms necessary to collect household goods productivity data are contained in the Appendix. Form 6 is an equipment list containing information similar to records maintained by most movers. This form should be prepared by the cost study analyst from company records. It is used to classify vehicles for the preparation of the vehicle fixed cost. A summary of the forms will produce a fixed cost on any basis desired. The forms also can be used in software programs such as Lotus or Excel. The information can be retrieved by fuel type, year, make, whether the vehicle was acquired new or used, or by any other basis required. A review of the vehicle fixed cost discussion in this chapter will help the analyst determine the necessary data sorts.

Form 7 is used to acquire information about the distance move operation. When completed, these forms will provide all the productivity data necessary to construct the cost study. A sufficient number of forms must be completed in order to reflect the mover's entire distance operation. If only three or four shipments of this type are handled each week, several weeks of forms will be required to obtain a sufficient sample. If the mover handles shipments of this type routinely, less time will be necessary.

The objective is to make the sample sufficiently representative of the entire operation. The study should include shipments of various sizes, all drivers and all vehicles used in this type of service, and all operating techniques. Shipments should not be preselected for purposes of the study. All distance shipments transported during the test period must be represented. Otherwise, the study will be biased.

The study will be used to collect factual data for pricing purposes; it is not intended to be a comparison of individual drivers. Drivers should be instructed to perform their operations with no changes from routine handling. They should clearly understand the study's purpose to ensure their full cooperation. When properly constructed, the resulting rate structure will contribute to company longevity and job security.

Table 11.9 illustrates an outline of data format to be recorded and subsequently sorted for study design purposes.

TABLE 11.9

TRIP REPORT WORKSHEET

Line No.

1. Date .... _____

2. Vehicle number .... _____

3. Vehicle type (a) .... _____

4. Driver name .... _____

5. Leave terminal:

   Time .... _____

   Odometer reading .... _____

6. Arrive load or unload point: (check one)

   ☐ Load   ☐ Unload

   Time .... _____

   Odometer reading .... _____

   Shipment actual weight .... _____

7. Leave load or unload point: (check one)

   ☐ Load   ☐ Unload

   Time .... _____

   Odometer reading .... _____

8. Arrive load, unload, or terminal: (check one)

   ☐ Load   ☐ Unload   ☐ Terminal

   Time .... _____

   Odometer reading .... _____

   Shipment actual weight .... _____

   (a) Vehicle codes:

Gas bobtail	1
Diesel bobtail	2
2-axle gas tractor with semitrailer	3
2-axle diesel tractor with semitrailer	4

The data recorded in Table 11.9 will furnish all productivity necessary to construct pickup and delivery and line-haul costs. Pickup and delivery information is sorted by weight bracket; line-haul measurements are sorted by the length of haul. The use of the resulting figures is discussed in connection with the development of the cost for each operating process.

Platform handling cost (discussed later in the chapter) employs Form 8 to develop underlying productivity for handling small shipments at mover facilities.

When all of the field work is completed and the data summarized, the analyst is prepared to begin a cost study construction and rate design.

Cost Study - Distance Moves

Discussion of the labor cost in distance moving begins with different classifications of labor from those discussed for other trucking systems. Smaller movers often construct pay scales so that employees performing different functions are paid the same rate. An employee can be a driver on a specific shipment and the packer on another, or can perform both functions on still another. To accommodate this situation, one of the classifications in the development of labor cost is "Driver and Packer." This classification was selected to illustrate the point that not all labor classifications are distinct in daily operations.

The illustration includes separate wage levels for extra helpers and line drivers because most local movers pay helpers a lower rate and drivers who work in longer haul service a higher rate. Movers preparing this type of study may designate different classifications. It is important, however, that these classifications be determined in advance as they are basic to the entire cost study preparation.

TABLE 11.10

LABOR COST PER HOUR - DISTANCE BASIS

Line No.	Item	Local Driver & Packer	Helper	Line Driver
1.	Base Rate Per Hour	$ 10.463	$ 8.591	$ 10.823
2.	Vacation, Holidays, and Sick Leave	.817	.951	.648
3.	Subtotal	$ 11.280	$ 9.542	$ 11.471
4.	Workers Compensation	2.837	2.400	2.855
5.	Payroll Taxes	.997	.930	.976
6.	Health, Welfare, and Pension	1.100	1.193	.843
7.	Subtotal	$ 16.214	$ 14.065	$ 16.145
8.	Non-revenue Time	2.108	1.828	2.133
9.	Total Hourly Labor Cost	$ 18.322	$ 15.893	$ 18.278
10.	Annual Hours Worked	1,628	1,149	2,124
11.	Vacation, Holidays, and Sick leave (15.9 days = 127.2 hours)	7.81%	11.07%	5.99%
12.	Workers Compensation	25.15%	25.15%	25.15%
13.	FICA = 7.65%; SUI 2.3% of $7,000; FUF .8% of $7,000.	—	—	—
14.	Health, Welfare, and Pension	—	—	—
	$119.63 per month times 12 divided by annual hours worked			

As the subject of labor cost was discussed at length in Chapter 4, the concepts will not be repeated here. Simply stated, however, wage rates are weighted within work classifications to obtain a single rate for each category.

The calculation of vacation, holidays, and sick leave employs 7.9 days for vacation pay, 6 holidays, and 2 days for sick leave. The total of 15.9 days equates to 127.2 hours, which is then divided by the annual hours worked in each employee classification. The resulting percentage is multiplied by the base rate per hour to determine the figures on line 2.

Workers compensation is 25.15% of the subtotal on line 2 because workers compensation in most states is paid on all wages except the penalty portion of overtime.

FICA is 7.65% of line 2 because the annual hours worked times line 2 is less than the statutory wages subject to tax. If the wages earned exceeded the taxable wage, the 7.65% would be applied only to the taxable wage. State and federal unemployment insurance is generally based upon $7,000 of annual wages. In the illustration, the state unemployment rate is 2.3% and the federal is .8%. The annual cost of these taxes is 3.1% of the first $7,000 in wages, or $217 annually. The hourly cost is calculated by adding the FICA annual cost to the unemployment insurance figure of $217 and dividing that result by the annual hours worked.

To determine the annual health, welfare, and pension costs, multiply the monthly employer cost by 12. The annual cost is then divided by the annual hours worked to obtain the cost per hour.

For a detailed discussion of issues involving the vehicle fixed cost, review Chapter 5. For these purposes, an analysis of such cost in connection with the rate structure is sufficient. Table 11.11 illustrates how the vehicle fixed cost is determined so that the results can be carried forward to the operating processes necessary for proper rate construction.

TABLE 11.11

VEHICLE FIXED COST DEVELOPMENT FOR DISTANCE RATED SHIPMENTS

Line No.	Item	2-Axle Diesel Tractor	2-Axle Gas Tractor	2-Axle Truck	2-Axle Van Semitrailer
1.	Historical Cost	$50,850	$40,850	$28,950	$19,850
2.	Salvage Value	7,628	6,128	4,343	2,978
3.	Service Value	$43,222	$34,722	$24,607	$16,872
4.	Vehicle Life	10 yrs	10 yrs	10 yrs	12 yrs
5.	Annual Vehicle Cost	$4,322	$3,472	$2,461	$1,406
6.	Vehicle License Fees:				
7.	Registration Fees	$23	$23	$23	$23
8.	Weight Fees	450	450	400	300
9.	License Fees	550	500	350	250
10.	Annual License Fees	$1,023	$973	$773	$573
11.	Other Vehicle Fixed Cost:				
12.	Federal Hwy Use Tax	550	550	550	-
13.	Van Equipment	-	-	480	660
14.	Insurance	5,488	4,388	3,526	1,040
15.	Annual Vehicle Fixed Cost	$11,383	$9,383	$7,790	$3,679
16.	Annual Hours Worked	1,500	1,500	1,500	1,500
17.	Fixed Cost Per Hour	$7.589	$6.255	$5.193	$2.453

Examples in Table 11.11 can be easily expanded to include more detailed vehicle descriptions, when necessary. If the mover engages in electronics transportation as well as household goods moving, it may be useful to calculate the cost of vans with lift gates separately from the traditional drop-floor trailers. Or, if the mover transports a significant number of storage vaults on flatbeds, the analyst may want to include that operation here, although a separate scale of rates can be developed. The organization of the cost development as shown is highly flexible, and it can be adjusted to fit any trucking circumstances. All vehicle cost decisions in connection with the study design should be based on the vehicle inventory forms described earlier.

Vehicle running cost may also be developed for any predetermined equipment categories, but these same categories should be used throughout the study. When properly constructed, all vehicle direct cost is sufficiently detailed to provide accuracy, but not so detailed as to be overly burdensome with unnecessary information. The details of running cost in Chapter 6 should be reviewed in connection with study design. In this chapter, it is important to note that the vehicle classifications selected for inclusion in the vehicle fixed cost analysis are the same as those employed in the vehicle running cost analysis.

TABLE 11.12

VEHICLE RUNNING COST DEVELOPMENT FOR DISTANCE — RATED SHIPMENTS

Line No.	Item	2-Axle Diesel Tractor	2-Axle Gas Tractor	2-Axle Truck	2-Axle Van Semitrailer
1.	Fuel Cost				
2.	Cost Per Gallon	$ 1.26	$ 1.28	$ 1.28	$ -
3.	Miles Per Gallon	6.40	5.90	7.00	-
4.	Cost Per Mile	$ .197	$ .217	$ .183	-
5.	Oil Cost Per Mile	.002	.002	.002	-
6.	Tire Cost Per Mile	.044	.036	.040	.023
7.	Repair Cost Per Mile	.166	.197	.220	.042
8.	Running Cost Per Mile	$ .409	$ .452	$ .445	$ .065

The final element of operating cost is termed "indirect." It includes those costs not determined in connection with the direct cost construction. Indirect cost preparation was discussed in Chapter 7, and should be reviewed before summarizing the actual cost. The process for measuring indirect cost is done in the same manner, but the expense account design and ratio results are substantially different for household goods transportation. Table 11.13 provides a method to determine the indirect ratio for household goods carriers.

TABLE 11.13

DEVELOPMENT OF INDIRECT COST - HOUSEHOLD GOODS

Line No.	Item	Direct	Indirect	Total
1.	Supervisory Salaries	$ -	$ 55,000	$ 55,000
2.	Clerical Salaries	-	128,491	128,491
3.	Sales Salaries	-	99,424	99,424
4.	Officers Salaries	-	55,000	55,000
5.	Driver & Helper, Interstate	27,975	-	27,975
6.	Driver & Helper, Intrastate	24,669	-	24,669
7.	Driver & Helper, Local	478,251	-	478,251
8.	Commissions	-	23,938	23,938
9.	Group Insurance	31,120	18,569	49,689
10.	Workers Compensation	30,964	5,265	36,229
11.	Uniforms	-	732	732
12.	Payroll Taxes	31,812	19,820	51,632
13.	Fuel & Oil, Line haul	20,392	-	20,392
14.	Fuel & Oil, Local	39,585	1,023	40,608
15.	Tires & Tubes, Line haul	10,898	-	10,898
16.	Tires & Tubes, Local	10,792	485	11,277
17.	Office Supplies	-	26,092	26,092
18.	Packing Materials	178,486	-	178,486
19.	Vehicle Repairs - Line haul	12,382	-	12,382
20.	Vehicle Repairs - Local	34,727	1,623	36,350
21.	Building Repairs	-	6,083	6,083
22.	Janitorial Services	-	1,456	1,456
23.	Watch & Alarm	-	2,165	2,165
24.	Professional Services	-	6,226	6,226
25.	Advertising	-	3,348	3,348
26.	Utilities	-	6,214	6,214
27.	Communications	-	23,448	23,448
28.	Equipment Rental	28,081	2,938	31,019
29.	Purchased Labor	115,106	-	115,106
30.	Driver Travel Expense	8,698	-	8,698
31.	Travel & Entertainment	-	35,659	35,659
32.	Dues & Subscriptions	-	6,398	6,398

(continued)

33. Postage	-	5,964	5,964
34. Depreciation, Vehicles	17,900	-	17,900
35. Depreciation, Warehouse	-	1,416	1,416
36. Depreciation, Office	-	1,124	1,124
37. Rent	-	71,364	71,364
38. Property Taxes	-	968	968
39. Vehicle Taxes	11,797	350	12,147
40. Other Taxes	-	200	200
41. Claims	-	28,135	28,135
42. Insurance	44,198	4,196	48,394
Total Expense	$ 1,157,833	$ 643,114	$ 1,800,947
Ratio	64.29	35.71	100.00

Similar indirect ratios can be developed from an analysis of individual expense accounts in the income statement. The objective is to determine the ratio of expenses not included in the determination of the direct cost set (Tables 11.10 through 11.12) to the total expenses. In some cases, the expense accounts from an income statement or a general ledger will not be constructed in sufficient detail to allocate the entire account totals to either direct or indirect cost. For example, the account for employee payroll taxes might need to be analyzed to determine what portion of the total is incurred for direct employees as opposed to indirect employees. Table 11.10 only illustrates the cost development for drivers, packers, and helpers because these are the employee classifications directly involved in producing transportation service. Employees such as clerks, secretaries, and dispatchers are not included in the table; their wages are classified as indirect. Payroll tax allocation must follow the same distribution.

In another example, line 14 in Table 11.13 indicates an amount for both direct and indirect fuel and oil. The fuel cost is incurred for both revenue-producing equipment and service cars such as sales vehicles and shop pickup trucks. The cost classified as indirect results from fuel purchased for company cars and pickups. Since this expense was not measured in the direct cost, and does not vary by shipment, it is an indirect cost.

The array of accounts in Table 11.13 portrays a logical and detailed distribution of mover expenses. Lines 1 through 4 are expenses incurred for clerical and management personnel not measured as a part of direct cost: dispatchers, clerks, shop supervisors, mechanics, and others. All such wages in the table are shown as an indirect expense.

Mechanics are included as a direct cost if the carrier employs them for an in-house shop. In this circumstance, and when the maintenance cost included in the running cost is determined from time sheets and work orders, mechanics become direct employees because both parts and labor are recorded in individual vehicle records from which the direct cost for maintenance is determined. The tables in this chapter presume that maintenance is done outside, and that there are no shop employees. Clearly, the proper handling of mechanic or shop wages is dependent upon a carrier's individual circumstances and study design.

Lines 5 through 7 include all direct employees who perform transportation service. The commissions in line 8 are classified as an indirect cost because they are paid to people who perform no transportation function. Group insurance and Workers Compensation (lines 9 and 10) are costs incurred in circumstances similar to payroll taxes. When expense accounts do not provide separate totals for direct and indirect employees, the analyst must separate them to avoid duplicating the cost. The cost will be duplicated if an expense is included in both the direct and indirect cost measurement.

Uniforms in line 11 are normally worn by drivers and packers to present a professional image for the firm. Because the direct cost development did not include such an item, they are included as an indirect cost in Table 11.13.

The vehicle expenses in lines 13 through 16 are typical of accounts that contain a mixture of both direct and indirect costs. These accounts include the cost incurred in connection with company cars, an indirect cost, and the cost incurred in connection with revenue-producing equipment, a direct cost.

Office Supplies in line 17 were not measured in the development of the direct cost and are included, therefore, as an indirect cost.

Packing materials (line 18) are a direct cost because a separate accessorial charge is built into the rate structure. The materials are purchased for resale, and vary according to the service provided. If packing materials were included as an indirect cost, all customers would pay for a portion of that cost in the transportation rates. This would be inappropriate and unfair to customers not requiring packing services.

Vehicle repairs (lines 19 and 20) are similar to fuel, oil, and tires in that the cost of repairs for vehicles are included in the running cost, except for those costs incurred in connection with company cars.

The items listed in lines 21 through 27 are clearly overhead costs that do not vary with each service provided by the firm, and cannot be measured as direct costs.

The Rental Services in lines 28 and 29 relate primarily to rental of services to provide transportation. In this case, a small portion is devoted to office equipment rental. The work function of rental vehicles or drivers does not change simply because they are not company-owned or employed. The work is performed in transportation service, and all such expenses are direct.

Driver travel expense (line 30) is incurred in connection with layovers during long-haul transportation. While this cost is not measured in developing the direct labor cost, it will be included as a part of line-haul cost. When such cost is measured as a direct cost, it cannot be included in the indirect ratio.

The revenue-producing vehicle portions of insurance, licenses, and depreciation are all considered direct expenses when determining the indirect cost ratio. All of these costs were measured in connection with development of the vehicle fixed cost in Table 11.11.

The remaining expense accounts are indirect costs because none of them are directly incurred as the result of a particular transportation service.

From this array of expenses and distributions of cost, the indirect ratio is determined to be 36%, a figure that is quite similar to actual industry studies of the household goods moving subindustry.

The analyst can begin to formulate actual tables for construction of the cost study once the underlying data is collected and summarized. All of the direct costs and productivity elements are organized in a fashion that will produce the total cost by the length of the haul. In the tables that follow, the direct cost for three operating processes are prepared. From these tables the direct cost is summarized, and the total cost calculated at cost points and weight brackets selected in the study design.

Platform Cost

Platform cost is the first operating process to be evaluated. The purpose of measuring this process is to provide for the cost of handling small shipments from a pickup and delivery vehicle to the line-haul vehicle, or vice versa, at the warehouse staging area. The illustration in Table 11.14 utilizes only two weight brackets because an underlying study found that only shipments weighing less than 2,000 pounds receive this handling. Shipments weighing in excess of that amount are loaded and delivered directly.

Secondly, in the illustration, it was determined that not all smaller shipments are handled at the mover's warehouse. Of shipments weighing 1,000 pounds or less, 75% were handled at the warehouse, and just 32% of shipments weighing between 1,000 and 2,000 pounds were handled in this manner. Finally, the illustration found that shipments handled at the warehouse were transferred equally by all three employee classifications. Accordingly, the wage used in the measurement of the platform cost is a weighted wage using one-third weighting for each employee classification.

TABLE 11.14

DIRECT PLATFORM COST PER 100 POUNDS

Line		WEIGHT GROUP	
No.	Item	Less than 1,000 Pounds	1,000-1,999 Pounds
1.	Platform Pounds Per Man Hour	625	675
2.	Labor Cost Per Hour	$17.498	$17.498
3.	Labor Cost Per 100 Pounds	$ 2.800	$ 2.592
4.	Percent Over Platform	75%	32%
5.	Direct Cost Per 100 Pounds	$ 2.100	$ .829

Pounds per man hour was determined from a field study using Form 8 in the Appendix. Pounds per man hour is divided into the labor cost per hour to obtain the labor cost per 100 pounds on line 3. Since not all shipments are handled on the platform, the labor cost per 100 pounds is reduced accordingly in lines 4 and 5. Direct cost per 100 pounds in both columns will be brought forward to schedules determining the total cost.

Pickup and Delivery Cost

The construction of the cost incurred as a result of varying shipment distances requires some preliminary data because the servicing of those shipments is done by a variety of vehicle combinations. The mixture of vehicles changes as the distance increases. More shipments are handled on bobtail trucks in shorter lengths of haul. Heavier vehicles are used as the length of the haul increases because shipments are more frequently combined. Since more shipments are combined in the longer hauls, the load weight increases also, which requires heavier equipment.

The analyst will need to determine the combined cost of the vehicle fixed cost and the vehicle running cost at each of the cost points selected for the study. Underlying data necessary to make this determination is available from the field study and Form 7. The data in Form 7 is first sorted by the length of the haul. Then the vehicles employed to provide service within each mileage bracket are categorized and averaged to determine the mix of the vehicles used. The result of that process is reflected in Table 11.15, which is designed to provide, at each mileage point, a weighted vehicle cost based upon the hourly or the mileage cost of individual vehicles in Tables 11.11 and 11.12. Cost per hour for each unit is combined and weighted according to use in each distance bracket.

TABLE 11.15

WEIGHTING OF VEHICLE FIXED AND RUNNING COST

Line No.	Item	LENGTH OF HAUL (miles)				
		50	100	250	400	600
1.	Weighting					
2.	Truck	63%	36%	12%	10%	-
3.	2-Axle Diesel Tractor and 2-Axle Semitrailer	32%	59%	83%	85%	95%
4.	2-Axle Gas Tractor and 2-Axle Semitrailer	5%	5%	5%	5%	5%
5.	Fixed Cost Per Hour					
6.	Truck ($5.193)	$ 3.272	$ 1.869	$ .623	$ .519	$ -
7.	Diesel Tractor and Trailer ($10.042)	3.213	5.925	8.335	8.536	9.540
8.	Gas Tractor and Trailer ($8.708)	.435	.435	.435	.435	.435
9.	Fixed Cost Per Hour	$ 6.920	$ 8.229	$ 9.393	$ 9.490	$ 9.975
10.	Running Cost Per Mile					
11.	Truck ($.445)	$ .280	$ .160	$ .053	$ .045	$ -
12.	Diesel Tractor and Trailer ($.474)	.152	.280	.393	.403	.450
13.	Gas Tractor and Trailer ($.517)	.026	.026	.026	.026	.026
14.	Running Cost Per Hour	$ .458	$ .466	$ .472	$ .474	$ .476

The figures developed in Table 11.15 will be used in following tables to measure the cost of pickup and delivery service and the actual line-haul transportation cost by the length of the haul.

Determination of the cost for pickup and delivery of household goods shipments involves several concepts that must be considered prior to actual construction. Though industry practice and simple economics explain much of the table format and objectives, many of these conditions are worthy of additional discussion. The conditions would include distance variations, loading and unloading characteristics, and the use of helpers in various situations.

The construction of the line-haul cost includes only actual transportation between the point of origin and the point of destination. This conforms with the distance used in the Household Goods Carrier's Bureau Mileage Guide. The distances in the guide do not include additional miles necessary to service various types of shipment. The line-haul cost does not include shipment loading and unloading; those costs are included in the pickup and delivery compilations. Accordingly, the pickup and delivery cost includes additional distances not included in the origin-to-destination distances as well as the loading and unloading cost.

In some cases, additional miles are traveled to pick up or deliver small shipments to or from the mover's facility to await further transportation. In other cases, mover vehicles travel to or from their facility for loading or unloading and transportation. All of the costs incurred in these circumstances must be recovered in the rate structure. The following tables are constructed to capture the pickup and delivery cost as an operating process. The line-haul cost will be discussed later.

There is another basic difference between pickup and delivery cost and line-haul cost. Pickup and delivery cost is expressed as a cost per 100 pounds for the average weight per shipment in each weight bracket. Line-haul cost, on the other hand, is a function of the average load, not the average shipment weight. Average weight per load in the line-haul operating process is a method to spread the transportation cost over the entire weight transported so that each shipment bears its fair share. The greater the load factor, the lower the cost per 100 pounds. To be competitive, movers strive to load vehicles to capacity in order to reduce the cost per 100 pounds.

Illustrations of cost preparation, beginning with Table 11.16, are designed to measure the pickup and delivery cost in a fashion that considers all operating characteristics. Table 11.16 illustrates a cost development for the pickup and delivery of shipments moving distances of less than 100 miles from the origin to the destination. The pickup and delivery cost for shipments moving over 100 miles from the point of origin to the point of destination is shown in Table 11.17.

The reason for separate tables by length of line haul reflects the difference in the pickup and delivery performance. Shipments moving over 100 miles incur travel time from the origin of the shipment to the mover's facilities and from the destination mover's facilities to the point of destination. Furthermore, the pickup and delivery of shipments moving distances in excess of 100 line-haul miles involves travel between two or more loading or unloading points. This can be observed by reviewing the en route hours in each of the tables.

The major reason for the difference is that shipments moving distances in excess of 100 miles from the origin to the destination are not handled directly. This concept was explained in connection with the industry fragmentation between local carriers and van line. The pickup and delivery cost illustrated for shipments moving under 100 miles indicates that the local mover transports most of these shipments directly: it loads the vehicle, transports the shipment, and delivers it with no additional miles except the mileage from the mover's facilities to the point of origin. Shipments of a longer length of haul incur greater miles than distance from shipment origin to destination because the shipments are combined to achieve efficiency. To accomplish the improved productivity, higher miles are traveled in the pickup and delivery process but the higher mileage cost is more than offset by the improved load factor in the line-haul operation.

Another way to view the pickup and delivery concept is in terms of stem miles (discussed in connection with pricing of other specialized carrier service in Chapter 9). Rates expressed on a distance basis for both carrier groups are predicated upon the distance from the shipment origin to the shipment destination. When rate construction is built only upon these distances, the cost and the rate are understated because the carrier must be compensated for getting to and from the work location. In the case of household goods transportation, the method to accomplish this objective is the pickup and delivery analysis; in other specialized carrier transportation, the method is that described as "stem miles" in Chapter 9.

Other observations on the pickup and delivery cost tables include the addition of En Route Hours in lines 1 and 2 to Hours at Stops in line 3 to achieve the total hours per shipment, the increasing use of helpers as the shipment weight increases, and the use of local drivers for pickup and delivery handling for short line-haul shipments versus using line drivers for longer hauls. The vehicle cost in each table is averaged to obtain one figure for spreading throughout the weight brackets. The average weight per shipment in each weight bracket is used to convert a shipment cost to a cost per 100 pounds, a figure that will decrease as the shipment weight increases. Each of these performance characteristics and cost elements may be determined from the field study or from previous cost schedules illustrated in this chapter.

The ratio of helpers in each shipment weight group is determined from the field study in Form 7 and summarized as indicated in Table 11.9. The objective is to include the additional cost of helpers as the shipment weight increases. The example determined that local drivers handle shipments within 100 miles and line drivers handle shipments in excess of that distance. This is indicated where the hourly labor rate is shown on line 6 in Tables 11.16 and 11.17. The productivity form should include the driver's name to identify the wage classification. (Actual operational analysis will disclose the true facts.)

Trip summaries, such as that illustrated in Table 11.9, must be sorted to provide the distance between the starting and the ending of the line-haul operation. The concept is that all loading, unloading, and travel time to and from carrier facilities is included in the pickup and delivery; travel time in line-haul service is recorded separately.

TABLE 11.16

DIRECT COST FOR PICKUP OR DELIVERY OF SHIPMENTS TRANSPORTED 50 AND 100 MILES

Line No.	Item	SHIPMENT WEIGHT GROUP (Pounds)						
		Less than 1,000	1,000- 1,999	2,000- 4,999	5,000- 7,999	8,000- 11,999	12,000 15,999	16,000 And Over
1.	En route Hours (23 miles @ 27 mph)	.85	.85	-	-	-	-	-
2.	En route Hours (12 miles @ 23 mph)	-	-	.52	.52	.52	.52	.52
3.	Hours at Stops (Pickup or Delivery)	1.27	2.25	4.45	7.05	10.20	14.00	18.28
4.	Hours Per Shipment	2.12	3.10	4.97	7.57	10.72	14.52	18.80
5.	Ratio, Helpers to Driver	1.00	1.00	1.25	1.50	1.67	1.67	1.75
6.	Driver Cost ($18.322)	$ 38.843	$ 56.798	$ 91.060	$ 138.698	$ 196.412	$ 266.035	$ 344.454
7.	Helper Cost ($15.893) (Line 4 x 5)	33.693	49.268	98.735	180.465	284.523	385.379	522.879
8.	Vehicle Fixed Cost ($7.575)*	16.059	23.483	37.648	57.343	81.204	109.989	142.410
9.	Vehicle Running Cost ($.462 x 23 miles)**	10.626	10.626	-	-	-	-	-
10.	Vehicle Running Cost ($.462 x 12 miles)**	-	-	5.544	5.544	5.544	5.544	5.544
11.	Total Cost Per Shipment	$ 99.221	$ 140.175	$ 232.987	$ 382.050	$ 567.683	$ 766.947	$1,015.287
12.	Average Weight Per Shipment	550	1,500	3,665	6,195	9,365	13,165	17,500
13.	Cost Per 100 Pounds	$ 18.040	$ 9.345	$ 6.357	$ 6.167	$ 6.062	$ 5.826	$ 5.802

*   Average fixed cost in columns 1 and 2, Table 11.13.

**   Average running cost in columns 1 and 2, Table 11.13.

TABLE 11.17

DIRECT COST FOR PICKUP OR DELIVERY OF SHIPMENTS TRANSPORTED 250, 400, AND 600 MILES

Line No.	Item	SHIPMENT WEIGHT GROUP (Pounds)						
		Less than 1,000	1,000- 1,999	2,000- 4,999	5,000- 7,999	8,000- 11,999	12,000 15,999	16,000 And Over
1.	En route Hours (23 miles @ 27 mph)	1.70	1.70	1.70	1.70	1.70	1.70	1.70
2.	En route Hours (12 miles @ 23 mph)	-	-	-	-	-	-	-
3.	Hours at Stops (Pickup or Delivery)	1.27	2.25	4.45	7.05	10.20	14.00	18.28
4.	Hours Per Shipment	2.97	3.95	6.15	8.75	11.90	15.70	19.98
5.	Ratio, Helpers to Driver	1.00	1.00	1.25	1.50	1.67	1.67	1.75
6.	Driver Cost ($18.322)	$ 54.416	$ 72.372	$ 112.680	$ 160.318	$ 218.032	$ 287.655	$ 366.074
7.	Helper Cost ($15.893) (Line 4 x 5)	47.202	62.777	122.178	208.596	315.842	416.698	555.699
8.	Vehicle Fixed Cost ($9.619)*	28.568	37.995	59.157	84.166	114.466	151.018	192.188
9.	Vehicle Running Cost ($.474 x 46 miles)*	21.804	21.804	21.804	21.804	21.804	21.804	21.804
10.	Vehicle Running Cost ($.474 x 12 miles)**	-	-	-	-	-	-	-
11.	Total Cost Per Shipment	$151.990	$194.948	$ 315.819	$ 474.884	$ 670.144	$ 877.175	$1,135.765
12.	Average Weight Per Shipment	550	1,500	3,665	6,195	9,365	13,165	17,500
13.	Cost Per 100 Pounds	$ 27.635	$ 12.997	$ 8.617	$ 7.666	$ 7.156	$ 6.663	$ 6.490

*   Average fixed cost in columns 3, 4 and 5, Table 11.13.

**   Average running cost in columns 3, 4 and 5, Table 11.13.

The difference between Tables 11.16 and 11.17 is described in the table headings. Table 11.16 is the pickup and delivery cost of shipments moving up to 100 miles from the point of origin to the point of destination. Table 11.17 includes the cost points over 100 miles.

Pickup and delivery costs in these tables are organized in a way that will yield the direct cost per 100 pounds for the average shipment weights in the preselected weight brackets. These tables are prepared from the trip summaries in Table 11.9.

For emphasis, one additional table illustrates the various components of productivity necessary for the ultimate cost development. Table 11.18 demonstrates the data sorts and calculations that can be created from the information recorded in Table 11.9. These calculations can be made after the initial sort into shipment weight brackets.

TABLE 11.18

PRODUCTIVITY MEASUREMENTS FROM TABLE 11.9

Line No.	Item
1.	Average weight per shipment. Add all weights in the bracket and divide by the number of weights.
2.	Distance in pickup and delivery operation. Add all pickup and delivery distances and divide the result by the number of observations.
3.	Load time. Add all load times and divide the result by the number of observations.
4.	Unload time. Add all unload times and divide the result by the number of observations. To obtain the load and unload times as illustrated in the pickup and delivery tables, add the average of lines 3 and 4.
5.	Running speed in pickup and delivery service. Determine the time en route for performing the pickup and delivery service. Divide the result by the distance in line 2 above.

Lines 2 and 5 in Table 11.18 require additional consideration. In the illustration, small shipments moving in line-haul operations under 100 miles were found, in the illustration, to travel relatively more pickup and delivery miles than larger shipments moving the same line-haul distance. This is because these shipments are returned to the carrier facilities for cross-vehicle loading. These small shipments are also taken to carrier facilities at the destination when the length of line-haul is over 100 miles. Accordingly, small shipments moving over 100 miles are handled twice at carrier facilities. This phenomenon may be observed in line 1 of Tables 16 and 17.

Also, shipments weighing in excess of 2,000 pounds and traveling over 100 miles in line-haul operations require pickup and delivery operations at both ends of the service. These shipments are not operated radially on local agent equipment; they are turned over to van lines or hauling carriers for the route-type work. Conditions discussed in this chapter and in Chapter 10 will differ from actual practice but the study analysts will be able to determine the proper methodology.

Line-haul Cost

Line-haul cost, as described earlier, is a function of load and distance. The parameters of the line-haul function are determined from the data collected through the use of the forms in the Appendix. Analysts using the described methods must determine from the trip data when the line-haul function begins and ends. A review of each operation performed by the driver and equipment will provide the information. Line-haul operations exceed 50 miles in distance and include the time the equipment leaves the last point of origin until it arrives at the first point of destination. All times and distances before and after those points are included in the pickup and delivery operation.

Weights transported in line-haul operations can be obtained by adding the shipment load weights on board or by using the actual scale weights. Once load weights are determined for each operation, they are plotted on a scatter-gram, as illustrated in Graph 11.1. The vertical plane is weight and the horizontal plane is distance. After all weights are posted to the scattergram, a trend line representing the dispersal of weights is drawn. If the study has been properly constructed, the weight will increase with the distance. The trend line may be read at any distance to obtain the average weight per load. Our illustrations were read from the graph at 50, 100, 250, 400, and 600 miles, which were the points chosen as the study points in the cost study.

GRAPH 11.1

LINE HAUL — AVERAGE WEIGHT PER TRIP

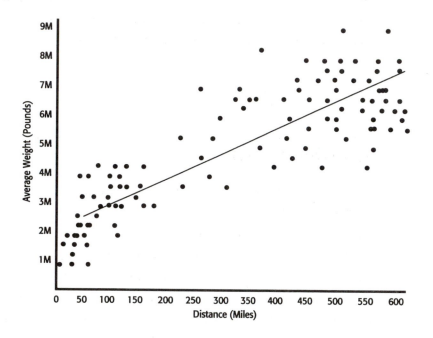

The running speed, which determines the trip time and the trip cost as functions of the distance, can be calculated with a scattergram. The vertical plane is speed and the horizontal plane is distance. The speed is posted on the scattergram for each trip. A trend line is drawn, similar to Graph 11.2, and the speed is read from the line at various cost points.

GRAPH 11.2

LINE HAUL — RUNNING SPEED

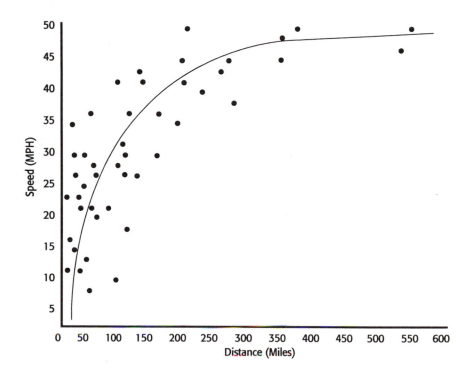

Table 11.19 illustrates the method for capturing line-haul cost using the methods described.

TABLE 11.19

LINE HAUL COST

Line No.	Item	LENGTH OF HAUL - Miles				
		50	100	250	400	600
1.	Average Speed	23	33	45	48	49
2.	Running Time Per Trip	2.17	3.03	5.56	8.33	12.24
3.	Equipment Cost Per Trip					
4.	Fixed Cost Per Hour	$ 6.920	$ 8.229	$ 9.393	$ 9.490	$ 9.975
5.	Fixed Cost Per Trip	$ 15.016	$ 24.934	$ 52.225	$ 79.052	$ 122.094
6.	Running Cost Per Mile	$ .458	$ .466	$ .472	$ .474	$ .476
7.	Running Cost Per Trip	$ 22.900	$ 46.600	$ 118.000	$ 189.600	$ 285.600
8.	Labor Cost Per Trip					
9.	Driver Cost ($18.322)	$ 39.759	$ 55.516	-	-	-
10.	Driver Cost ($18.278)	-	-	$ 101.626	$ 152.256	$ 223.723
11.	Helper Cost ($15.893)	34.488	48.156	-	-	-
12.	Subsistence	-	-	30.000	45.000	60.000
13.	Direct Cost Per Trip	$ 112.163	$ 175.206	$ 301.851	$ 465.908	$ 691.417
14.	Average Load	2,325	3,000	4,900	6,100	7,400
15.	Cost Per 100 Pounds	$ 4.824	$ 5.840	$ 6.160	$ 7.638	$ 9.343

In Table 11.19, the running time is determined by dividing the speed into the one-way trip distance. For example, a 50-mile haul time is determined by dividing 50 miles by 23 miles per hour. Since loading and unloading is included in pickup and delivery, no time is imputed for such cost. The vehicle fixed cost is a function of time, so the hourly cost is multiplied by the hours per trip. The running cost is a function of distance, so the running cost per mile is multiplied by the number of miles. The running cost per mile varies by the distance because Table 11.15 showed that different types of vehicles operate at different lengths of haul. The labor cost is a function of time, so the hourly cost is multiplied by the trip time. Subsistence is added at the 250-mile length of haul to illustrate that this cost is incurred at longer lengths of haul.

A total of these costs gives the cost per trip for line-haul operations moving various distances. The final calculation is to determine the cost per 100 pounds because rates will be expressed in that unit of measure. In most operations, the average load is relatively small. Our illustration uses one-half of the actual one-way average loads to illustrate the significance of the load factor. We assume the vehicle will return empty because none of the operations are in traffic lanes where return loads are readily acquired. If return loads were achievable, the average trip weight would nearly **double**. That word is emphasized because in actual operation not all vehicles are loaded to capacity. When the average load is increased, the cost per 100 pounds is reduced. It follows that the resulting rates can also be reduced.

The final illustration brings together all of the costs incurred in the transportation of household goods on a distance basis. Table 11.20 accumulates the various cost and operational processes by weight bracket and distance cost points. From this information, cost-based rates are structured.

TABLE 11.20

DEVELOPMENT OF TOTAL COST PER 100 POUNDS

Line		LENGTH OF HAUL - Miles				
No.	Item	50	100	250	400	600
1.	Less Than 1,000 Pounds:					
2.	Pickup and Delivery Cost	$ 18.040	$ 18.040	$ 27.635	$ 27.635	$ 27.635
3.	Platform Cost	2.100	2.100	2.100	2.100	2.100
4.	Line-haul Cost	4.824	5.840	6.160	7.637	9.343
5.	Total Direct Cost	$ 24.964	$ 25.980	$ 35.895	$ 37.372	$ 39.078
6.	Cost at 100 O. R.	$ 39.006	$ 40.594	$ 56.086	$ 58.394	$ 61.059
7.	1,000 - 1,999 Pounds:					
8.	Pickup and Delivery Cost	$ 9.345	$ 9.345	$ 12.997	$ 12.997	$ 12.997
9.	Platform Cost	.829	.829	.829	.829	.829
10.	Line-haul Cost	4.824	5.840	6.160	7.637	9.343
11.	Total Direct Cost	$ 14.998	$ 16.014	$ 19.986	$ 21.463	$ 23.169
12.	Cost at 100 O.. R.	$ 23.434	$ 25.022	$ 31.228	$ 33.536	$ 36.202
13.	2,000 - 4,999 Pounds:					
14.	Pickup and Delivery Cost	$ 6.357	$ 6.357	$ 8.617	$ 8.617	$ 8.617
15.	Line-haul Cost	4.824	5.840	6.160	7.637	9.343
16.	Total Direct Cost	$ 11.181	$ 12.197	$ 14.777	$ 16.254	$ 17.960
17.	Cost at 100 O. R.	$ 17.470	$ 19.058	$ 23.089	$ 25.397	$ 28.063
18.	5,000 - 7,999 Pounds:					
19.	Pickup and Delivery Cost	$ 6.167	$ 6.167	$ 7.666	$ 7.666	$ 7.666
20.	Line-haul Cost	4.824	5.840	6.160	7.637	9.343
21.	Total Direct Cost	$ 10.991	$ 12.007	$ 13.826	$ 15.303	$ 17.009
22.	Cost at 100 O. R.	$ 17.173	$ 18.761	$ 21.603	$ 23.911	$ 26.577
23.	8,000 - 11,999 Pounds:					
24.	Pickup and Delivery Cost	$ 6.062	$ 6.062	$ 7.156	$ 7.156	$ 7.156
25.	Line-haul Cost	4.824	5.840	6.160	7.637	9.343
26.	Total Direct Cost	$ 10.886	$ 11.902	$ 13.316	$ 14.793	$ 16.499
27.	Cost at 100 O. R.	$ 17.009	$ 18.597	$ 20.806	$ 23.114	$ 25.780

(continued)

28.	12,000 - 15,999 Pounds:					
29.	Pickup and Delivery Cost	$ 5.826	$ 5.826	$ 6.663	$ 6.663	$ 6.663
30.	Line-haul Cost	4.824	5.840	6.160	7.637	9.343
31.	Total Direct Cost	$ 10.650	$ 11.666	$ 12.823	$ 14.300	$ 16.006
32.	Cost at 100 O. R.	$ 16.641	$ 18.228	$ 20.036	$ 22.344	$ 25.009
33.	16,000 Pounds and Over:					
34.	Pickup and Delivery Cost	$ 5.802	$ 5.802	$ 6.490	$ 6.490	$ 6.490
35.	Line-haul Cost	4.824	5.840	6.160	7.637	9.343
36.	Total Direct Cost	$ 10.626	$ 11.642	$ 12.650	$ 14.127	$ 15.833
37.	Cost at 100 O. R.	$ 16.603	$ 18.191	$ 19.766	$ 22.073	$ 24.739

Table 11.13 demonstrated a method to determine the indirect ratio. The example found that indirect cost is 36% of the total cost for household goods carrier operations. To determine the total cost at 100 operating ratio, the complement of the indirect ratio is divided into the direct cost. The complement of 36% is 64%, so each direct cost is divided by that figure. The result is the total cost at the break-even point.

Rate Structure - Distance Basis

Preparation of a rate structure at levels higher than break-even will return some increment of profit at the cost points. However, proper rate construction reflects considerations other than cost, although operating cost is the overriding consideration. Other considerations include income tax consequences, cost of borrowed funds, return on equity, and technical rate design issues. Except for the technical rate issues, all of the considerations are included in the profit margin.

The profit margin in our illustrations is 7%. It recovers the carrier's cost of borrowed funds and considers income taxes and return on equity. The selection of the 7% figure is based solely upon historical usage; most regulatory agencies use that figure in setting rates but it does not follow that the figure would be correct for every carrier. Each carrier has different tax issues and a different level of borrowed funds. Accordingly, the rate structures should be predicated upon the actual carrier cost, and should consider profit needs.

Competitive conditions also impact the level of profit imputed into the rate structure. Rates upon which the company will base its marketing activity consider all of these matters. If specific competitive conditions dictate a reduction of rates below an adequate profit margin, it means that unless other rates subsidize the lower rates the company endangers its operation.

Technical aspects of rate design will be discussed in connection with the rate scales developed to illustrate the procedure. The rate design will show the importance of a relationship between weight brackets. It will also show a smooth flow of rates through all distances by maintaining a continuing relationship to cost.

Table 11.21 is an abbreviated rate scale showing how rates are projected from the cost study. The table indicates what the rates would be at each point in the cost study after two adjustments to the cost. As the total cost in Table 11.20 is at a break-even point, we increased costs by 7% to build a margin of profit into our construction of rates. Each of the mileage brackets in the rate scale straddle the specific mileage points in the cost study. Accordingly, each of the mileage brackets in the rate scale are slightly higher or lower than the actual cost. For example, the cost including profit at 50 miles on shipments rated as Any Quantity in Table 11.20 is $41.74 ($39.006 x 1.07 = $41.74). The rates at that point in Table 11.21 are $41.70 between 40 and 50 miles, and $41.80 from 50 to 60 miles. The $41.70 rate applying to distances between 40 and 50 miles should be slightly less than the specific 50-mile rate because the rate applies at lower distances (under 50 miles) where cost is less. The rate between 50 and 60 miles is slightly higher than the cost at 50 miles because it applies to longer distances and must compensate for the additional cost.

TABLE 11.21A

ILLUSTRATED RATE TABLE LAYOUT AT COST POINTS - (Rates in dollars per 100 pounds)

MILES	AQ	BREAK POINT	1000 POUNDS	BREAK POINT	2000 POUNDS	BREAK POINT	5000 POUNDS	BREAK POINT
					MINIMUM WEIGHT			
40-50	41.70		25.00		18.60		18.25	
50-60	41.80		25.15		18.75		18.40	
90-100	42.35		25.65		19.30		18.95	
100-120	42.50		26.00		19.65		19.15	
225-250	47.70		28.85		24.70		23.30	
250-275	48.80		29.65		25.35		23.70	
375-400	50.70		31.35		27.10		25.40	
400-425	51.10		31.80		27.40		25.85	
550-600	53.35		34.20		30.00		28.20	
600-650	53.80		34.65		30.50		28.55	

TABLE 11.21B

ILLUSTRATED RATE TABLE LAYOUT AT COST POINTS - (In dollars per 100 pounds)

MILES	8000 POUNDS	BREAK POINT	12000 POUNDS	BREAK POINT	16000 POUNDS
		MINIMUM WEIGHT			
40-50	18.15		17.75		17.70
50-60	18.25		17.85		17.80
90-100	18.75		18.40		18.35
100-120	18.85		18.50		18.45
225-250	22.60		21.70		21.45
250-275	22.80		21.95		21.70
375-400	24.60		23.75		23.50
400-425	24.95		24.15		23.85
550-600	27.40		26.60		26.30
600-650	27.85		27.10		26.85

TABLE 11.22A

ILLUSTRATED RATE TABLE LAYOUT - (Rates in dollars per 100 pounds)

| | | | | | | MINIMUM WEIGHT | | | | |
| MILES | | | BREAK | 1000 | BREAK | 2000 | BREAK | 5000 | BREAK |
OVER	NOT OVER	AQ	POINT	POUNDS	POINT	POUNDS	POINT	POUNDS	POINT
0	10	40.30		24.65		18.15		17.90	
10	20	40.40		24.70		18.20		17.95	
20	30	40.50		24.80		18.30		18.05	
30	40	40.60		24.90		18.45		18.15	
40	50	41.70		25.00		18.60		18.25	
50	60	41.80		25.15		18.75		18.40	
60	70	41.95		25.25		18.85		18.50	
70	80	42.10		25.35		19.00		18.60	
80	90	42.20		25.50		19.15		18.75	
90	100	42.35		25.65		19.30		18.95	
100	120	42.50		26.00		19.65		19.15	
120	140	43.10		26.40		20.20		19.60	
140	160	43.80		26.80		21.00		20.35	
160	180	44.60		27.30		22.10		21.10	
180	200	45.60		27.80		23.00		21.85	
200	225	46.60		28.30		23.90		22.60	
225	250	47.70		28.85		24.70		23.30	
250	275	48.80		29.65		25.35		23.70	
275	300	49.40		30.00		25.80		24.10	
300	325	49.80		30.30		26.25		24.45	
325	350	50.10		30.60		26.60		24.80	
350	375	50.40		30.95		26.85		25.10	
375	400	50.70		31.35		27.10		25.40	
400	425	51.10		31.80		27.40		25.85	
425	450	51.40		32.30		27.85		26.35	
450	475	51.90		32.80		28.50		26.85	
475	500	52.40		33.30		29.10		27.30	
500	550	52.90		33.75		29.55		27.75	
550	600	53.35		34.20		30.00		28.20	
600	650	53.80		34.65		30.50		28.55	
650	700	54.40		35.15		31.05		29.95	
700	750	55.10		35.70		31.60		30.50	
750	800	55.70		36.30		32.20		31.05	
800	850	56.40		37.00		32.80		31.60	
850	---								
		.70		.65		.60		.55	

TABLE 11.22B

ILLUSTRATED RATE TABLE LAYOUT - (Rates in dollars per 100 pounds)

MILES		8000	BREAK	MINIMUM WEIGHT 12000	BREAK	16000
OVER	NOT OVER	POUNDS	POINT	POUNDS	POINT	POUNDS
0	10	17.80		17.50		17.45
10	20	17.85		17.55		17.50
20	30	17.95		17.60		17.55
30	40	18.00		17.65		17.60
40	50	18.10		17.75		17.70
50	60	18.25		17.85		17.80
60	70	18.35		17.95		17.90
70	80	18.45		18.05		18.00
80	90	18.60		18.20		18.15
90	100	18.75		18.40		18.35
100	120	18.85		18.50		18.45
120	140	19.25		18.80		18.70
140	160	19.90		19.40		19.20
160	180	20.60		20.00		19.70
180	200	21.35		20.60		20.25
200	225	21.95		21.20		20.80
225	250	22.60		21.70		21.45
250	275	22.80		21.95		21.70
275	300	23.30		22.40		22.05
300	325	23.60		22.70		22.50
325	350	23.95		23.05		22.80
350	375	24.25		23.40		23.15
375	400	24.60		23.75		23.50
400	425	24.95		24.15		23.85
425	450	25.35		24.55		24.25
450	475	25.80		25.00		24.70
475	500	26.20		25.50		25.25
500	550	26.90		26.05		25.80
550	600	27.40		26.60		26.30
600	650	27.85		27.10		26.85
650	700	28.25		27.60		27.35
700	750	28.75		28.10		27.85
750	800	29.25		28.60		28.35
800	850	29.75		29.10		28.85
850	---					
		.50		.50		.50

Table 11.22 uses the same format as Table 11.21 except that rates have been computed for distances up to 850 miles and weights up to 16,000 pounds. In feathering the rates through the rate design, the objective is to maintain an even flow as distance increases so that cost relationships are consistent. The rate relationship between rate brackets is also necessary. This relationship is checked and improved when the break-back points are calculated in Table 11.23.

TABLE 11.23A

ILLUSTRATED RATE TABLE LAYOUT - (Rates in dollars per 100 pounds)

						MINIMUM WEIGHT			
MILES OVER	NOT OVER	AQ	BREAK POINT	1000 POUNDS	BREAK POINT	2000 POUNDS	BREAK POINT	5000 POUNDS	BREAK POINT
0	10	40.30	612	24.65	1,472	18.15	4,931	17.90	7,866
10	20	40.40	611	24.70	1,474	18.20	4,931	17.95	7,866
20	30	40.50	612	24.80	1,476	18.30	4,932	18.05	7,867
30	40	40.60	613	24.90	1,482	18.45	4,919	18.15	7,934
40	50	40.70	614	25.00	1,488	18.60	4,906	18.25	7,934
50	60	40.80	616	25.15	1,491	18.75	4,907	18.40	7,935
60	70	41.00	616	25.25	1,493	18.85	4,907	18.50	7,935
70	80	41.40	612	25.35	1,499	19.00	4,895	18.60	7,935
80	90	41.80	610	25.50	1,502	19.15	4,896	18.75	7,936
90	100	42.15	609	25.65	1,505	19.30	4,909	18.95	7,916
100	120	42.50	612	26.00	1,512	19.65	4,873	19.15	7,875
120	140	43.10	613	26.40	1,530	20.20	4,851	19.60	7,857
140	160	43.80	612	26.80	1,567	21.00	4,845	20.35	7,823
160	180	44.60	612	27.30	1,619	22.10	4,774	21.10	7,810
180	200	45.60	610	27.80	1,655	23.00	4,750	21.85	7,817
200	225	46.60	607	28.30	1,689	23.90	4,728	22.60	7,770
225	250	47.70	605	28.85	1,712	24.70	4,717	23.30	7,760
250	275	48.80	608	29.65	1,710	25.35	4,675	23.70	7,696
275	300	49.40	607	30.00	1,720	25.80	4,671	24.10	7,734
300	325	49.80	608	30.30	1,733	26.25	4,657	24.45	7,722
325	350	50.10	611	30.60	1,739	26.60	4,662	24.80	7,726
350	375	50.40	614	30.95	1,735	26.85	4,674	25.10	7,729
375	400	50.70	618	31.35	1,729	27.10	4,686	25.40	7,748
400	425	51.10	622	31.80	1,723	27.40	4,717	25.85	7,721
425	450	51.40	628	32.30	1,724	27.85	4,731	26.35	7,696
450	475	51.90	632	32.80	1,738	28.50	4,711	26.85	7,687
475	500	52.40	635	33.30	1,748	29.10	4,691	27.30	7,678
500	550	52.90	638	33.75	1,751	29.55	4,695	27.75	7,755
550	600	53.35	641	34.20	1,754	30.00	4,700	28.20	7,773
600	650	53.80	644	34.65	1,760	30.50	4,680	28.55	7,804
650	700	54.40	646	35.15	1,767	31.05	4,662	28.95	7,807
700	750	55.10	648	35.70	1,770	31.60	4,668	29.50	7,797
750	800	55.70	652	36.30	1,774	32.20	4,666	30.05	7,787
800	850	56.40	656	37.00	1,773	32.80	4,665	30.60	7,778
850	---								
		.70		.65		.60		.55	

TABLE 11.23B

ILLUSTRATED RATE TABLE LAYOUT - (Rates in dollars per 100 pounds)

MILES		8000	BREAK	MINIMUM WEIGHT 12000	BREAK	16000
OVER	NOT OVER	POUNDS	POINT	POUNDS	POINT	POUNDS
0	10	17.80	11,932	17.50	15,954	17.45
10	20	17.85	11,932	17.55	15,954	17.50
20	30	17.95	11,899	17.60	15,955	17.55
30	40	18.00	11,767	17.65	15,955	17.60
40	50	18.10	11,768	17.75	15,955	17.70
50	60	18.25	11,737	17.85	15,955	17.80
60	70	18.35	11,738	17.95	15,955	17.90
70	80	18.45	11,740	18.05	15,956	18.00
80	90	18.60	11,742	18.20	15,956	18.15
90	100	18.75	11,776	18.40	15,956	18.35
100	120	18.85	11,777	18.50	15,957	18.45
120	140	19.25	11,719	18.80	15,915	18.70
140	160	19.90	11,698	19.40	15,835	19.20
160	180	20.60	11,650	20.00	15,760	19.70
180	200	21.35	11,578	20.60	15,728	20.25
200	225	21.95	11,590	21.20	15,698	20.80
225	250	22.60	11,522	21.70	15,816	21.45
250	275	22.80	11,553	21.95	15,818	21.70
275	300	23.30	11,536	22.40	15,750	22.05
300	325	23.60	11,542	22.70	15,859	22.50
325	350	23.95	11,549	23.05	15,826	22.80
350	375	24.25	11,579	23.40	15,829	23.15
375	400	24.60	11,585	23.75	15,832	23.50
400	425	24.95	11,615	24.15	15,801	23.85
425	450	25.35	11,621	24.55	15,804	24.25
450	475	25.80	11,628	25.00	15,808	24.70
475	500	26.20	11,679	25.50	15,843	25.25
500	550	26.90	11,621	26.05	15,846	25.80
550	600	27.40	11,650	26.60	15,820	26.30
600	650	27.85	11,677	27.10	15,852	26.85
650	700	28.25	11,724	27.60	15,855	27.35
700	750	28.75	11,729	28.10	15,858	27.85
750	800	29.25	11,733	28.60	15,860	28.35
800	850	29.75	11,738	29.10	15,863	28.85
850	---					
		.50		.50		.50

The purpose of calculating the break-back is to simplify the shipment rating process. When break-back points are included in the rate structure, the rate clerk or billing clerk knows immediately which assessed rate would afford the customer the lowest charge. To find the break-back weight in each bracket, multiply the next higher minimum weight by the rate at that weight. For example, the rate for a minimum weight shipment of 5,000 pounds moving 165 miles would be $21.10 per 100 pounds, or $1,055.00. That number is then divided by the rate at the next lower weight bracket, which is $22.10 per 100 pounds. The result is the break-back weight of 4,774 pounds.

At a shipment weight of 4,774 pounds, the shipment can be rated at $22.10, which produces $1,055.00, or it can be rated using the next higher minimum weight of 5,000 pounds at the lower rate of $21.10 per 100 pounds, which also produces a total charge of $1,055.00. Shipments weighing between 2,000 pounds and 4,774 pounds would be rated at $22.10 per 100 pounds. Shipments weighing between 4,774 pounds and 5,000 pounds would be rated at $21.10 per 100 pounds on a minimum weight of 5,000 pounds. This method produces the lowest charge for the customer.

Accessorial Rates

Household goods carriers offer their customers a full range of services. They provide both warehousing services and auxiliary services such as placement of furniture in the home. It is not unusual for drivers and helpers to move items within the household as a customer service. Other services include carrying items for long distances, up stairways, or in and out of elevators. Rates must be developed for all of these services.

Accessorial service rates in this section apply only to shipments moving under rates other than hourly. Hourly rates are applied to all services provided on shipments moving less than 50 miles. As transportation rates on shipments moving over 50 miles only include loading and unloading and transportation, the cost of additional services must be recovered in additional rate assessments.

Stop in Transit

Split pickup or delivery service is common to most of the industry. In household goods transportation, customers often want the carrier to pick up or drop a few items at the residence of a relative. Where practical, household goods carriers provide this service at an additional charge. Table 11.24 illustrates how a split pickup or delivery rate might be determined.

TABLE 11.24

SPLIT PICKUP — SPLIT DELIVERY - (Per 100 pounds)

Line No.	Item	Unit Cost	Amount Per Stop
1.	Off-route Hours (10 miles @ 23 mph)		.43
2.	Time at Stop - 10 Minutes		.17
3.	Split Pickup or Delivery Time		.60
4.	Driver Cost ($18.278)		$ 10.967
5.	Helper Cost ($15.893)		9.536
6.	Vehicle Fixed Cost		
7.	Gas Tractor and Semitrailer	$ 8.708	
8.	Diesel Tractor and Semitrailer	10.042	
9.	Truck	5.193	
10.	Sum For Units	$ 23.943	
11.	Average For Equipment	$ 7.981 x L3	4.789
12.	Vehicle Running Cost		
13.	Gas Tractor and Semitrailer	$ .517	
14.	Diesel Tractor and Semitrailer	.474	
15.	Truck	.445	
16.	Sum For Units	$ 1.436	
17.	Average For Equipment	$ .479 x 10 miles	4.790
18.	Total Direct Cost		$ 30.082
19.	Indirect Cost		16.921
20.	Total Cost Per Stop		$ 47.003

The example shows that the carrier traveled 5 miles one-way off-route to service split pickup or delivery portions of shipments. The example also indicates that the average stop created an additional 10 miles to service the split. Together these operations added an additional .6 of an hour to service the shipment.

The example shows that a riding helper accompanied the driver on the trip. From Table 11.10, the cost per hour of $18.278 for the driver and $15.893 for the helper were obtained. These figures were multiplied by the .6 of an hour to determine the labor cost for the stop.

The vehicle fixed cost per combination unit of equipment was brought forward from Table 11.15. On lines 6 through 11 in Table 11.24 the cost for each of the units was averaged to determine the cost per stop. The example assumes that all vehicles in the fleet share the split pickup and delivery operation equally. That determination is made from the analysis of driver trip reports in the field study supporting the overall cost study.

The vehicle running cost per stop was accomplished using the same technique as that described for the vehicle fixed cost. However, the running cost per mile was multiplied by the number of miles instead of hours as the running cost is measured as a cost per mile.

The sum of labor, vehicle fixed cost, and vehicle running cost comprise the direct cost. We added the indirect cost to the direct cost to determine the total cost at a 100 operating ratio, the break-even point. The ratio of the indirect cost to the direct cost is 36%, the same figure that was used in earlier household goods transportation illustrations. To do the calculation, we divided the complement of the indirect ratio into the direct cost ($30.082 \div .64 = 47.003).

A profit factor must be added to the break-even cost to determine the applicable rate. The factor of 7% used in the split pickup and delivery illustration results in a rate of $50.30.

Service at Other Than Ground Floor

Many customers of household goods carriers reside in apartments above ground level. The illustrations of loading and unloading time to determine the transportation cost in Tables 11.16 and 11.17 included only shipments serviced at ground level. The reason for this construction is to prevent all of the customers from bearing a part of the cost to service shipments at higher than ground level. It would be unreasonable for single-family residents to share the cost of shipment handling above ground floor. To compensate for this, household goods carriers must construct a separate rate for these shipments. Table 11.25 illustrates a method to determine the proper rate level for this service.

TABLE 11.25

PICKUP/DELIVERY AT OTHER THAN GROUND FLOOR - (Per 100 pounds)

Line No.	Item	Amount
1.	Man Hours Per 100 Pounds - One Flight	.088
2.	Man Hours Per 100 Pounds - Ground Floor	.077
3.	Added Man Hours Per 100 Pounds for One Flight	.011
4.	Driver Cost ($18.278)	$ .201
5.	Helper Cost ($15.893)	.175
6.	Vehicle Fixed Cost ($7.981)	.088
7.	Direct Cost Per 100 Pounds	$ .464
8.	Indirect Cost	.261
9.	Total Cost Per 100 Pounds	$ .725

In this illustration, the pickup or delivery time per 100 pounds at ground level is determined first. That time is then subtracted from the total time per 100 pounds for handling shipments at one level above the ground. The difference is the added time required to handle shipments to the second floor. Accordingly, the rate charged to the customer must be assessed on the basis of 100 pounds for each floor above ground level.

Various cost elements shown in Table 11.25 are the same as those used in Table 11.24 for split pickup and delivery. Each hourly cost is multiplied by the fraction of an hour indicated in line 3 of Table 11.25. The sum of the individual direct costs is added to the indirect cost by the same method as that discussed in connection with Table 11.24. When the profit is included, the correct rate to assess would be $.775 per 100 pounds.

Long Carry

Sometimes household goods carriers can drive right up to buildings, but often they are called upon to pick up or deliver shipments where their vehicles must remain a distance away. Transportation rates in Table 11.23 do not include the additional cost of employees carrying goods to or from the residence. In our example, the transportation costs and rates were constructed considering that an employee carries distances up to 75 feet, a figure that would cover most shipments and locations.

Where carriers are required to provide longer carries, an additional rate is necessary to recover the added cost. To assess a charge for this service, the underlying field study trip forms were analyzed to determine the time necessary for the service and the average additional distance required for the final delivery. From this analysis, it was determined that it would be appropriate to prepare a rate per 100 pounds for each 50 feet the goods are carried beyond the first 75 feet. Table 11.26 illustrates how that rate was determined.

TABLE 11.26

COST FOR EXCESSIVE CARRY DISTANCE - (Per 100 pounds)

Line No.	Item	Amount
1.	Man Minutes Per 100 Pounds	.51
2.	Man Hours Per 100 Pounds	.0085
3.	Driver Cost Per 100 Pounds ($18.278 x L2)	$ .155
4.	Helper Cost Per 100 Pounds ($15.893 x L2)	.135
5.	Vehicle Fixed Cost Per 100 Pounds ($7.981 x L2)	.068
6.	Total Direct Cost	$ .358
7.	Indirect Cost	.201
8.	Total Cost At 100 O. R.	$ .559

No vehicle running cost is included in Tables 11.25 and 11.26. In both flight carry and long carry, the vehicle is not operating. However, the vehicle is being used to house goods while they are loaded or unloaded. Therefore, a vehicle fixed cost is included in the rate assessed.

Warehouse Handling

An important profit center for household goods carriers is offering storage facilities. The storage of household goods is an integral part of the carrier service. Householders store their goods for many reasons, including a change in moving plans. The scheduled move includes planning and preparation by the mover, real estate people, attorneys, escrow holders, repair people, and so on. If any of these vendors fail to perform, the schedule fails, and goods must be stored in transit.

Storage in transit involves two operating processes. Transportation employees load or unload the goods at the carrier storage facility. The cost for this part of the transportation process is included in the transportation rate. However, transferring of the goods to or from the warehouse staging area to storage vaults and other containers is performed by warehousemen who are not part of the actual transportation service. This handling cost is usually recovered in a rate termed "Warehouse Handling."

The second operating process is the charge for storage, a subject that is not covered in this book. Storage rates are predicated upon local rental rates and property values. To provide examples of a specific rate construction would not be useful. It is common for the industry to assess storage rates on a per-vault basis. The rates depend upon square footage and the number of vaults stacked in the warehouse.

In the example below, Warehouse Handling rates were based upon the Helper hourly labor cost.

TABLE 11.27

WAREHOUSE HANDLING

Line No.	Item	Amount
1.	Pounds Per Man Hour	850
2.	Labor Cost Per 100 Pounds ($15.893 x Line 1)	$1.870
3.	Indirect Cost	1.052
4.	Total Cost Per 100 Pounds	$2.922

The total Warehouse Handling rate including profit would be $3.13 per 100 pounds. The pounds per man hour is determined from the field study in Table 11.14, Platform Handling.

Summary

The household goods transportation industry is perhaps the most highly competitive sub-industry in trucking. It is also more inclined to include price-takers, rather than price-makers. Industry practice is to match the rates of competitors with little regard for the cost incurred to provide specific moves. However, many of these carriers provide services other than household goods transportation.

When the information provided in this chapter is used properly, carriers will be able to establish cost-based rates at compensatory levels.

Less-Than-Truckload Carriers

Often referred to as common carriers or certificated carriers, less-than-truck-load carriers have been clearly defined by both federal and state law. Within these definitions, LTL carriers were described as those who operated on regular schedules between two or more fixed terminals and transported shipments weighing less than 10,000 pounds.

This short description also suggests something different about these carriers in the context of the overall industry structure: they are the only sub-industry that regularly operates between fixed terminals. All of the carrier types discussed in earlier chapters operate radially from a single terminal on an irregular basis.

The LTL carrier system presents some unique requirements that must be met when the determination of operating cost for pricing purposes is the objective. These carriers must operate in a structured fashion, in the sense that they must pick up and deliver shipments in daily or weekly route operations. They must transfer shipments across platforms, or docks, between pickup and delivery route vehicles and line-haul vehicles. They also cater to a large number of commercial shippers tendering small shipments.

These specific operating processes are well-defined, and analysts who develop cost statements for LTL carriers are required to specifically measure each operation as a separate function.

In addition to the intricacies of cost construction, rate design is also more specific than it is for other types of carriers. As stated in the National Motor Freight Classification, LTL carrier rates are created not only by distance and weight, but also by taking into account the transportation characteristics of nearly all of the commodities shipped. Commodities are classified according to packaging, density, susceptibility to damage, and so on, and rates are applied within classification groups. This classification system requires the designers of rate structures to prepare several rates in the same weight bracket for moves of the same distance.

Since passage of the Motor Carrier Act in 1980, LTL carriers have practiced a policy of rate discounts through so-called "contract" transportation. During the period of rate discounting, published rates were increased to somewhat offset the rate reductions. Interstate published rates in today's market have little relation to reality in terms of carrier operating cost.

With the demise of economic regulation within each state, carriers no longer can compare the current intrastate rate levels of rivals, for comparison purposes. Accordingly, it has become more difficult for firms to follow the "price-taker" strategy of simply meeting the rates of competitors. As price-competitive markets are developing, and the information base is diminishing, carriers need to improve information systems to remain competitive.

The cost study and rate design discussed in this chapter will provide individual carriers with a basis for determining productivity, operating cost, and rates justified by such cost. The procedures described are time-tested. Properly constructed studies will provide management with a full range of rates upon which the firm can organize its pricing policy.

LTL cost studies and investigations rely upon the same elements of operating cost as those developed in previous chapters. Direct cost consists of labor cost, vehicle fixed cost, and vehicle running cost. The methods used to construct these costs will not be repeated except when necessary to provide details so that readers can follow the flow of information. For example, because LTL carriers employ several classifications of direct labor, some discussion of labor cost is necessary to define the work of each classification.

Labor Cost

Prior to 1980, many LTL general freight carrier employees were members of the Teamsters Union. According to their contracts, all operating employees were paid a specified wage according to job classification. Benefits were defined in the contracts and applied across the board.

At about the same time, discussions of regulatory change and the eventual passage of the Motor Carrier Act of 1980 created downward pricing pressure and similar suppression of wage rates. Carriers began discarding union contracts, and wage rates were reduced in response to heavy rate discounting.

The structure of employment packages has remained somewhat the same in the sense that a large number of pay rates and job classifications continue to exist. To construct a cost analysis predicated partially upon labor cost, the firm's employment package must be analyzed. This becomes the starting point of the total labor cost determination.

The illustrated analysis of operating cost for pricing purposes will be based upon a two-terminal operation because it is the simplest way to demonstrate the procedure without burdening the discussion. Clearly, LTL carriers operating more than two terminals can expand this study to include the required number of terminals.

Illustrations of labor cost for LTL carriers begin with Table 12.1, which is an abstract of the wage package to be used in cost development. The abstract is an orderly method to summarize and record the various factors that make up the total package.

TABLE 12.1

WAGE PACKAGE ABSTRACT — LOCAL EMPLOYEES

Line No.	Item	Terminal A	Terminal B
1.	Wages:		
2.	Driver - Truck	$ 12.275	$ 12.475
3.	Driver - Doubles	12.525	12.725
4.	Driver - Heavy Duty	12.525	-
5.	Helper	12.275	12.475
6.	Platform		
7.	a) Day Shift	12.350	12.550
8.	b) Night Shift	12.500	12.700
9.	Lift Truck Operator		
10.	a) Day Shift	12.400	12.600
11.	b) Night Shift	12.550	12.750
12.	Hostler		
13.	a) Day Shift	12.550	12.750
14.	b) Night Shift	12.700	12.900
15	Other Benefits		
16	Insurance And Welfare (Man/month)	$ 300.00	$ 325.00
17.	Paid Holidays (Days/Year)	8	8
18.	Vacation Allowance	1 Yr. – 10 Days	1 Yr. – 10 Days
		5 Yrs. – 15 Days	5 Yrs. – 15 Days
		15 Yrs. – 20 Days	15 Yrs. – 20 Days
19.	Retirement Fund (Man/month)	$ 100.00	$ 100.00
20.	Sick Leave (Days/year)	6	6
21.	Premium Pay	1.5 after 8 Hrs.	1.5 after 8Hrs.

Table 12.1 indicates the labor package for local employees. Some LTL carriers maintain a different package for line drivers because they are either paid on a mileage basis or receive different benefits as a matter of policy. Table 12.2 illustrates a line driver wage package.

TABLE 12.2

WAGE PACKAGE ABSTRACT — LINE DRIVERS

Line No.	Item	Amount
1.	Wages	
2.	Hourly Rate	$ 13.00
3.	Mileage Rate	$ .325
4.	Other Benefits	
5.	Insurance and Welfare (Man/month)	$ 300.00
6.	Paid Holidays	8
7.	Vacation Allowance	1 Yr. - 10 Days
		5 Yrs. - 15 Days
		15 Yrs. - 20 Days
8.	Retirement Fund (Man/month)	$ 100.00
9.	Sick Leave (Days/year)	6
10.	Premium Pay	N. A.

The data in Tables 12.1 and 12.2 is the foundation for the calculation of total hourly labor cost. This information, together with payroll taxes and workers compensation, make up the total for each wage classification. Our examples include Social Security taxes of 7.65% on the first $56,000 in wages. State payroll taxes are predicated upon 3.5% of the first $7,000 in wages, and the federal unemployment tax is .8% of that same taxable wage. Workers compensation is assumed to be 15% of straight time wage after adjustment for the employer's loss experience, if any.

Additional information needed for the preparation of the total labor cost is a summary of tenure of employment and the annual hours worked for each work classification. Tenure of employment is used to determine a weighted vacation pay allowance for each work classification. Line 18 of Table 12.1 and line 7 in Table 12.2 describe the company vacation policy, but they do not disclose the number of employees earning each allowance. Once the number of employees qualifying for the various vacation allowances is determined, each group is weighted on a percentage basis to determine the number of annual vacation hours actually earned in each wage classification.

Annual hours worked is the factor used to convert labor cost items paid by the company on a monthly or yearly basis to a cost per hour. Lines 16 and 19 of Table 12.1 and lines 5 and 8 of Table 12.2 indicate the amounts paid each month for employee welfare programs. These monthly costs must be annualized, and that result divided by the annual hours worked to obtain the cost per hour.

Table 12.3 may be constructed to determine the vacation pay allowance, based upon the number of years employees in each work classification have been employed.

TABLE 12.3
SUMMARY OF EMPLOYMENT TENURE — (All terminals)

Line No.	Seniority	Local Employees	Line Drivers
1.	Less Than 1 Year	0.0	0.0
2.	1 Year	27.2	31.0
3.	2 Years	11.6	14.3
4.	3 Years	9.6	8.8
5.	4 Years	6.6	6.1
6.	5 Years	6.1	5.7
7.	6 Years	5.4	5.9
8.	7 Years	3.6	3.2
9.	8 Years	3.5	3.5
10.	9 Years	4.6	3.9
11.	10 Years	3.6	3.2
12.	11 Years	2.9	2.7
13.	12 Years	1.7	1.5
14.	13 Years	2.9	1.7
15.	14 Years	2.7	2.3
16.	15 Years	1.9	1.8
17.	Over 15 Years	6.1	4.4
18.	Total	100.0	100.0
19.	1 - 5 Years	61.1	65.9
20.	6 - 15 Years	32.8	29.7
21.	16 Years and Over	6.1	4.4
22.	Total	100.0	100.0

The tenure of employment includes both line drivers and local employees at both terminals. Local employees in both terminals are included in the first column, line drivers in the second. Lines 19 through 22 summarize the tenure into annual groups consistent with the vacation benefit indicated in Tables 12.1 and 12.2. The final calculation in connection with vacation pay is to weight the vacation allowance by the percentages of employees in each group. This can be accomplished as follows:

Local Employees

Tenure of Employment	Vacation Hours	Weighted Hours
61.1	80	48.9
32.8	120	39.4
6.1	160	9.8
100.0		98.1

Line Drivers

Tenure of Employment	Vacation Hours	Weighted Hours
65.9	80	52.7
29.7	120	35.6
4.4	160	7.0
100.0		95.3

Local employees, weighted by seniority, received 98.1 hours of vacation pay each year; line drivers received 95.3 hours.

Our example showed that no employees had been with the firm less than one year. If such employees were included in payroll figures, the annual cost of vacation pay would be less as they receive no pay.

Annual hours worked, the final ingredient in development of the total hourly labor cost, is also obtained from employee payroll records. According to the Wage Package Abstracts, the firm pays overtime after 8 hours per day. As such cost must be recovered in the rate structure, a collection of individual straight time and overtime hours is required. Table 12.4 accomplishes that objective.

TABLE 12.4

EMPLOYEE ANNUAL HOURS WORKED

Line No.	Item	Terminal A	Terminal B	Line Drivers
1.	Local Drivers			
2.	Straight Time Hours	1,995	2,060	-
3.	Overtime Hours	155	190	-
4.	Total Hours	2,150	2,250	-
5.	Helpers			
6.	Straight Time Hours	1,805	1,850	-
7.	Overtime Hours	145	150	-
8.	Total Hours	1,950	2,000	-
9.	Day Platform Workers			
10.	Straight Time Hours	1,935	1,962	-
11.	Overtime Hours	115	88	-
12.	Total Hours	2,050	2,050	-
13	Day Lift Truck Operators			
14.	Straight Time Hours	1,960	1,915	-
15.	Overtime Hours	90	135	-
16.	Total Hours	2,050	2,050	-
17.	Day Hostlers			
18.	Straight Time Hours	1,910	1,855	-
19.	Overtime Hours	140	195	-
20.	Total Hours	2,050	2,050	-
21.	Night Platform Workers			
22.	Straight Time Hours	1,950	1,954	-
23.	Overtime Hours	100	96	-
24.	Total Hours	2,050	2,050	-
25.	Night Lift Truck Operators			
26.	Straight Time Hours	1,965	1,906	-
27	Overtime Hours	85	144	-
28.	Total Hours	2,050	2,050	-
29.	Night Hostlers			
30.	Straight Time Hours	1,910	1,855	-
31	Overtime Hours	140	195	-
32.	Total Hours	2,050	2,050	-
33.	Line Drivers			
34.	Straight Time			2,400
35.	Annual Miles			96,000

All of the labor components are now in place to begin construction of the total hourly labor cost. Before actual figures for cost per hour or cost per mile are processed, a table to summarize the benefit and tax cost to the firm will facilitate additional analysis. Tables 12.5 through 12.7 bring together these various cost elements. Table 12.5 shows the labor cost elements for Terminal A, Table 12.6 for Terminal B, and, Table 12.7 for line drivers.

TABLE 12.5

SUMMARY OF PAYROLL FACTORS — TERMINAL A

Line No.	Item	Vacation, Holidays, Sick Lv. % of C.1	Premium Earnings % of Column 1	Workers Compensation % of Column 3	Payroll Taxes % of Column 3+5
1.	Classification				
2.	Driver - Truck	8.58	7.77	15	8.63
3.	Driver - Doubles	8.58	7.77	15	8.61
4.	Driver - Heavy Duty	8.58	7.77	15	8.61
5.	Helpers	9.46	8.03	15	8.72
6.	Platform				
7.	Day Platform	9.00	5.94	15	8.69
8.	Day Lift Truck Operator	9.00	4.59	15	8.70
9.	Day Hostler	9.00	7.33	15	8.66
10.	Night Platform	9.00	5.13	15	8.68
11.	Night Lift Truck Operator	9.00	4.33	15	8.68
12.	Night Hostler	9.00	7.33	15	8.64

TABLE 12.6

SUMMARY OF PAYROLL FACTORS — TERMINAL B

Line No.	Item	Vacation, Holidays, Sick Lv. % of C.1	Premium Earnings % of Column 1	Workers Compensation % of Column 3	Payroll Taxes % of Column 3+5
1.	Classification				
2.	Driver - Truck	8.20	9.22	15	8.57
3.	Driver - Doubles	8.20	9.22	15	8.55
4.	Driver - Heavy Duty	8.20	9.22	15	8.55
5.	Helpers	9.23	8.11	15	8.68
6.	Platform				
7.	Day Platform	9.00	4.49	15	8.68
8.	Day Lift Truck Operator	9.00	7.05	15	8.66
9.	Day Hostler	9.00	10.51	15	8.62
10.	Night Platform	9.00	4.91	15	8.67
11.	Night Lift Truck Operator	9.00	7.56	15	8.64
12.	Day Hostler	9.00	10.51	15	8.60

TABLE 12.7

SUMMARY OF PAYROLL FACTORS — LINE DRIVERS

Line No.	Item	Vacation, Holidays, Sick Lv. % of Line 1	Premium Earnings Percent of Line 1	Workers Compensation Percent of Line 3	Health Pension Percent of Line 1	Payroll Taxes Percent of Line 3
1.	Line Driver - Hour	7.57	-	15	15.38	8.54
2.	- Mile	7.57	-	15	16.00	8.57

Column 1 in the preceding tables shows the factor to be applied to the base hourly wage for vacation, holidays, and sick leave. From the tenure of employment, it was determined that local employees receive 98.1 hours of vacation pay each year. It was also determined, in Tables 12.1 and 12.2, that all employees receive pay for 8 hours per day for 8 holidays, for a total of 64 hours. The company also has a sick leave policy that pays 8 hours per day for up to 6 days each year. The payroll analysis indicated that employees take 2.8 sick days per year on the average. At a rate of 8 hours per day, 2.8 days convert to 22.4 hours each year.

Adding the hours for vacation, holidays, and sick leave allowances produces a total of 184.5 hours per year per employee for which the company pays and the employee does not work. The cost of these hours must be recovered in a cost-justified rate structure. This is done by dividing 184.5 hours by the annual hours worked in Table 12.4. For example, local drivers in Terminal A worked a total of 2,150 hours per year, according to the payroll records. The calculation of unworked hours to hours worked produces a factor of 8.58 (184.5 ÷ 2,150 = 8.58) for local drivers in Terminal A, as shown in Table 12.5.

A similar calculation is made for each employee classification in Tables 12.5 through 12.7. The result of this calculation is multiplied by the base wage rate for each job classification, and the result is entered in the column headed Vacation, Holidays, and Sick Leave in Tables 12.8 through 12.10. When the result in column 2 in these tables is added to the base wage rate, each hour worked by the employee included in the rate structure will recover a sufficient amount to recover the cost of these fringe benefits on an annualized basis. The third column in Tables 12.8 through 12.10 is a subtotal of base wage rate and vacation, holidays, and sick leave. This subtotal (cost of base wage rates plus the cost of fringe benefits in column 1) is used to calculate other labor costs.

The second column in Tables 12.5 through 12.7 is a factor to determine the cost per hour for premium pay, or overtime. The figures in that column were obtained from the figures in Table 12.4. The overtime hours were divided by the straight time hours for each wage classification and the result was posted in the second column of Tables 12.5 through 12.7, Premium Earnings.

This calculation produces a factor that, when multiplied by the base hourly wage rate, produces a cost per hour that will recover the cost of overtime on an annualized basis. It assumes that no separate rate will be assessed for overtime work. If overtime rates are to be assessed, no factor for such cost is added to the base hourly wage rate. It would be necessary to determine separate rates for work performed at straight time and overtime.

The result of the overtime determination is indicated in column 5 of the Total Hourly Labor Cost tables for local employees. Line drivers received no overtime pay in our illustrations of total hourly labor cost development.

Workers compensation was assumed to be 15% of figures indicated as subtotals in Tables 12.8 through 12.10. In most states, manual rates are published that specify the rate for all job classifications of employees within the state's jurisdiction. These rates are then adjusted by the experience rating of individual companies. Workers compensation net rates vary widely; to calculate a specific rate would be meaningless. The figure of 15% is assumed to be in the range of most rates in the country. The 15% rate is applied to the subtotal in Tables 12.8 through 12.10 because premiums are paid on all wages except the penalty portion of overtime in many states.

Health, Welfare, and Retirement cost is determined by dividing the annual cost of the benefit by the annual hours worked. The Wage Package Abstract in Table 12.1 shows that the company paid $300 per month for insurance and welfare and $100 per month for retirement for employees working in Terminal A. The total cost of $400 per month produces an annual cost of $4,800.00. Local Drivers in Terminal A worked 2,150 annual hours. The hourly cost for these benefits is $2.233 ($4,800 ÷ 2,150 = $2.233).

The last column in Tables 12.5 through 12.7 is the factor used to determine the cost per hour for payroll taxes. Since none of the employees in the example earned sufficient wages to reach the maximum taxable wage for FICA purposes, this cost was determined by multiplying 7.65% times the subtotal in column 3 of Tables 12.8 through 12.10 plus the cost of overtime pay. FICA is paid on all wages earned.

The illustration assumed that state unemployment taxes were paid at a rate of 3.5% of the first $7,000 in annual wages. It also assumed that federal unemployment taxes were paid at a rate of .8% of the first $7,000 in annual earnings. These taxes cost the employer $301 per year for each employee who earned $7,000 or more.

More than one calculation was necessary to determine one factor to reflect the cost of payroll taxes. To illustrate the procedure, we will use the truck driver in Terminal A. The Base Wage Rate plus Vacation, Holidays, and Sick Leave cost per hour was $13.328, as shown in line 1 of Table 12.8. This figure plus the Premium Earnings in column 5 of $.954 produces a total of $14.282 per hour in actual earnings. These drivers worked 2,150 hours annually.

The annual wage for these employees was $30,706.30 ($14.282 x 2,150 = $30,706.30). The total cost per year for FICA was $2,349.03 ($30,706.30 x .0765 = $2,349.03).

State and federal unemployment taxes per year in the amount of $301 were added to the annual cost of Social Security. Accordingly, the annual payroll tax cost for each employee was $2,650.03. Annual payroll taxes divided by annual earnings produces the figures in the last columns of Tables 12.5 through 12.7 ($2,650.03 ÷ $30,706.30 = 8.63).

Cost per hour for payroll taxes is 8.63% of the total of columns 3 and 5 in Tables 12.8 and 12.9 ($13.328 + $.954 = $14.282, $14.282 x 8.63 = $1.233). The same procedure is followed for calculating all wage classifications except line drivers who earned no overtime pay. The calculation for line drivers is the tax factor in Table 12.7 multiplied by the subtotal in Table 12.10.

TABLE 12.8

TOTAL HOURLY LABOR COST — TERMINAL A

Line No.	Item	Base Wage Rate (1)	Vacation Holidays Sick Lv. (2)	Sub. Total (3)	Comp. Insurance (4)	Premium Earnings (5)	Health Welfare Pension (6)	Payroll Taxes (7)	Total Hourly Cost (8)
1.	Local Driver								
2.	Truck	$ 12.275	1.053	$ 13.328	1.999	.954	2.233	1.233	$ 19.747
3.	Tractor-semi	$ 12.525	1.075	$ 13.600	2.040	.973	2.233	1.255	$ 20.101
4.	Tractor - Doubles	$ 12.525	1.075	$ 13.600	2.040	.973	2.233	1.255	$ 20.101
5.	Heavy Duty	$ 12.525	1.075	$ 13.600	2.040	.973	2.233	1.255	$ 20.101
6.	Helpers	$ 12.275	1.161	$ 13.436	2.015	.986	2.462	1.258	$ 20.157
7.	Day Terminal								
8.	Platform	$ 12.350	1.112	$ 13.462	2.019	.734	2.341	1.234	$ 19.790
9.	Lift Truck	$ 12.400	1.116	$ 13.516	2.027	.569	2.341	1.225	$ 19.678
10.	Hostler	$ 12.550	1.130	$ 13.680	2.052	.920	2.341	1.264	$ 20.257
11.	Night Terminal								
12.	Platform	$ 12.500	1.125	$ 13.625	2.044	.641	2.341	1.238	$ 19.889
13.	Lift Truck	$ 12.550	1.130	$ 13.680	2.052	.543	2.341	1.235	$ 19.851
14.	Hostler	$ 12.700	1.143	$ 13.843	2.076	.931	2.341	1.277	$ 20.468

TABLE 12.9

TOTAL HOURLY LABOR COST — TERMINAL B

Line No.	Item	Base Wage Rate (1)	Vacation Holidays Sick Lv. (2)	Sub. Total (3)	Comp. Insurance (4)	Premium Earnings (5)	Health Welfare Pension (6)	Payroll Taxes (7)	Total Hourly Cost (8)
1.	Local Driver								
2.	Truck	$ 12.475	1.023	$ 13.498	2.025	1.150	2.267	1.255	$ 20.195
3.	Tractor-semi	$ 12.725	1.043	$ 13.768	2.065	1.173	2.267	1.277	$ 20.550
4.	Tractor - Doubles	$ 12.725	1.043	$ 13.768	2.065	1.173	2.267	1.277	$ 20.550
5.	Heavy Duty	$ 12.725	1.043	$ 13.768	2.065	1.173	2.267	1.277	$ 20.550
6.	Helpers	$ 12.475	1.151	$ 13.626	2.044	1.012	2.550	1.271	$ 20.503
7.	Day Terminal								
8.	Platform	$ 12.550	1.130	$ 13.680	2.052	.563	2.488	1.237	$ 20.020
9.	Lift Truck	$ 12.600	1.134	$ 13.734	2.060	.888	2.488	1.266	$ 20.436
10.	Hostler	$ 12.750	1.148	$ 13.898	2.085	1.340	2.488	1.313	$ 21.124
11.	Night Terminal								
12.	Platform	$ 12.700	1.143	$ 13.843	2.076	.624	2.488	1.254	$ 20.285
13.	Lift Truck	$ 12.750	1.148	$ 13.898	2.085	.964	2.488	1.284	$ 20.719
14.	Hostler	$ 12.900	1.161	$ 14.061	2.109	1.356	2.488	1.326	$ 21.340

TABLE 12.10

TOTAL LABOR COST PER HOUR AND PER MILE — LINE DRIVERS

Line No.	Item	Amount Per Hour	Amount Per Mile
1.	Base Wage Rate	$ 13.000	$ .325
2.	Vacation, Holidays, and Sick Leave	.984	.025
3.	Subtotal	$ 13.984	$ .350
4.	Compensation Insurance	2.098	.053
5.	Premium Earnings	-	-
6.	Health, Welfare, and Pension	2.000	.052
7.	Payroll Taxes	1.195	.030
8.	Total Labor Cost	$ 19.277	$ .485

The base wage rates, fringe benefits, and taxes total the figures shown in the last column of Tables 12.8 and 12.9 and in line 8 of Table 12.10. It is interesting to note that, in the illustrations, the hourly base wage rates must be increased approximately 65% to cover related labor cost for each employee.

Vehicle Fixed Cost

Chapter 5 discussed the circumstances surrounding the cost of vehicles and the other ownership or leased cost related to those vehicles. In this chapter, the illustrations will summarize the cost of vehicles in different categories from those provided in the earlier chapters. The difference in vehicle categories reflects the types of equipment used by LTL carriers in their performance of service.

In addition to differences in vehicle configurations, there are also differences in economic life, salvage value, and original cost. Local vehicles working in pickup and delivery operations incur shorter lives because they are used almost daily. The operation involves many starts and stops, heavy traffic congestion at times, and several shipment loadings and unloadings each day. In short, vehicles used by LTL carriers in route work take a beating.

For this reason, trade-in values are less than some other types of carriage. Just as with other carrier vehicles, these trade-in values depend upon outside market conditions but on a relative basis, the trade-in value of pickup and delivery vehicles is less.

Line-haul tractors of LTL carriers, on the other hand, experience similar lives and salvage values to other carrier types, although trailers are generally operated over shorter life spans.

In earlier chapters, liability and fleet insurance were included as a part of the vehicle fixed cost. Though many specialized carriers are quoted rates per unit of equipment, this is not necessarily true of LTL carriers. The illustrations in this chapter will record insurance cost as an indirect expense to reflect a practice different from specialized carriers. Such treatment will provide analysts an opportunity to consider both methods.

Form 4 in the Appendix is an inventory of vehicles to use in preparing the underlying historical fleet cost. The form provides all of the information necessary to prepare the following tables. Completed forms can be summarized by vehicle type according to actual company use. Most data base software provide spreadsheets to accomplish this objective.

Table 12.11 illustrates a method to determine vehicle historical cost for typical vehicles operated by LTL carriers.

TABLE 12.11

HISTORICAL COST OF EQUIPMENT — (Excluding tires - in dollars)

Line No.	Year	Straight Truck	Tractor 2-Axle Gas	Tractor 2-Axle Diesel	Tractor 3-Axle Diesel	Semi-Trailer 2-Axle 1-Axle	Semi-Trailer 1-Axle Short	Converter Gear Long
1.	1985	$ 29,970	$ 34,930	$ 46,160	$ 59,590	$ 24,830	$ 27,165	$ 11,765
2.	1986	29,830	34,750	45,800	59,295	24,770	27,050	11,740
3.	1987	29,685	34,565	45,445	58,975	24,715	26,945	11,710
4.	1988	29,550	34,385	45,090	58,660	24,655	26,850	11,685
5.	1989	29,375	34,250	44,450	58,350	24,695	26,750	11,660
6.	1990	29,220	33,960	44,050	58,040	24,625	26,560	11,645
7.	1991	-	-	43,750	57,750	24,500	26,450	11,600
8.	1992	-	-	43,500	57,545	24,445	26,390	11,595
9.	1993	-	-	-	-	24,400	26,300	11,580
10.	1994	-	-	-	-	24,385	26,260	11,570
11.	Total	$177,630	$206,840	$358,245	$468,205	$246,020	$266,720	$116,550
12.	Avg.	$ 29,605	$ 34,473	$ 44,781	$ 58,526	$ 24,602	$ 26,672	$ 11,655

Table 12.11 summarizes the historical cost of vehicles within selected types. Vehicles purchased in each year of the vehicle's lives are averaged. These yearly averages are posted to a table similar to Table 12.11. The figures for all the years are then added and averaged. The result is average cost of vehicles in the fleet by type. As with all examples in the book, the actual figures in this illustration do not represent a particular carrier or group of carriers.

Inflationary influence is not an important consideration in Table 12.11 as opposed to earlier examples in the book. In fact, historical cost actually declined over the life of vehicles in Table 12.11. These declining values show that when inflation is not present, historical cost can actually reflect current cost. When this is true, no adjustment to historical cost is necessary, unless it is anticipated that future vehicle acquisitions will be more costly.

Chapter 5 discussed at length some of the other considerations involved in the determination of vehicle historical cost.

TABLE 12.12

DETERMINATION OF VEHICLE FIXED COST — (Excluding tires - in dollars)

Line No.	Year	Straight Truck	Tractor 2-Axle Gas	Tractor 2-Axle Diesel	Tractor 3-Axle Diesel	Semi-Trailer 2-Axle 1-Axle	Semi-Trailer 1-Axle Short	Converter Gear Long
1.	Historical Cost	$ 29,605	$ 34,475	$ 44,780	$ 58,525	$ 24,600	$ 26,675	$ 11,650
2.	Salvage Value	2,960	3,450	4,475	5,850	2,460	2,670	1,165
3.	Economic Value	$ 26,645	$ 31,025	$ 40,305	$ 52,675	$ 22,140	$ 24,005	$ 10,485
4.	Economic Life	6 Yrs	6 Yrs	8 Yrs	8 Yrs	10 Yrs	10 Yrs	10 Yrs
5.	Annual Cost	$ 4,441	$ 5,171	$ 5,038	$ 6,584	$ 2,214	$ 2,401	$ 1,049
6.	Licenses							
7.	Registration	$ 25	$ 25	$ 25	$ 25	$ 25	$ 25	$ 25
8.	Weight	240	280	320	450	240	300	20
9.	License Fee	260	340	450	750	240	250	24
10.	Total License Fees	$ 525	$ 645	$ 795	$ 1,225	$ 505	$ 575	$ 69
11.	Federal Highway Use Tax	-	550	550	550	-	-	-
12.	Total Annual Cost	$ 4,966	$ 6,366	$ 6,383	$ 8,359	$ 2,719	$ 2,976	$ 1,118

The figures in line 1 of Table 12.12 are brought forward from the average cost in Table 12.11 to indicate the current original cost of the fleet. On line 2, the table uses a salvage value, or expected trade-in value, of 10% of the acquisition cost. When this value is subtracted from the historical cost, the result is the net vehicle fixed cost to be recovered in the price structure over the life of the vehicle. Between the amount received at the retirement of the vehicle and the amount recovered in the cost-justified rate structure, the carrier will recover the full acquisition cost.

Dividing the Economic Value on line 3 by the Economic Life on line 4 produces the cost per year to be recovered in the rate structure. This result is indicated on line 5 of Table 12.12.

Vehicle licenses and Federal Highway Use Tax figures provided in Table 12.12 are estimates based upon a variety of assumptions. First, we assumed that license fees were based upon a flat registration fee of $25 per vehicle, a weight fee, and another fee based upon the value of the vehicle. Secondly, the Highway Use Tax amounts were not applied to bobtails. Either one or both of these assumptions may be invalid in particular circumstances, but the methods used are flexible enough to provide an accurate format. We also believe that the figures are sufficiently accurate to provide a reliable cost development framework.

Addition of the annual fees to the annual vehicle cost produces the cost per year for vehicle fixed cost by type of unit. This result is indicated on line 12 of Table 12.12. (These annual costs are converted to productivity units in the following tables.)

The final determination in the construction of vehicle fixed cost for LTL carriers is to find the cost of vehicle combinations normally used in the service. In Tables 12.11 and 12.12, the cost for power units was determined separately from the cost of trailing equipment. In Tables 12.13 and 12.14, the individual unit costs are combined to get the total operating unit cost.

The vehicle fixed cost per year is converted to a cost per hour by dividing the annual vehicle use hours into the annual cost. Vehicle use hours may be determined from a variety of sources, including the maintenance cost records for each unit, a sampling of vehicle hours from a field study period, and summaries of pickup and delivery and line-haul trips during the study period. Vehicle hours per year should be developed with care as they are the basis for the vehicle cost per hour.

TABLE 12.13

ANNUAL FIXED COST FOR VEHICLE COMBINATIONS
PICKUP AND DELIVERY OPERATION — (In dollars)

Line No.	Item	Straight Truck	Local Trac. 1-Axle Trailer	Local Trac. 1-Axle Doubles	Local Trac. 2-Axle Trailer	Line Trac. 1-Axle Doubles	Line Trac. 2-Axle Trailer
1.	Power Unit Annual Cost	$ 4,966	$ 6,366	$ 6,366	$ 6,366	$ 6,383	$ 8,359
2.	Use Factor (Hours Per Year)	1,525	1,525	1,525	1,525	2,190	2,190
3.	Power Unit Per Hour	$ 3.256	$ 4.174	$ 4.174	$ 4.174	$ 2.915	$ 3.817
4.	Trailer Per Year	$ -	$ 2,719	$ 2,719	$ 2,976	$ 2,719	$ 2,976
5.	Use Factor (Hours Per Year)	-	1,680	1,680	2,020	1,680	2,020
6.	Trailer Per Hour	$ -	$ 1.618	$ 1.618	$ 1.473	$ 1.618	$ 1.473
7.	Number of Trailers	-	1	2	1	2	1
8.	Trailers Per Hour	$ -	$ 1.618	$ 3.236	$ 1.473	$ 3.236	$ 1.473
9.	Converter Gear Per Year	$ -	$ -	$ 1,118	$ -	$ 1,118	$ -
10.	Use Factor (Hours Per Year)	-	-	1,450	-	1,450	-
11.	Converter Gear Per Hour	$ -	$ -	$ .771	$ -	$ 771	$ -
12.	Fixed Cost Per Hour	$ 3.256	$ 5.792	$ 7.410	$ 5.647	$ 6.151	$ 5.290

Table 12 .13 reflects the vehicle fixed cost per hour in local pickup and delivery operations. In this example, pickup and delivery includes all operations where shipments, regardless of weight, are picked up and/or delivered and handled "through the terminal." This means that the shipment is brought to or taken from the terminal and is also handled as a line-haul shipment. It is not the same term as shipments "across the platform," which obviously means, for our purposes, the shipment is handled across the carrier platform.

Shipments handled through the terminal are a part of the local operation because, in many cases, the operation requires trailers to be spotted at the shipper or receiver facilities for loading or unloading. This activity also accounts for the difference in the Use Factor set forth in lines 2 and 5 of the table. Use hours are higher for trailers to reflect the time they are spotted off carrier premises for loading or unloading. In some operations, local drivers spot and pick up trailers before or after line-haul transportation, which means that the operation must be included in local cost development.

The example also uses only gasoline-powered tractors in the local operation, except when double trailers are used. If the carrier uses diesel or other types of tractor fuel in route work, an additional determination must be made. To achieve a vehicle fixed cost for route operations to be developed later in this chapter, a weighting of vehicle types should be used in place of the single figure indicated in Table 12.13 when tractors of varying fuel types are used to pull single short trailers.

Previous tables in this book developed the vehicle fixed cost per hour for local pickup and delivery operations. It is also necessary to accomplish the same objective for vehicles operated in line-haul service. A separate table for the vehicle fixed cost in line-haul operations is necessary to highlight two additional concepts in cost determination.

Typically, LTL carriers operate a large number of trailers in comparison with the number of power units. The high, ratio of trailers is necessary to provide trailing equipment to be spotted at loading and unloading facilities of both the carrier and its customers as well as at break-bulk locations where shipment transfers are accomplished. The cost to be recovered in the rate structure for the additional vehicles may be accomplished in a fashion similar to that illustrated in Table 12.14.

The second concept in line-haul operations as it relates to vehicle fixed cost is that, in longer lengths of haul, distance rather than time is the appropriate measure of cost. Vehicles operating on a regular schedule in line-haul operations between distant terminals incur increasing vehicle cost as distance increases, not necessarily as time increases. Accordingly, the vehicle fixed cost for equipment used in line-haul service is developed on both an hourly basis and a mileage basis.

TABLE 12 .14

ANNUAL FIXED COST IN VEHICLE COMBINATIONS — SHORT LINE HAUL OPERATIONS

Line No.	Item	2-Axle Tractor And Doubles	3-Axle Tractor And 2-Axle Semi
1.	Tractor	$ 6,383	$ 8,359
2.	Trailer(s)	5,438	2,976
3.	Tractor-trailer Ratio	1.8	1.4
4.	Trailers(s) Total	$ 9,788	$ 4,166
5.	Converter Gear	1,118	-
6.	Total Unit Fixed Cost	$ 16,171	$ 12,525

Table 12.14 completes construction of the vehicle fixed cost on an annual basis in line-haul service when the cost is to be expressed in terms of time. Short line-haul service under 700 miles (in our example) is measured in terms of time, and line hauls of 700 miles or more are expressed on a per-mile basis. In addition, each length of haul in the line-haul portion of the study uses different annual vehicle hours to convert the annual cost to a cost per hour.

LTL carriers operate on a schedule between fixed terminals. Accordingly, it is appropriate to determine annual vehicle hours for the selected lengths of the line-haul because each length of haul represents an operation between two terminals instead of a random radial operation. This determination will be demonstrated later in this chapter in the discussion of line-haul cost.

Tables 12.15A and B illustrate the other method to prepare vehicle fixed cost when the one-way length of haul equals or exceeds 700 miles. As indicated earlier, such cost is expressed on a per-mile basis. This is, however, only true for the power unit. In this example, the power unit cost is expressed per mile while the trailer cost is expressed on an hourly basis. The theory is that tractors in daily operations of over 700 miles one-way are expended as a result of miles traveled, not of age. On the other hand, trailers containing only limited moving parts are not depleted as a result of miles operated. Tables 12.15A and B illustrate a method to express fixed cost in terms of these consumption systems.

TABLE 12.15A

ANNUAL VEHICLE FIXED COST IN COMBINATIONS — LONG LINE OPERATIONS

Line No.	Item	2-Axle Tractor	3-Axle Tractor
1.	Cost Per Mile		
2.	Vehicle Historical Cost (See Table 12.11)	$ 44,780	$ 58,525
3.	Salvage Value	4,475	5,850
4.	Economic Value	$ 40,305	$ 52,675
5.	Economic Life	800,000 miles	800,000 miles
6.	Fixed Cost Per Mile	$ .050	$ 066

TABLE 12.15B

ANNUAL VEHICLE FIXED COST IN COMBINATIONS

Line No.	Item	2-Axle Tractor	3-Axle Tractor
1.	Taxes and Licenses	$ 1,345	$ 1,775
2.	Trailers(s)	9,788	4,166
3.	Converter Gear	1,118	-
4.	Annual Vehicle Fixed Cost	$ 12,251	$ 5,941

This method allows for the recovery of the historical cost of power units in the rate structure based upon miles operated in long-haul service, while vehicle taxes for the power unit, fixed cost for the trailers, and taxes for the trailers are all recovered on an hourly basis. Use of these illustrations will become more apparent in connection with the discussion of the operating processes.

In summary, vehicle fixed costs for LTL operations are determined for pickup and delivery service and short- and long- haul operations between terminals. This system produces an accurate total cost for pricing purposes that reflects actual carrier operations.

Vehicle Running Cost

As discussed in Chapter 6, the vehicle running cost includes fuel, oil, tires, and maintenance, which is, in fact, the cost of operating the motor vehicles. An LTL carrier's total operating cost is heavily impacted by this vehicle cost because of pickup and delivery and line-haul operations.

Many carriers operate their own repair facilities and perform most, if not all, maintenance operations in-house. As a rule, records of these costs on a per-unit basis reflect accurate and detailed information about each vehicle operated. In addition, cost studies may be readily developed for pricing purposes. This type of cost construction generally results in more accurate results than those obtained from outside vendors.

The application of vehicle running cost in this chapter assumes that the firm maintains a full repair shop with separate facilities and supervision. When such facilities are maintained, cost records are somewhat inconsistent in the handling of overhead cost. Some shops include an increment of overhead in each work order to reflect a total shop cost in each repair. If this system is maintained, some of the following discussion will not apply.

The illustrations that follow assume that repair orders do not contain overhead cost. In this situation, it is necessary to add overhead to the direct maintenance cost per mile. We selected this method in order to illustrate cost construction in more detail. The methods described will give carriers a way to add overhead to work orders.

If fuel cost-per-mile records are not maintained, such costs can be obtained by using the methods described in Chapter 6. Tire costs can also be obtained in the same manner.

Table 12.16 lists the various components of vehicle running cost that will be used to construct the total cost in the various operating processes. As with other costs in this book, the levels of cost do not reflect a particular operation, but illustrate cost relationships incurred by LTL carriers.

TABLE 12.16

DETERMINATION OF VEHICLE RUNNING COST PER MILE

Line No.	Item	Straight Truck Gas	Tractor 2-Axle Gas	Tractor 2-Axle Diesel	Tractor 3-Axle Diesel	Semi-Trailer 1-Axle Short	Semi-Trailer 2-Axle Long	Converter Gear 1-Axle
1.	Local and Short Haul							
2.	Fuel Cost Per Gallon	$ 1.25	$ 1.25	$ 1.23	$ 1.23	-	-	-
3.	Miles Per Gallon	7.6	6.0	6.6	6.4	-	-	-
4.	Cost Per Mile	$ .164	$ .208	$ .186	$ .192	$ -	$ -	$ -
5.	Oil Cost Per Mile	.002	.003	.004	.004	-	-	-
6.	Tire Cost Per Mile	.050	.055	.059	.072	.018	.036	.009
7.	Repair Cost Per Mile	.096	.124	.110	.135	.022	.039	.007
8.	Running Cost Per Mile	$ .312	$ .390	$.359	$ .403	$ .040	$.075	$ .016
9.	Long Haul							
10.	Fixed Cost	-	-	.050	.066	-	-	-
11.	Vehicle Cost Per Mile	$ .312	$ .390	$ .409	$ .469	$ .040	$ .075	$ .016

Figures indicated on line 8 are used in the development of local pickup and delivery and short line-haul services. Figures on line 12 include the historical cost of long line power units to be recovered in longer line-haul service.

Individual vehicle running costs may be combined to form operating units just as was done with vehicle fixed costs. The combinations of vehicles must be the same as those used in the construction of fixed cost so that continuity will be preserved throughout the study. Table 12.17 provides a method to accumulate the cost of individual units into operating combinations of vehicles used in pickup and delivery service.

TABLE 12 17

VEHICLE RUNNING COST PER MILE IN COMBINATIONS

Line No.	Item	Straight Truck	Local Trac. 1-Axle Trailer	Local Trac. 1-Axle Doubles	Local Trac. 2-Axle Trailer	Line Trac. 1-Axle Doubles	Line Trac. 2-Axle Trailer
1.	Power Unit Per Mile	$ .312	$ .390	$ .390	$ .390	$ .359	$ .403
2.	Trailer(s)	-	.040	.080	.075	.080	.075
3.	Converter Gear	-	-	.016	-	.016	-
4.	Direct Cost	$ .312	$ .430	$ .486	$ .465	$ .455	$ .478
5.	Indirect Cost	.031	.043	.049	.047	.046	.048
6.	Running Cost Per Mile	$ .343	$ .473	$ .535	$ .512	$ .501	$ .536
7.	Long Haul						
8.	Fixed Cost (Table 12.15A)	-	-	-	-	.050	.066
9.	Operating Cost Per Mile	$ .343	$ .473	$ .535	$ .512	$ .551	$.602

The illustrations of running cost for LTL carriers assume that the carrier maintains a repair facility to maintain company vehicles. To remain efficient, these facilities generate indirect cost, including management, supervision, clerical labor, office supplies, and rent. These costs, however, are not added to the economic value of power units shown on line 8 of Table 12.17. Line 8 is added to Table 12.17 after the total running cost per mile, including overhead, is determined.

Table 12.17 accounts for such overhead, or indirect, cost by adding 10% to the direct cost. This percentage was determined from accounting records, as follows:

Item	Direct	Indirect	Total
Supervision	-	.42	.42
Office and Other Expenses	-	04	.04
Repair and Service	8.15	-	8.15
Employees Welfare	.13	-	.13
Tires and Tubes - Rev. Equip.	1.70	-	1.70
Other Maintenance Expense	-	.46	.46
Operating Rent	-	.11	.11
Total	9.98	1.03	11.01

The figures above are expressed in terms of a percentage of the total expenses. To determine the indirect ratio for the vehicle repair facility, divide the amount of indirect expense by the amount of direct expense. In the illustration above, the indirect ratio is 10.32. For purposes of adding shop overhead to the direct cost, we rounded this figure to 10%.

When the overall company overhead, or indirect factor, is developed, the total expense of the shop facility is treated as a direct expense since all of that cost has been included in the vehicle running cost.

The elements of direct cost are now in place and ready to use in the development of cost to provide the various operating processes.

Platform Handling

The objective of this section is to measure the cost of labor to transfer shipments over the carrier platform. It is accomplished by time and motion studies of a sampling of shipments accorded such handling, an analysis of all platform labor hours during the study period, and an analysis of all shipments moving over the platform for the same period.

The time and motion study is conducted by trained observers to measure the exact time necessary to move shipments of various sizes across the platform. Such shipments are moved either directly or indirectly between vehicles. For example, shipments on line vehicles may be unloaded with some shipments moving directly to the local pickup and delivery vehicles and others coming to rest on the platform for later handling to the local vehicle. Conversely, shipments arriving on pickup and delivery vehicles are transferred to line vehicles or to the platform floor for later loading.

The only direct cost included in the platform operating process is the labor to handle the shipments. Platform rent or ownership costs and the cost of such handling equipment as forklifts are treated as indirect expense. There is no vehicle cost incurred in the platform-handling process.

Preparation of the platform-handling cost begins with a selection of shipment weight brackets. These brackets are used to establish costs at specific points. The average weight per shipment within each weight group is determined from a freight bill analysis of shipments moving through the terminal. The freight bill analysis also determines the number of shipments moving through the terminal, and the amount of weight and the number of shipments moving across the platform within each weight group.

Form 2-B in the Appendix is a sample form that will produce the information necessary to conduct the freight bill analysis. Compilation of data from this type of form will produce the information necessary to determine the overall platform handling performance in connection with volume.

Form 2-A in the Appendix records the number of hours that all dock workers spend in platform handling. A summary of data derived from these forms will produce the gross number of hours necessary to handle the number of shipments and amount of weight that moved across the platform during the study. Employees should make an entry on this form each time they leave and re-enter the platform. When related to the weight and the number of shipments, the gross hours determine the overall pounds per man hour.

Both the freight bill and the labor studies must be conducted for exactly the same time period so that the pounds per man hour will be accurate.

The study period for the freight bill and labor analysis should be of sufficient length to assure that the results will be representative of the overall operation. It is also suggested that studies be conducted periodically in an ongoing effort to update the statistical base to determine accurate cost-based pricing.

The shipment volume analysis may be constructed in a fashion similar to Table 12.18 for any number of terminals.

TABLE 12.18

OVERALL PLATFORM PERFORMANCE — ANALYSIS OF INDIVIDUAL TERMINALS

Line No.	Item	Terminal A	Terminal B	Total
1.	Total Weight Across Platform	28,443,191	42,337,984	70,781,175
2.	Total Weight Around Platform	31,251,667	40,208,240	71,459,907
3.	Total Weight Through Terminal	59,694,858	82,546,224	142,241,082
4.	Number of Shipments Across Platform	79,353	124,158	203,511
5.	Number of Shipments Around Platform	5,771	6,910	12,681
6.	Number of Shipments Through Terminal	85,124	131,068	216,192
7.	Average Weight Per Shipment Across Platform	358.44	341.00	347.80
8.	Average Weight Per Shipment Around Platform	5,415.29	5,818.85	5,635.19
9.	Average Weight Per Shipment Overall	701.27	629.80	657.94
10.	Man Hours On Platform	19,045.9	27,315.8	46,361.7
11.	Pounds Per Man Hour Across Platform	1,493.4	1,549.9	1,526.7

Table 12.18 is an overall summary of shipment activity and labor hours for two terminals during the selected test period. This table sets the stage for additional analysis to determine the cost per 100 pounds for platform handling of shipments of varying weights. The information in Table 12.18 may also be used to measure productivity among the carrier's terminals. Pounds per man hour across the dock is an accurate productivity measurement.

Form 2 in the Appendix is compiled for each employee who worked on the platform in connection with the study. Form 2-A provides a complete record of the hours worked, wage rates paid, and employee classification. Compilation of these forms produces the total platform hours required to handle shipments during the study.

The following tables are necessary to achieve the average weight per shipment, percentage of weight, and number of shipments in each bracket receiving platform handling. The source of the information for these tables is also the freight bill study conducted during the period.

TABLE 12.19

SUMMARY OF TRAFFIC MOVING THROUGH TERMINALS

Line No.	Weight Group	Total Wt. of Shipments Thru Terminal	No. of Shipments Terminal	Total Wt. of Shipments Over Plat. (lbs)	No. of Shipments Over Plat.	Wt. Over Plat. in Each Group (%)
1.	0 - 24	147,777	9,919	142,810	9,486	96.64
2.	25 - 49	903,485	24,228	882,629	23,667	97.69
3.	50 - 74	1,662,543	27,648	1,626,661	27,051	97.84
4.	75 - 99	1,681,611	19,677	1,641,713	19,214	97.63
5.	0 - 99	4,395,416	81,472	4,293,813	79,418	97.69
6.	100 -149	3,641,210	30,558	3,549,739	29,799	97.49
7.	150 - 199	3,144,150	18,434	3,046,082	17,862	96.88
8.	200 - 249	3,098,777	14,078	2,995,545	13,611	96.67
9.	250 - 299	2,629,571	9,714	2,530,737	9,351	96.24
10.	300 - 349	2,519,690	7,877	2,425,385	7,582	96.26
11.	350 - 399	2,146,971	5,782	2,058,640	5,545	95.89
12.	400 - 449	2,065,673	4,913	1,986,077	4,724	96.15
13.	450 - 499	1,914,562	4,064	1,828,863	3,882	95.52
14.	100 - 499	21,160,604	95,420	20,421,068	92,356	96.51
15.	500 - 599	3,451,947	6,388	3,294,984	6,099	95.45
16.	600 - 699	2,902,139	4,522	2,719,426	4,238	93.70
17.	700 - 799	2,422,505	3,260	2,275,318	3,062	93.92
18.	800 - 899	2,202,671	2,611	2,053,951	2,435	93.25
19.	900 - 999	2,078,359	2,204	1,917,877	2,034	92.28
20.	500 - 999	13,057,621	18,985	12,261,556	17,868	93.90
21.	1,000 - 1,999	12,944,961	9,489	11,410,358	8,421	88.15
22.	2,000 - 4,999	19,215,937	6,335	12,873,64	4,443	66.99
23.	5,000 - 9,999	14,103,655	2,068	4,990,742	750	35.39
24.	10,000 - 19,999	17,121,195	1,275	2,406,954	185	14.06
25.	20,000 - 29,999	11,908,680	511	975,271	43	8.19
26.	30,000 - 39,999	10,096,760	293	469,342	14	4.65
27.	40,000 - 49,999	10,486,016	245	352,481	8	3.36
28.	50,000 and Over	7,750,237	99	325,947	5	4.21
29.	Total	142,241,082	216,192	70,781,175	203,511	49.76

TABLE 12.19 (Continued)
SUMMARY OF TRAFFIC MOVING THROUGH TERMINALS

Line No.	Weight Group	Relation To Total Term. Wt. (%)	Total Wt. Over Plat. (%)	Average Weight Per Shipment Over Plat. Ea. Grp. (Lbs)	Through Terminal Each Group (Lbs)
1.	0 - 24	.10	.20	15.05	14.90
2.	25 - 49	.64	1.25	37.29	37.29
3.	50 - 74	1.17	2.30	60.13	60.13
4.	75 - 99	1.18	2.32	85.44	85.46
5.	0 - 99	3.09	6.07	54.07	53.95
6.	100 -149	2.56	5.02	119.12	119.16
7.	150 - 199	2.21	4.30	170.53	170.56
8.	200 - 249	2.18	4.23	220.08	220.11
9.	250 - 299	1.85	3.58	270.64	270.70
10.	300 - 349	1.77	3.42	319.89	319.88
11.	350 - 399	1.51	2.91	371.26	371.32
12.	400 - 449	1.45	2.81	420.42	420.45
13.	450 - 499	1.35	2.58	471.11	471.10
14.	100 - 499	14.88	28.85	221.11	221.76
15.	500 - 599	2.43	.66	540.25	540.38
16.	600 - 699	2.04	3.84	641.68	641.78
17.	700 - 799	1.70	3.21	743.08	743.10
18.	800 - 899	1.55	2.90	843.51	843.61
19.	900 - 999	1.46	2.71	942.91	942.99
20.	500 - 999	9.18	17.32	686.23	687.79
21.	1,000 - 1,999	9.10	16.12	1,354.99	1,364.21
22.	2,000 - 4,999	13.51	18.19	2,897.51	3,033.30
23.	5,000 - 9,999	9.91	7.05	6,654.32	6,819.95
24.	10,000 - 19,999	12.04	3.40	13,010.56	13,428.39
25.	20,000 - 29,999	8.37	1.38	22,680.72	23,304.66
26.	30,000 - 39,999	7.10	.66	33,524.43	34,459.93
27.	40,000 - 49,999	7.37	.50	44,060.13	42,800.07
28.	50,000 and Over	5.45	.46	65,189.40	78,285.22
29.	Total	100.00	100.00	347.80	657.94

TABLE 12.19 (Concluded)

SUMMARY OF TRAFFIC MOVING THROUGH TERMINALS

Line No.	Weight Group	Total No. of Through Terminal	Shipments Over Platform	Shpts. Over Plat. in Each Group (%)	Relation To	
					Total Term. Shpts. (%)	Total Shpts. Over Plat. (%)
1.	0 - 24	9,919	9,486	95.63	4.59	4.66
2.	25 - 49	24,228	23,667	97.68	11.21	11.63
3.	50 - 74	27,648	27,051	97.84	12.79	13.29
4.	75 - 99	19,677	19,214	97.65	9.10	9.44
5.	0 - 99	81,472	79,418	97.48	37.69	39.02
6.	100 - 149	30,558	29,799	97.52	14.13	14.64
7.	150 - 199	18,434	17,862	96.90	8.53	8.78
8.	200 - 249	14,078	13,611	96.68	6.51	6.69
9.	250 - 299	9,714	9,351	96.26	4.49	4.59
10.	300 - 349	7,877	7,582	96.25	3.64	3.73
11.	350 - 399	5,782	5,545	95.90	2.67	2.72
12.	400 - 449	4,913	4,724	96.15	2.27	2.32
13.	450 - 499	4,064	3,882	95.52	1.88	1.91
14.	100 - 499	95,420	92,356	96.79	44.12	45.38
15.	500 - 599	6,388	6,099	95.48	2.95	3.00
16.	600 - 699	4,522	4,238	93.72	2.09	2.08
17.	700 - 799	3,260	3,062	93.93	1.51	1.50
18.	800 - 899	2,611	2,435	93.26	1.21	1.20
19.	900 - 999	2,204	2,034	92.29	1.02	1.00
20.	500 - 999	18,985	17,868	94.12	8.78	8.78
21.	1,000 - 1,999	9,489	8,421	88.74	4.39	4.14
22.	2,000 - 4,999	6,335	4,443	70.13	2.93	2.18
23.	5,000 - 9,999	2,068	750	36.27	.96	.37
24.	10,000 - 19,999	1,275	185	14.51	.59	.10
25.	20,000 - 29,999	511	43	8.41	.24	.02
26.	30,000 - 39,999	293	14	4.78	.14	.01
27.	40,000 - 49,999	245	8	3.27	.11	.00
28.	50,000 and Over	99	5	5.05	.05	.00
29.	Total	216,192	203,511	94.13	100.00	100.00

The key data compiled in Table 12.19 is the average weight per shipment in each weight group, the relation of weight and number of shipments in each group to the total, and the amount of weight receiving platform handling in each group. With the labor hours, productivity, and labor cost per hour, the cost per 100 pounds for handling shipments of any weight may be determined.

Productivity for platform handling of 100 pounds is expressed in terms of man-seconds. Man-seconds per 100 pounds is observed and recorded as the actual operation occurs. A form for this specific purpose is not provided because measurement is not precise in terms of format. Employees performing this process move quickly, and it is difficult to find a specific point in a form, record the time, and still closely observe the operation. The only data recorded is the weight moved, the time the operation begins, and the time it is completed. The shipment weight can be taken from shipping documents, or it can be estimated by the employee. The actual shipment weight on documentation is preferable.

At the end of the day, the observations are summarized to show the weight and elapsed handling time for each shipment. The analyst posts the observations to a scattergram with pounds per shipment on the horizontal plane and man-seconds per 100 pounds on the vertical plane.

All observations should be posted on the graph. Once all observations are marked on the graph, a trend line representing all the points is drawn similar to that shown in Graph 12.1.

GRAPH 12.1

DISTRIBUTION CURVE SHOWING PLATFORM PERFORMANCE IN MAN-SECONDS PER 100 POUNDS

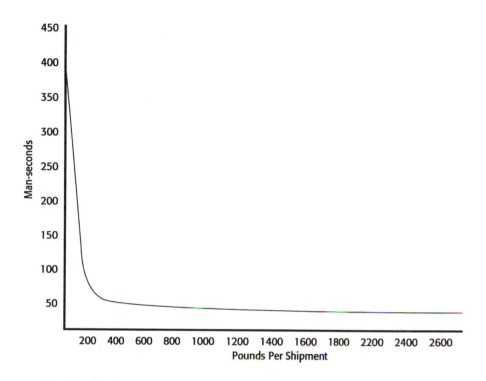

The line in Graph 12.1 represents productivity in terms of man-seconds per 100 pounds to handle shipments across the carrier's platform. The labor cost per hour applied to the handling times of average shipment weights within each group produces the cost per 100 pounds. One method to determine cost per 100 pounds for platform handling is illustrated in Table 12.20.

TABLE 12.20

DIRECT COST PER 100 POUNDS FOR PLATFORM HANDLING

Line No. Item	0-99	100-499	500-999	1000-1999	2000-4999	5000-9999	10,000+
1. Average Weight Per Shipment	54.1	221.1	686.2	1,355.0	2,897.5	6,654.3	17,764.7
2. Weight Over Platform	4,293,813	20,421,068	12,261,556	11,410,358	12,873,643	4,990,742	4,529,995
3. Percent of Weight Over Platform	6.07	28.85	17.32	16.12	18.19	7.05	6.40
4. Man-seconds Per 100 Pounds							
5. a) Graph	151	72	51	40	36	36	36
6. b) Weighted Portion	9.17	20.77	8.83	6.45	6.55	2.54	2.30
(Line 3 x Line 5 ÷ 100)							
7. c) Weighted Average	57	57	57	57	57	57	57
8. Ratio (Line 5 ÷ Line 7)	2.65	1.26	.89	.70	.63	.63	.63
9. Labor Cost Per 100 Pounds	$3.220	$1.531	$1.081	$ .851	$ .765	$ .765	$ .765
(Weight Basis)							
(Line 8 x $1.215 Per 100 Pounds)							
10. Ratio of Shipments in Each Weight Group To Total Shipments Across Platform - Percent	39.02	45.38	8.78	4.14	2.18	.37	.13
11. Labor Cost Per 100 Pounds (Shipment Basis)	$ .771	$ .189	$ .061	$ .031	$ .014	$ .006	$ .002
(Line 10 ÷ Line 3 x $.120 Per 100 Pounds)							
12. Cost Per 100 Pounds	$3.991	$1.720	$1.142	$ .882	$ .779	$ .771	$ .767
13. Ratio of Weight Over Platform To Total Weight in Each Group - Percent	97.69	96.51	93.90	88.15	66.99	35.39	7.90
14. Total Platform Cost Per 100 Pounds	$3.899	$1.660	$1.072	$ .777	$ .522	$ .273	$ .061

Overall Performance = 235.8 Man-seconds/100 Pounds

Weighted Labor Cost Per Hour - $20.387

Cost Per 100 Pounds = $1.335

Cost Allocated on Shipment Basis (9%) = $.120

Cost Allocated on Weight Basis (91%) = $1.215

Discussion of Table 12.20 begins with the notations at the bottom of the table where overall performance and costs are indicated. The overall performance, in terms of man-seconds per 100 pounds, is determined from data in Table 12.18. Pounds per man hour on line 11 of that table is divided into 3,600 seconds to find the number of seconds required to move 100 pounds across the platform. Since pounds per man hour is expressed per pound and man-seconds are expressed per 100 pounds, it is necessary to move the decimal two places to the right to obtain man-seconds per 100 pounds.

Labor cost per hour, at the bottom of Table 12.20, is obtained from the figures in Tables 12.8 for Terminal A and 12.9 for Terminal B. The platform wages in each table were averaged. Each resulting hourly wage rate was weighted according to tonnage moved across each platform, as indicated in Table 12.18. The average hourly labor cost was $19.989 for Terminal A and $20.654 for Terminal B. Weights across the platform, line 1 of Table 12.18, show that Terminal A handled 40.18% of the total weight and Terminal B handled 59.82%. These calculations produced a total hourly labor cost figure of $20.387.

Cost per 100 pounds for platform handling is determined by dividing the cost per hour by the productivity per hour. In the example, the cost per hour was $20.387, and in that hour 1,526.7 pounds were handled across the platform. Using these figures, the cost per 100 pounds was $1.335.

The time and motion study of productivity found that platform handling requires more than simply moving freight. Platform workers must be certain that each carton of each shipment is handled as a unit. It requires that workers match shipping document count of items with the count actually handled. The time spent coordinating these shipments is called shipment time.

The example found that 9% of platform handling was devoted to shipment time, while the other 91% was devoted to actual shipment transfer. Accordingly, 9% of the $1.335 cost per 100 pounds, or $.120, was the cost for shipment identification. The remaining cost per 100 pounds of $1.2115 was for actual platform handling.

Determination of the cost per 100 pounds over the platform of $1.335 does not complete the process of cost development for pricing purposes because not all shipments moving across the carrier's platforms receive the same type of handling. Small shipments are handled along with other shipments. As the weight increases and the number of shipments handled decreases, the cost circumstances change. As the weight increases, more mechanical handling by four-wheel carts and forklifts is used. When these mechanical means are employed, the cost per 100 pounds decreases because the weight handled at one time increases. Though there are a myriad of reasons why the cost per 100 pounds changes as the shipment weight increases, these changes must be reflected in the pricing structure so that small shipments receive their fair share of the cost burden, and large shipments receive the economies of scale they deserve.

Table 12.20 is designed to accomplish these objectives. Line 1 of the table is the average weight per shipment within the weight groups selected to reflect a sound rate structure. The figures on this line are reproduced from the freight bill analysis in Table 12.19. Since rates will be expressed in terms of 100-pound increments, the cost study is prepared with the same units of measure. It is, however, relatively simple to convert that cost to a cost per shipment: divide the cost per 100 pounds by the average shipment weight, and move the decimal accordingly. This calculation serves a valuable purpose in connection with small shipments where assessment of rates on a hundredweight basis might be replaced with a charge per shipment so that the relatively high cost of handling small shipments may be reflected in the overall rate design.

Line 2 of Table 12.20 is the total weight across the platform in each weight group. The totals on this line are equal to the weight totals in Tables 12.18 and 12.19. The purpose of recording these weights in line 2 is to find the weighted average weight in line 3.

Line 3 indicates the percentage of total weight in each weight group. The totals on line 3 add to 100.

Beginning on line 4, the productivity in each weight group is determined. Line 5 represents the productivity of labor determined from Graph 12.1, where all observations of productivity were recorded. The graph was read at each average shipment weight to find the man-seconds per 100 pounds. For example, shipments with an average weight of 54.1 pounds took 151 man-seconds to handle. As the shipment weight increases, time decreases because of the mechanical handling discussed earlier.

In line 6, the man-seconds in each weight group are weighted according to the weight in each group. The purpose of this calculation is to find a weighted average number of man-seconds. Line 7 of the example shows that the weighted average man-seconds were found to be 57. This figure is obtained by adding the figures on line 6. The 57 man-seconds per 100 pounds reflects the mixture of weight among the weight groups. Line 8 is determined by finding the ratio of line 7 to line 5: divide the figures on line 7 by the figures on line 5. For example, 57 weighted average man-seconds divided by 151 man-seconds for shipments weighing 54.1 pounds is 2.65 times greater than the overall average. From this calculation, it was determined that such shipments should receive 2.65 times the cost of overall platform handling.

This method allocates cost consistent with changes in productivity. The example determined that shipments weighing an average of 54.1 pounds took 2.65 times longer than the average of all shipments across the platform. Accordingly, these shipments incurred 2.65 times the average cost of platform handling. To accomplish this, the overall labor cost per 100 pounds was multiplied by 2.65, which produced the figures on line 9. For example, a labor cost of $1.215 times 2.65 for shipments weighing 54.1 produces a cost per 100 pounds of $3.220, while shipments weighing over 10,000 pounds would cost just $.765 per 100 pounds.

Discussion of calculations in Table 12.20 to this point have explained the determination of cost for platform handling during the time shipments are actually being transferred. The remainder of the discussion will describe the incurred cost for shipment identification.

In Table 12.19, we determined the number of shipments receiving platform handling in each weight group out of all shipments moved by the company across its platforms. A review of that table will confirm the figures on line 10 of Table 12.20. For example, 39.02% of all shipments transferred across platforms that weighed an average of 54.1 pounds received platform handling.

Now it is necessary to allocate overall platform cost per 100 pounds on a shipment basis to each of the shipment weight groups. To accomplish this, the percentage of shipments receiving platform handling is divided by the percentage of weight receiving platform handling, as shown in line 3. This weighted percentage is multiplied by the cost per 100 pounds indicated in the title of line 11. For example, 39.02 divided by 6.07 produces 6.428. This figure times $.120 results in a cost per 100 pounds of $.771 for shipments weighing 54.1 pounds. The cost per 100 pounds for shipment identification on the platform in each weight group is indicated on line 11.

Line 12 of Table 12.20 results from the addition of the figures on line 9 and line 11. The cost per 100 pounds on line 12 must be modified to include only those shipments that received platform handling. Weightings of cost and productivity to this point have been based upon the total weight in each weight group as compared to the total weight handled over the platform. However, not all shipments in each weight group receive platform handling. For example, of all shipments weighing an average of 54.1 pounds, only 97.69% received platform handling. To compensate for this condition, it is necessary to reduce the cost per 100 pounds by this percentage.

The reduction in cost is reflected in line 14 of Table 12.20. Figures on line 12, the cost per 100 pounds for all shipments, are multiplied by the figures in line 13, the percentage of shipments receiving platform handling in each weight group. The figures on line 14 represent the cost per 100 pounds to handle shipments of varying weights across the carrier's platform.

The cost per 100 pounds for handling shipments of any weight may be determined by reading from a line graph based upon the cost points in line 14 of

Table 12.20. Graph 12.2 illustrates the flow of cost for handling shipments across the carrier platform. In this graph, the average weight per shipment is on the vertical plane and the cost per 100 pounds is on the horizontal plane.

GRAPH 12.2

PLATFORM HANDLING COST PER 100 POUNDS

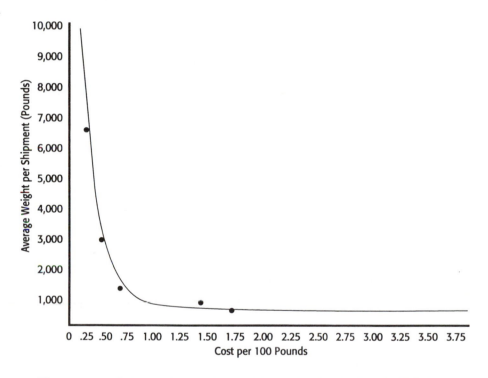

The cost per 100 pounds may be read from the line in Graph 12.2 for any weight per shipment. For illustration purposes, the graph goes only to 10,000 pounds. Actual studies can determine whether extending the graph for greater weights is appropriate.

Pickup and Delivery

The cost to provide pickup and delivery of shipments transported by LTL carriers begins with collection of data on Form 12E. The form is designed to obtain all the information required to compile such cost for shipments of varying weights expressed in terms of cost per 100 pounds.

The number of trips to be represented in the study varies by the size of the carrier, the number of terminals, the number of routes, and the volume of shipments transported. In many cases, a sample period of one week for each terminal is sufficient. If volume fluctuates seasonally, the period selected should be representative of the average volume during the year.

Carriers that use the methods described in this book to establish cost-based pricing will explore ways to prepare study segments on an on-going basis. For example, pickup and delivery studies might be conducted semiannually as a method to monitor changes in productivity that affect price levels or company efficiency. Between these studies, platform performance can be monitored through procedures described above.

Form 1 must be summarized by software programs or spreadsheets in several ways. The first summary should produce information about the terminal location, the vehicle types in terms of power units and trailing equipment, and the auxiliary equipment.

The second summary should provide data about commodities transported, packaging, and overall hours worked on the route.

The final summary is productivity. All times during the trip are recorded, and elapsed times for each segment are calculated. Each stop is described in terms of number of helpers, types of power equipment, number of shipments, weight, and pieces. When trips make more then two stops, the last line of the form and the first line in Shipment Information on the following page are left blank. The driver should number the pages when more than one form is used per day to describe all stops.

Before beginning the discussion of cost calculation, it is helpful to outline the pickup and delivery operation. There are two types of routes in LTL service. Single-stop service is where the vehicle and driver leave the terminal, go to a single stop, and return to the terminal. Similar to a truckload operation, this procedure is conducted within the context of a predominately LTL operation.

The second pickup and delivery operation is a multiple-stop service. Here, the vehicle functions in a route where more than one stop is made to pick up or deliver shipments.

Stops are also defined in terms of the operating process. There are single-shipment stops and multiple-shipment stops. For example, a shipper may tender 10 shipments destined for 10 different consignees in different locations. In a multiple-shipment stop it is normal for all shipments to contain different weights and pieces. In a single-shipment stop a single shipment is picked up or delivered at the stop.

We will explore methods to accumulate cost for these operations into a single figure for an overall pickup and delivery service. It is important to remember that rates are not quoted separately for multiple-stop service, single-stop service, multiple-shipment stops, or single-shipment stops. A single rate to recover the cost for all of these operating processes is the objective.

It is equally significant that pickup and delivery cost is incurred on a stop basis and on an en route basis. Part of the pickup and delivery cost is incurred while the vehicle and driver are moving between stops, and part is incurred while the vehicle and driver are at the stop while the vehicle is being loaded or unloaded.

To begin the cost-finding procedure for pickup and delivery service, certain underlying data must be recorded and accumulated from the trip reports. The first is the mixture of equipment employed in each operation.

TABLE 12.21

PICKUP AND DELIVERY — EQUIPMENT WEIGHTING FACTORS (In percent)

Line No.	Item	WEIGHT GROUP - Pounds						
		0- 99	100 - 499	500 - 999	1000 - 1999	2000 - 4999	5000 - 9999	10000 And Over
1.	Single-stop Service:							
2.	Local Truck	79.0	71.9	58.4	47.9	27.1	14.1	-
3.	Tractor and 1-Axle							
	Semitrailer	16.2	24.1	30.2	42.5	59.3	67.1	-
4.	Tractor and 2							
	1-Axle Semitrailers	-	-	-	.5	2.6	1.1	-
5.	Tractor and 2-Axle							
	Semitrailer	4.8	4.0	11.4	9.1	11.0	17.7	-
6.	Multiple-stop Service:							
7.	Local Truck	87.2	85.8	80.7	72.3	48.5	20.1	-
8.	Tractor and 1-Axle							
	Semitrailer	11.7	12.9	17.0	23.4	41.5	62.2	54.0
9.	Tractor and 2							
	1-Axle Semitrailers	-	-	-	.9	1.9	5.8	23.5
10.	Tractor and 2-Axle							
	Semitrailer	1.1	1.3	2.3	3.4	8.1	11.9	22.5

The figures for less-than-truckload service in Table 12.21 are weighted on the basis of the type of vehicle used for single and multiple stops. Figures for both the single-stop service and multiple-stop service add to 100 in each column. The weighting is for equipment used at the stops in the field study. The purpose of these figures is to determine the vehicle cost of performing stops of varying sizes, and the cost of traveling between stops.

Results shown in Table 12.21 are as expected. As stop weight increases, and vehicles are expected to carry greater weight, lighter vehicles tend to drop off in quantity and heavier equipment utilization increases. The result of this distribution is that vehicle cost increases as weight increases.

Similar determinations are necessary for truckload shipments. The major difference between the LTL and the truckload operation is that the example found no significant multiple-stop service or multiple-shipment stops in the truckload sector. The cost calculations for truckload pickup and delivery are, therefore, less complex.

TABLE 12.22

PICKUP AND DELIVERY EQUIPMENT — WEIGHTING FACTORS (In percent)

Line No.	Item	WEIGHT GROUP - Pounds			
		10,000- 19,999	20,000- 29,999	30,000- 39,999	40,000- And Over
1.	Tractor and 1-Axle Semitrailer	71.6	46.1	-	-
2.	Tractor and 2 1-Axle Semitrailers	7.7	24.3	70.6	88.7
3.	Tractor and 2-Axle Semitrailer	20.7	29.6	29.4	11.3

The figures in Table 12.22 continue the trend found in the LTL equipment weighting. As weight increases, the use of heavier equipment increases. Though the figures in both tables are not representative of a particular circumstance, they illustrate possible methods and results.

Table 12.13 prepared the cost per hour for vehicles used in the pickup and delivery operation. Figures in that table, and in Tables 12.21 and 12.22, will provide the vehicle fixed cost per hour for handling of various numbers of stops and sizes of shipments. The actual numbers to represent this cost may be constructed as indicated in Tables 12.23 and 12.24.

TABLE 12.23

PICKUP AND DELIVERY EQUIPMENT — WEIGHTING FACTORS (In dollars)

Line No.	Item	WEIGHT GROUP - Pounds						
		0-99	100-499	500-999	1000-1999	2000-4999	5000-9999	10000 And Over
Vehicle Fixed Cost Per Hour								
1.	Single-stop Service:							
2.	Local Truck	$2.572	$2.341	$1.902	$1.560	$.882	$.459	$ -
3.	Tractor and 1-Axle Semitrailer	.938	1.396	1.749	2.462	3.435	3.886	-
4.	Tractor and 2 1-Axle Semitrailers	-	-	-	.037	.193	.082	-
5.	Tractor and 2-Axle Semitrailer	.271	.226	.644	.514	.621	1.000	-
6.	Total	$3.781	$3.963	$4.295	$4.573	$5.131	$5.427	$ -
7.	Multiple-stop Service:							
8.	Local Truck	$2.839	$2.794	$2.628	$2.354	$1.579	$.654	$ -
9.	Tractor and 1-Axle Semitrailer	.678	.747	.985	1.355	2.404	3.603	3.128
10.	Tractor and 2 1-Axle Semitrailers	-	-	-	.067	.141	.043	1.741
11.	Tractor and 2-Axle Semitrailer	.062	.073	.130	.192	.457	.672	1.271
12.	Total	$3.579	$3.614	$3.743	$3.968	$4.581	$4.972	$6.140
Vehicle Running Cost Per Mile								
1.	Single-stop Service:							
2.	Local Truck	$.271	$.247	$.200	$.164	$.093	$.048	$ -
3.	Tractor and 1-Axle Semitrailer	.077	.114	.143	.201	.280	.317	-
4.	Tractor and 2 1-Axle Semitrailers	-	-	-	.003	.014	.006	-
5.	Tractor and 2-Axle Semitrailer	.025	.020	.058	.047	.056	.091	-
6.	Total	$.373	$.381	$.401	$.415	$.443	$.462	$ -
7.	Multiple-stop Service:							
8.	Local Truck	$.299	$.294	$.277	$.248	$.166	$.069	$ -
9.	Tractor and 1-Axle Semitrailer	.055	.061	.080	.111	.196	.294	.255
10.	Tractor and 2 1-Axle Semitrailers	-	-	-	.005	.010	.031	.126
11.	Tractor and 2-Axle Semitrailer	.006	.007	.012	.017	.04	.061	.115
12.	Total	$.360	$.362	$.369	$.381	$.413	$.455	$.496

TABLE 12.24

PICKUP AND DELIVERY EQUIPMENT — WEIGHTING FACTORS (In dollars)

Line No.	Item	WEIGHT GROUP - Pounds			
		10,000-19,999	20,000-29,999	30,000-39,999	40,000-And Over
Vehicle Fixed Cost					
1.	Tractor and 1-Axle Semitrailer	4.147	2.670	-	-
2.	Tractor and 2 1-Axle Semitrailers	.571	1.801	5.231	6.573
3.	Tractor and 2-Axle Semitrailer	1.169	1.672	1.660	.638
4.	Total	5.887	6.143	6.891	7.211
Vehicle Running Cost					
5.	Tractor and 1-Axle Semitrailer	.339	.218	-	-
6.	Tractor and 2 1-Axle Semitrailers	.041	.130	.378	.475
7.	Tractor and 2-Axle Semitrailer	.106	.152	.151	.058
8.	Total	.486	.500	.529	.533

Upon completion of these tables, the vehicle fixed cost per hour to handle various stops in pickup and delivery service is calculated. As the cost analysis is developed further, a similar process is necessary to find the labor cost and the vehicle running cost to handle similar stops.

The process to determine weighted labor cost per hour is somewhat different from previous examples because there is more than one unit of cost. This is because the carrier in the illustrations operates two terminals and employees are paid different wages. Before the labor cost can be weighted to find the cost per stop, it is necessary to find the weighted pickup and delivery labor cost for the company system. The cost at each terminal must be combined into one cost for each driver and helper classification.

Data about the quantity of stops and their distribution is found in the field study. The trip reports indicate the nature of each stop in terms of weight handled, vehicles used, and driver pay rates. To determine the weighted carrier system labor cost per hour for each wage classification, this data is summarized in a table similar to Table 12.25.

TABLE 12.25

DEVELOPMENT OF AVERAGE WEIGHT PER STOP (Multiple-stop service)

Line No.	Weight Group	No. Of Stops	Total Weight (Pounds)	Average Weight Per Stop
1.	0 - 24	1,887	29,013	15.4
2.	25 - 49	4,729	174,559	36.9
3.	50 - 74	5,491	328,818	59.9
4.	75 - 99	3,893	332,169	85.3
5.	0 - 99	16,000	864,559	54.0
6.	100 - 149	6,938	824,274	118.8
7.	150 - 199	4,474	759,515	169.8
8.	200 - 249	3,709	815,390	219.8
9.	250 - 499	9,559	3,359,592	351.5
10.	100 - 499	24,680	5,758,771	233.3
11.	500 - 999	7,110	4,964,695	698
12.	1,000 - 1,999	4,256	5,833,031	1,371
13.	2,000 - 4,999	2,772	8,380,538	3,023
14.	5,000 - 9,999	720	4,881,682	6,780
15.	10,000 - and Over	400	7,147,491	17,869
16.	Total	55,938	37,830,767	676

This table describes the company-wide distribution of shipments through the same weight groups that were used in the development of the platform cost. The data must be distributed between the two terminals so that the labor cost in each terminal is related to total productivity. For this purpose, stops will be allocated between terminals, as shown in Table 12.26.

TABLE 12.26

DEVELOPMENT OF STOP ALLOCATION BETWEEN TERMINALS (Multiple-stop service)

Line No.	Weight Group	Terminal A No. Of Stops	Percent	Terminal B No. Of Stops	Percent	Total No. Of Stops
1.	0 - 24	844	44.7	1,043	55.3	1,887
2.	25 - 49	2,141	45.3	2,588	54.7	4,729
3.	50 - 74	2,531	46.1	2.960	53.9	5,491
4.	75 - 99	1,639	42.1	2,254	57.9	3,893
5.	0 - 99	7,155	44.7	8,845	55.3	16,000
6.	100 - 149	3,164	45.6	3,774	54.4	6,938
7.	150 - 199	2,036	45.5	2,438	54.5	4,474
8.	200 - 249	1,693	45.6	2,016	54.4	3,709
9.	250 - 499	4,282	44.8	5,277	55.2	9,559
10.	100 - 499	11,175	45.3	13,505	54.7	24,680
11.	500 - 999	3,249	45.7	3,861	54.3	7,110
12.	1,000 - 1,999	2,001	47.0	2,255	53.0	4,256
13.	2,000 - 4,999	1,322	47.7	1,450	52.3	2,772
14.	5,000 - 9,999	327	45.4	393	54.6	720
15.	10,000 - and Over	177	44.3	223	55.7	400
16.	Total	25,415	45.4	30,523	54.6	55,938

The number of stops in each weight group described above will be used to find the total labor cost per hour within each of the groups. Before that calculation can be made, it is necessary to determine the mixture of labor classifications used in each of the stop weight groups. We have already shown that different equipment is used as the weight-per-stop changes, with larger equipment used on heavier stops and shipments. We have indicated in the labor cost section of this chapter that drivers are classified according to the type of vehicle they operate. It follows that labor cost also changes as stop weight changes.

Normally, drivers operating larger vehicles earn higher wages than those using small units. When this is the case, the labor cost increases as the stop weight increases. There is another change in the application of labor as stop weight increases: as the weight of shipments and stops increase, the use of additional employees also increases. It many cases, a helper is required for safe and efficient operations.

These changes in operating cost must be reflected in the total cost and rate structure under development. To accomplish this objective, the field study is summarized again to determine the wage classification in the stop weight groups. That summary also determines the incidence of additional helpers.

The example in Table 12.27 uses the weighting of wage classifications within stop weight groups for the company system. In practice, the analyst should determine whether the mixture of employees within weight groups varies so significantly among terminals that a separate weighting should be used for each.

TABLE 12.27

DEVELOPMENT OF WEIGHTED LABOR COST (Multiple-stop service)
TERMINAL A

Line No.		Truck	Tractor-Semi	Tractor-Doubles	Heavy Duty	Helper	Weighted Cost
1.	Hourly Labor Cost	$ 19.747	$2 0.101	$ 20.101	$ 20.101	$ 20.157	-
2.	Weight Group (Pounds)						
3.	0 - 24	98.2	1.8	-	-	-	$ 19.754
4.	25 - 49	97.2	2.8	-	-	-	$ 19.757
5.	50 - 74	94.1	5.9	-	-	-	$ 19.768
6.	75 - 99	86.1	10.9	-	3.0	-	$ 19.796
7.	0 - 99	88.2	9.8	-	2.0	-	$ 19.789
8.	100 - 149	88.0	10.1	-	1.9	.1	$ 19.809
9.	150 - 199	86.3	10.5	-	3.2	.1	$ 19.816
10.	200 - 249	84.7	12.0	-	3.3	.4	$ 19.882
11.	250 - 499	83.8	12.2	-	4.0	.5	$ 19.905
12.	100 - 499	86.0	11.1	-	2.9	.4	$ 19.877
13.	500 - 999	81.3	16.0	-	2.7	2.2	$ 20.256
14.	1,000 - 1,999	71.3	22.6	.8	5.3	12.9	$ 22.449
15.	2,000 - 4,999	45.0	42.1	1.9	11.0	20.4	$ 24.054
16.	5,000 - 9,999	18.9	61.1	4.4	15.6	30.3	$ 26.142
17.	10,000 - and Over	-	53.8	22.6	23.6	31.1	$ 26.370
18.	10,000 - 19,999	-	56.1	23.3	20.6	30.7	$ 26.289
19.	20,000 - 29,999	-	54.1	23.9	22.0	32.1	$ 26.571
20.	30,000 - 39,999	-	16.8	33.6	49.6	33.9	$ 26.934
21.	40,000 and Over	-	-	49.7	50.3	35.6	$ 27.277

TABLE 12.28

DEVELOPMENT OF WEIGHTED LABOR COST (Multiple-stop service)
TERMINAL B

Line No.		Truck	Tractor- Semi	Tractor- Doubles	Heavy Duty	Helper	Weighted Cost
1.	Hourly Labor Cost	$ 20.195	$ 20.550	$ 20.550	$ 20.550	$ 20.503	-
2.	Weight Group (Pounds)						
3.	0 - 24	98.2	1.8	-	-	-	$ 20.201
4.	25 - 49	97.2	2.8	-	-	-	$ 20.205
5.	50 - 74	94.1	5.9	-	-	-	$ 20.215
6.	75 - 99	86.1	10.9	-	3.0	-	$ 20.245
7.	0 - 99	88.2	9.8	-	2.0	-	$ 20.237
8.	100 - 149	88.0	10.1	-	1.9	.1	$ 20.259
9.	150 - 199	86.3	10.5	-	3.2	.1	$ 20.265
10.	200 - 249	84.7	12.0	-	3.3	.4	$ 20.331
11.	250 - 499	83.8	12.2	-	4.0	.5	$ 20.355
12.	100 - 499	86.0	11.1	-	2.9	.4	$ 20.327
13.	500 - 999	81.3	16.0	-	2.7	2.2	$ 20.713
14.	1,000 - 1,999	71.3	22.6	.8	5.3	12.9	$ 22.941
15.	2,000 - 4,999	45.0	42.1	1.9	11.0	20.4	$ 24.574
16.	5,000 - 9,999	18.9	61.1	4.4	15.6	30.3	$ 26.695
17.	10,000 - and Over	-	53.8	22.6	23.6	31.1	$ 26.926
18.	10,000 - 19,999	-	56.1	23.3	20.6	30.7	$ 26.844
19.	20,000 - 29,999	-	54.1	23.9	22.0	32.1	$ 27.131
20.	30,000 - 39,999	-	16.8	33.6	49.6	33.9	$ 27.501
21.	40,000 and Over	-	-	49.7	50.3	35.6	$ 27.802

Each of the weight groups in Tables 12.27 and 12.28 contain percentages of each labor classification that performs pickup and delivery service within that group. Line 1 of each table is the applicable labor cost per hour for each terminal. The weighted labor cost in the last column is determined by accumulating the percentages of labor cost for each classification within the weight group. The following illustration, using the 1,000 - 1,999 pound weight group in Terminal A, will provide a detailed method to determine weighted labor cost:

Wage	Rate	Percent	Weighting
Truck	$ 19.747	71.3	$ 14.080
Tractor - Semitrailer	$ 20.101	22.6	4.543
Tractor - Doubles	$ 20.101	.8	.161
Heavy Duty	$ 20.101	5.3	1.065
Subtotal		100.0	$ 19.849
Helper	$ 20.157	12.9	$ 2.600
Total			$ 22.449

The percentages in each weight group total 100% within the weight group just for drivers because a driver is always with the vehicle at the stop. Helpers are added to the weighted cost when the field study indicates that they are used to load or unload shipments at the stops in the weight group. The weighted labor cost is the average cost of all employees at the terminal who are involved in the pickup and/or delivery of shipments.

The weighted labor cost in each weight group for each terminal is combined to achieve one labor cost per hour that represents both terminals. If, in practice, the carrier operates several terminals, the weighted labor cost would be combined for all terminals to develop one pickup and delivery cost for the company.

Table 12.26 developed the weighted distribution of stops in the carrier system. This weighting is an appropriate basis to accumulate the individual terminal weighted labor cost per hour into a system-wide labor cost per hour.

TABLE 12.29

DEVELOPMENT OF WEIGHTED LABOR COST IN PICKUP AND
DELIVERY SERVICE FOR CARRIER SYSTEM (Multiple-stop service)

Line No.	Weight Group	Terminal A Labor Cost	Percent	Terminal B Labor Cost	Percent	Labor Cost Per Hour
1.	0 - 24	$ 19.754	44.7	$20.201	55.3	$ 20.001
2.	25 - 49	$ 19.757	45.3	$20.205	54.7	$ 20.002
3.	50 - 74	$ 19.768	46.1	$20.215	53.9	$ 20.009
4.	75 - 99	$ 19.796	42.1	$20.245	57.9	$ 20.106
5.	0 - 99	$ 19.789	44.7	$20.237	55.3	$ 20.037
6.	100 - 149	$ 19.809	45.6	$20.259	54.4	$ 20.054
7.	150 - 199	$ 19.816	45.5	$20.265	54.5	$ 20.060
8.	200 - 249	$ 19.882	45.6	$20.331	54.4	$ 20.126
9.	250 - 499	$ 19.905	44.8	$20.355	55.2	$ 20.153
10.	100 - 499	$ 19.877	45.3	$20.327	54.7	$ 20.123
11.	500 - 999	$ 20.256	45.7	$20.713	54.3	$ 20.504
12.	1,000 - 1,999	$ 22.449	47.0	$22.941	53.0	$ 22.710
13.	2,000 - 4,999	$ 24.054	47.7	$24.574	52.3	$ 24.326
14.	5,000 - 9,999	$ 26.142	45.4	$26.695	54.6	$ 26.443
15.	10,000 and Over	$ 26.370	44.3	$26.926	55.7	$ 26.680
16.	10,000 - 19,999	$ 26.289	45.5	$26.844	54.5	$ 26.591
17.	20,000 - 29,999	$ 26.571	45.2	$27.131	54.8	$ 26.878
18.	30,000 - 39,999	$ 26.934	44.8	$27.501	55.2	$ 27.247
19.	40,000 and Over	$ 27.277	43.3	$27.802	56.7	$ 27.575

Table 12.23 showed the development and weighting of vehicle utilization and vehicle cost per hour in various stop weights. Table 12.29 calculated the labor cost. When these tables are combined they represent the direct cost per hour, by weight group to provide a portion of the pickup and delivery operating process. The portion that these direct costs represent is termed "stop time." It

is the time the vehicle, driver, and helpers, if any, are at the stop for the purpose of loading or unloading shipments. The vehicle is not moving during this period so the vehicle running cost is not included in the direct cost to provide the stop operation. Accordingly, the labor and the vehicle fixed costs are the only elements included in the direct cost for the operation.

Productivity during stop time may be determined using procedures illustrated in Table 12.30.

TABLE 12.30

DEVELOPMENT OF PRODUCTIVITY PER STOP (Multiple-stop service)

Line No.	Weight Group	No. of Stops	Total Weight (Pounds)	Man Hours	Vehicle Hours	Pounds Per Man Hour	Pounds Per Vehicle Hour
1.	0 - 24	1,887	29,013	48.4	48.4	600	600
2.	25 - 49	4,729	174,559	281.5	281.5	620	620
3.	50 - 74	5,491	328,818	534.7	534.7	615	615
4.	75 - 99	3,893	332,169	496.9	496.9	668	668
5.	0 - 99	16,000	864,559	1,361.5	1,361.5	635	635
6.	100 - 149	6,938	824,274	613.8	613.8	1,343	1,343
7.	150 - 199	4,474	759,515	561.5	561.5	1,353	1,353
8.	200 - 249	3,709	815,390	565.0	565.0	1,443	1,443
9.	250 - 499	9,559	3,359,592	1,892.7	1,892.7	1,775	1,775
10.	100 - 499	24,680	5,758,771	3,633.0	3,633.0	1,585	1,585
11.	500 - 999	7,110	4,964,695	1,757.4	1,732.9	2,825	2,865
12.	1,000 - 1,999	4,256	5,833,031	1,555.5	1,517.0	3,750	3,845
13.	2,000 - 4,999	2,772	8,380,538	1,677.8	1,603.9	4,995	5,225
14.	5,000 - 9,999	720	4,881,682	771.8	703.4	6,325	6,940
15.	10,000 and Over	400	7,147,491	805.4	644.2	8,875	11,095
16.	Total	55,938	37,830,767				

Figures in the first two columns of Table 12.30 are taken from Table 12.25, where the number of stops and amount of weight handled at the stops within each of the weight groups were developed. Vehicle and labor hours are taken from the field study. The pickup and delivery trip forms are summarized by stop weight group to show elapsed time and weight at each stop. The totals within each weight group produce the pounds per vehicle hour figure.

The summary of labor hours is slightly different because of helpers. All employee hours at the stop are added to obtain the pounds per man hour within the stop weight groups.

The preceding pickup and delivery discussion described the preparation of underlying data necessary to construct the direct cost for stops in various weight groups. One last cost distribution is necessary to construct the final cost for this segment.

Stop time is divided into two separate operations, much like platform handling. A certain amount of time is necessary to locate the shipment at the stop and to sign the shipping documents. This portion of stop time is referred to as "shipment time." In these illustrations, the shipment time is 15% of the total stop time.

The other 85% of the stop time is called "weight time." This is the time the driver and helpers, if any, are actually loading or unloading shipments at the stop.

Accurate cost development requires that these times be determined, and that the cost of each be determined separately. The reason is that labor productivity is different from vehicle productivity in terms of pounds per hour while at the stop. Vehicle pounds per hour are based upon the time the vehicle is at the stop, while labor productivity is all the time at the stop plus the time and productivity of helpers, where helpers are used. The result is that as the stop weight increases, the difference between pounds per vehicle hour and pounds per man hour also increases. This is because as the weight increases it becomes more likely that helpers will be involved.

The percentage, or allocation, of time at the stop is accomplished by a statistical equation that mathematicians call the "method of least squares." They define the method as being based upon the principle that "the best value of a quantity that can be deduced from a set of measurements or observations is that for which the sum of the squares of the deviations of the observed values is a minimum." Simply stated, what this procedure does is determine the impact of one variable upon another. An example is the allocation of stop cost to shipments and to weight. Use of this method in previous studies of over 200 carriers produced the results indicated in our examples.

For purposes of cost construction in this book, we will not analyze the mathematical procedure because we do not believe it is necessary. The allocations of both stop cost and en route costs are based upon large statistical universes. If individual carriers performed the math function, the same results would be achieved. Based upon these earlier studies, the stop cost is allocated on the basis of 15% to shipments and 85% to weight. En route cost is allocated as 46% on a stop basis and 54% on a weight basis. There are other methods to accomplish these allocations, but this one has been used for several years to allocate pickup and delivery cost.

The 15% of stop time referred to as "shipment time" does not vary with the size of the shipment. It takes the same amount of time to obtain the shipping documents no matter how large or small the shipment.

It is necessary to know the number of shipments at each stop so that the total time can be allocated to each. The illustrations in this chapter were based upon 413,941 shipments picked up and/or delivered during the study period. These shipments were picked up and/or delivered at 55,938 stops. Accordingly, 7.4 shipments were handled at each stop.

An example will illustrate the method to find the cost of shipment time at each stop. This explanation will track the calculations used in Table 12.31.

The labor cost per hour in the 0-99 stop weight group was \$20.037 in Table 12.29, and the vehicle cost in Table 12.23 was \$3.579. The total direct cost per hour was \$23.616. A cost per shipment may be determined by dividing the cost per hour by 7.4 shipments handled at the stops per hour. The result is a cost per shipment of \$3.191. This cost per shipment is then converted to a cost per 100 pounds by dividing the average weight per shipment into the cost per shipment (\$3.191 ÷ 54 = \$5.909). The cost per 100 pounds for the shipment time portion of the stops is \$5.909.

The cost per 100 pounds for shipment time at the stops requires one more sort of the underlying data collected from the field study. Dividing the total number of shipments in the study by the total number of hours at the stops results in the overall number of shipments handled per hour at the stops. This figure is then divided by the number of stops to obtain the number of shipments handled at each stop per hour. In our illustrations, these calculations produced 7.4 shipments per hour at the stops.

There are two sources for the average weight per shipment figures. The field study of pickup and delivery contains the number of shipments and the weight of each shipment within each stop weight group. These figures may be summarized in much the same fashion as the average weight per stop. The other source for average weight per shipment comes from the figures in Table 12.19 prepared in connection with platform handling. In either case, the average weight should be the same. For purposes of our illustrations, the average weights per shipment were taken from Table 12.19 for shipments moving through the terminal.

To this point, however, the cost of \$5.909 is a total shipment cost based upon the number of shipments and the average weight per shipment. Shipment time at the stops is 15% of the total time at the stop, with 85% devoted to handling pieces and weight. Fifteen percent of \$5.909 produces a shipment cost at the stop of \$.886.

Table 12.31 begins construction of pickup and delivery cost in multiple-stop service using the procedure just described.

TABLE 12. 31

DEVELOPMENT OF DIRECT COST PER 100 POUNDS FOR LESS THAN TRUCKLOAD STANDBY COST IN MULTIPLE-STOP PICKUP AND DELIVERY SERVICE

Line No.	Item	0- 99	100 - 499	500 - 999	1000- 1999	2000 - 4999	5000- 9999	10000 and Over	Average Cost Per 100 Lbs.
1.	Average Weight Per Stop	54	233	698	1,371	3,023	6,780	17,869	-
2.	Standby (Stop) Cost Per								
	100 Pounds - Shipment Basis:								
3.	Labor Cost Per Hour	$ 20.037	$20.123	$ 20.504	$ 22.710	$24.326	$ 26.443	$ 26.680	-
4.	Vehicle Fixed Cost Per Hour	3.579	3.614	3.743	3.968	4.581	4.972	6.140	-
5.	Direct Cost Per Hour	$ 23.616	$23.737	$ 24.247	$ 26.678	$28.907	$ 31.415	$ 32.820	-
6.	Shipments Per Hour	7.4	7.4	7.4	7.4	7.4	7.4	7.4	-
7.	Direct Cost per Shipment	$ 3.191	$ 3.208	$ 3.277	$ 3.605	$ 3.906	$ 4.245	$ 4.435	-
8.	Average Weight Per Shipment	54	222	688	1,364	3,033	6,820	23,674	-
9.	Cost Per 100 Pounds	$ 5.909	$ 1.445	$ .476	$ .264	$ .129	$ .062	$ .019	-
10.	Standby Cost,								
	Shipment Basis (15%)	$ .886	$ .217	$ .071	$ .040	$ .019	$ .009	$ .003	-
11.	Standby (Stop) Cost Per								
	100 Pounds - Weight Basis:								
12.	Standby Performance								
	a) Pounds Per Man Hour	635	1,585	2,825	3,750	4,995	6,325	8,875	-
	b) Pounds Per Vehicle Hour	635	1,585	2,865	3,845	5,225	6,940	11,095	-
13.	Labor Cost Per 100 Pounds								
	(l.3 + L12a)	$ 3.155	$ 1.270	$ .726	$ .606	$ .487	$ .418	$ .301	-
	(Line 3 + Line 12a)								
14.	Vehicle Fixed Cost Per								
	100 Pounds	.564	.228	.131	.103	.088	.072	.055	-
	(Line 4 + Line 12b)								
15.	Direct Cost Per 100 Pounds	$ 3.719	$ 1.498	$ .857	$ .709	$ .575	$ .490	$ .356	-
16.	Standby Cost -								
	Weight Basis (85%)	$ 3.161	$ 1.273	$ .728	$ .603	$ .489	$ .417	$ .303	-

Standby, or stop, time and cost is summarized on both a shipment and weight basis in Table 12.31. Cost on a weight basis is determined by dividing the pounds per man hour and the pounds per vehicle hour into the cost per hour for labor and the cost per hour for vehicle fixed cost.

Cost indicated on a weight basis represents the cost per stop, not the cost per shipment. The conversion will be made during the discussion of the other element of pickup and delivery cost, the en route portion.

Travel from the carrier terminal to the first stop, from the last stop to the carrier terminal, and between stops is called the "en route" portion of pickup and delivery operations. Cost for this operation is incurred because of weight and stops. If there were no weight or stops, there would be no en route time or cost.

The allocation of en route cost between stops and weight is accomplished by using the same method of "least squares" discussed in connection with the development of cost per shipment on a stop basis prepared in Table 12.31. In our illustrations, it was determined that 46% of en route cost should be allocated on a stop basis, and 54% should be allocated on a weight basis.

The method to accomplish the stop allocation is indicated in Table 12.32.

TABLE 12. 32

DEVELOPMENT OF DIRECT COST PER 100 POUNDS FOR LESS THAN TRUCKLOAD EN ROUTE COST ON A STOP BASIS IN MULTIPLE-STOP PICKUP AND DELIVERY SERVICE

Item	WEIGHT GROUP (Pounds)							Wtd. Avg. Cost Per 100 Lbs.
	0-99	100-499	500-999	1000-1999	2000-4999	5000-9999	10000 and Over	
1. Average Weight Per Stop	54	233	698	1,371	3,023	6,780	17,869	-
2. En route Cost Per 100 Pounds - Stop Basis:								
3. Labor Cost Per Hour	$ 20.037	$ 20.123	$ 20.504	$ 22.710	$ 24.326	$ 26.443	$ 26.680	-
4. Vehicle Fixed Cost Per Hour	3.579	3.614	3.743	3.968	4.581	4.972	6.140	-
5. Direct Cost Per Hour	$ 23.616	$ 23.737	$ 24.247	$ 26.678	$ 28.907	$ 31.415	$ 32.820	-
6. Stops Per En route Hour	5.9	5.9	5.9	5.9	5.9	5.9	5.9	-
7 Direct Cost Per Stop	$ 4.003	$ 4.023	$ 4.110	$ 4.522	$ 5.899	$ 5.325	$ 5.563	-
8. Cost Per 100 Pounds	$ 7.413	$ 1.727	$ .589	$ .330	$ .195	$ .079	$ .031	-
9. En route Cost - Stop Basis (46%)	$ 3.410	$ .794	$ .271	$ .152	$ .090	$ .036	$ .014	-
10. Standby Cost - Weight Basis (Table 12.31)	3.161	1.273	.728	603	.489	.417	.303	
11. Standby - Weight Basis, En route - Stop Basis	$ 6.571	$ 2.067	$ .999	$ .755	$ .579	$ .453	$ .317	

Lines 1 through 9 of Table 12.32 establish a procedure to determine the allocation of en route cost to stops for loading or unloading. The direct cost per hour for labor and the vehicle fixed cost is the same as those used in connection with standby cost in Table 12.31. Stops per en route hour is an overall figure determined from the field study of pickup and delivery performance. The total of the en route hours (time other than at stops) is divided by the number of stops, which was determined from the study of multiple-stop service.

The direct cost per hour for labor and the vehicle fixed cost in stop weight groups are established on lines 3 and 4. Line 5, which represents the total direct cost per hour in the various stop weight groups, is a total of the preceding lines.

The overall stops per en route hour figure of 5.9 is divided into the cost per hour to obtain the cost per stop on line 7. The cost per stop figure is then divided by the average weight per stop to obtain the cost per 100 pounds at each average stop weight.

The en route cost is allocated as 46% of the total to a stop basis and 54% to a weight basis. The calculation on line 9 means that the en route portion of pickup and delivery is impacted more by weight than by the number of stops. Line 9 shows the portion of the en route cost allocated on a stop basis, which is a cost per 100 pounds in each of the stop weight brackets.

Both the stop portion of the en route cost and the weight portion of the standby cost were calculated on a stop basis. The weight portion of the standby cost was determined by dividing the direct cost per hour by the pounds per man hour and the pounds per vehicle hour at the stop. Both of these costs must be converted to a cost per shipment because rates are assessed on shipments, not on stops.

The method to accomplish this conversion, a procedure called "shipment distribution," is shown on lines 12 through 19. The pickup and delivery field study recorded the number and weight of each shipment picked up or delivered at each stop.

To construct a computer-based shipment distribution, the software program should be set up to obtain the weight of each shipment picked up or delivered at each stop. From this source data, the software is able to sort shipments according to the weight of the stop where it was handled. The result is the number of shipments in each stop weight.

For example, line 12 indicates that 51.7% if all shipments weighing between 0 and 100 pounds were picked up or delivered in stops between 0 and 100 pounds. Similarly, 6.1% of shipments weighing between 0 and 100 pounds were picked up or delivered in stops of 2,000 to 5,000 pounds.

To convert the standby cost on a weight basis and the en route cost on a stop basis (line 11) to a cost per shipment, each stop amount is multiplied by the percentage of shipments in each weight group. These calculations are accumulated and recorded in the last column of Table 12.32. The figures in this column represent a cost per 100 pounds on a shipment basis for these portions of cost in the pickup and delivery operation.

The final portion of the pickup and delivery cost is the weight portion of the en route cost. This segment of cost is incurred as the vehicle is moving between its point of domicile and the route, or among stops along the route. The operating cost to be recovered includes the labor cost, the vehicle fixed cost, and the vehicle running cost.

Two additional concepts are introduced in connection with the en route portion of the pickup and delivery operation allocated on a weight basis.

The first concept is overall pounds per vehicle hour en route. The field study of the operating process recorded the overall hours the vehicles were traveling. It also indicated the weight picked up and/or delivered during the day. From this data, the analyst can determine the overall weight carried and the hours traveled by all vehicles in the study from the time they departed from the terminal until they returned to it. A software data base program can then calculate "pounds per vehicle hour-en route." The illustration that follows uses a figure of 3,980 pounds as the average pounds carried during en route hours. This weight becomes the productivity factor to convert the hourly cost of labor and vehicle fixed cost to a cost per 100 pounds.

The second concept is "pounds per vehicle mile." The vehicle running cost is incurred as each mile is traveled. Calculations of the running cost per mile in each of the weight groups was accomplished in Table 12.23.

The conversion to a vehicle running cost per 100 pounds is accomplished by dividing the pounds per vehicle mile into the cost per mile. The pounds per vehicle mile may be calculated by using the same weight as that described in connection with the pounds per vehicle hour. The total weight on the vehicles is divided by the total miles they traveled. In the illustrated cost study, we used 350 pounds per vehicle mile.

The en route cost on a weight basis, which is the last increment of the pickup and delivery cost, is calculated in Table 12.33.

TABLE 12. 33

DEVELOPMENT OF DIRECT COST PER 100 POUNDS FOR LESS THAN TRUCKLOAD — EN ROUTE COST ON A WEIGHT BASIS IN MULTIPLE-STOP PICKUP AND DELIVERY SERVICE

| | | WEIGHT GROUP (Pounds) | | | | | | Wtd. Avg. |
	Item	0-99	100-499	500-999	1000-1999	2000-4999	5000-9999	10000 and Over	Cost Per 100 Lbs.
1.	Average Weight Per Stop	54	233	698	1,371	3,023	6,780	17,869	-
2.	En route Cost - Weight Basis:								
3.	Labor Cost Per Hour	$20.037	$20.123	$20.504	$22.710	$24.326	$26.443	$26.680	-
4.	Vehicle Fixed Cost Per Hour	3.579	3.614	3.743	3.968	4.581	4.972	6.140	-
5.	Direct Cost Per Hour	$23.616	$23.737	$24.247	$26.678	$28.907	$31.415	$32.820	-
6.	Allocated Cost (54%)	$12.753	$12.818	$13.093	$14.406	$15.610	$16.964	$17.723	-
7.	Cost Per 100 Pounds (3,980 PPVH)	$ .320	$ .322	$ .329	$ .362	$ .392	$ .426	$ .445	-
8.	Vehicle Running Cost								
9.	Running Cost Per Mile	$ .360	$ .362	$ .369	$ .381	$ .413	$ .455	$ .496	-
10.	Weighted Portion (54%)	$ .194	$ .195	$ .199	$ .206	$ .223	$ .246	$ .268	-
11.	Running Cost Per 100 Pounds (350 Pounds Per Vehicle Mile)	$ .055	$ .056	$ .057	$ .059	$ .064	$ .070	$ .077	-
12.	Total En route Cost - Weight Basis (Line 7 + Line 11)	$ .375	$ .378	$ .386	$ .421	$ .456	$ .496	$ .522	-

Whether cost is expressed on the basis of stop or shipment is not relevant to cost in Table 12.33. Direct cost in both sections of the table were determined using overall productivity in connection with time and miles the vehicles were operating. A pounds per vehicle hour figure was used to convert the labor cost and the vehicle fixed cost per hour to a cost per 100 pounds because these costs are normally based upon a time increment, the hour.

Running cost, on the other hand, is a function of distance so the common denominator is pounds per vehicle mile. In Table 12.33, the running cost per mile is converted to cost per 100 pounds by dividing the pounds per vehicle mile into the cost per mile. For purposes of determining cost in Table 12.33, it does not matter how stop cost is determined because the en route cost is only developed while the vehicle is moving.

The development of en route cost on a stop basis in Table 12.32 received an allocation of 46%. The allocation of en route cost on a weight basis received the other 54%, as indicated on lines 6 and 10 of Table 12.33.

The final procedure blends all of the costs for pickup and delivery in multiple-stop service into a single cost per 100 pounds for shipments in various weight groups. This is accomplished in the following table.

TABLE 12. 34

DEVELOPMENT OF DIRECT COST PER 100 POUNDS FOR LESS THAN TRUCKLOAD MULTIPLE-STOP PICKUP AND DELIVERY SERVICE

		WEIGHT GROUP (Pounds)						Wtd. Avg.
Item	0-99	100-499	500-999	1000-1999	2000-4999	5000-9999	10000 and Over	Cost Per 100 Lbs.
1. Average Weight Per Stop	54	233	698	1,371	3,023	6,780	17,869	-
2. Standby Cost Per 100 pounds	$ .886	$ .217	$ .071	$ .040	$ .019	$ .009	$ .003	-
(Table 12.31, Shipment Basis)								
3. Standby Performance:								
4. a) Pounds Per Man Hour	635	1,585	2,825	3,750	4,995	6,325	8.875	-
5. b) Pounds Per Vehicle Hour	635	1,585	2,865	3,845	5,225	6,940	11,095	-
6. Cost Per 100 Pounds (Table 12.32)	$ 6.571	$ 2.067	$ .999	$ .755	$ .579	$ .453	$ .317	-
(Standby Weight Basis - En route - Stop Basis)								
12. Shipment Distribution (Pounds)								
13. 0 - 99	51.7%	21.4%	10.1%	8.2%	6.1%	1.8%	.7%	$4.048
14. 100 - 499		64.1	13.4	10.3	8.1	2.7	1.4	1.600
15. 500 - 999			67.5	15.8	10.6	3.6	2.5	.879
16. 1,000 - 1,999				76.1	15.6	5.2	3.1	.698
17. 2,000 - 4,999					87.9	7.9	4.2	.558
18. 5,000 - 9,999						92.2	7.8	.442
19. 10,000 and Over							100.0	.317
20. En route Cost - Weight Basis	$ .375	$ .378	$ .386	$ .421	$ .456	$ .496	$ .522	
(Table 12.33)								
21. Pickup and Delivery Cost	$ 5.309	$ 2.195	$1.336	$ 1.159	$1.033	$ .947	$ .842	
(Last Column, Plus Lines 2 and 20)								

Table 12.34 is the final table required to complete the cost development for pickup and delivery in multiple-stop service. The table summarizes the costs on a stop basis and on an en route basis for shipments in various weights. Costs are expressed in terms of 100 pounds since rates will be expressed in those increments.

Line 2 of the table is the standby cost on a shipment basis that was determined on line 10 of Table 12.31. This cost was allocated on the basis of the cost at the stop for paperwork, accounting for 15% of the cost on a shipment basis.

Line 6 of Table 12.34 is the other 85% of the stop cost allocated on the basis of weight. Here we see that most of the cost incurred at stops is caused by the weight handled. Line 6 also includes the 46% stop basis allocation of en route cost. Both of these cost allocations were determined in line 11 of Table 12.32.

At this point, the stop cost has been allocated on both a shipment basis and weight basis. The totals have been carried forward to Table 12.34. This is also true of the en route cost on a stop basis. The last part of pickup and delivery cost to be included in Table 12.34 is the en route cost allocated on a weight basis. This cost is shown on line 20 of Table 12.34. Finally, a cost per 100 pounds in multiple-stop service on a shipment basis is determined on line 21.

Single-stop service is the final operating process in pickup and delivery. The vehicle leaves the terminal, makes one stop to either load or unload, and returns to the terminal. Though single-stop service is not as widely used as multiple-stop service, it may arise when a shipper has an emergency, the carrier misses a stop, a shipper requires special equipment, or the location of the stop is off-route of the multiple-stop route. Costs and rates for single stops in regular truckload activities can be constructed as illustrated in Chapter 9.

The illustration demonstrates single-stop service where one shipment is picked up or delivered at each stop. In these circumstances, a shipment distribution similar to that shown in multiple-stop demonstrations is not necessary. In actual practice, single-stop service could include multiple-shipment stops. If that were a continuing practice, the analyst might prepare a shipment distribution by following earlier examples.

The study of single-stop service is similar to multiple-stop service in that the direct cost is prepared for both the cost at the stop and the cost en route. Direct stop cost includes only labor and vehicle fixed cost. Because the vehicle is not moving, no running cost is incurred.

En route cost includes all three elements of direct cost. The cost per hour in all cases is converted to a cost per 100 pounds in each weight group by productivity measurements of pounds per man hour or pounds per vehicle hour.

The field study is again summarized for all single-stop service routes to indicate the number of stops, the weight picked up or delivered, and the number of man hours expended at the stop. The analyst determines the average weight per stop, pounds per man hour at the stops, and pounds per vehicle hour at the stops in each weight group. The weight groups are the same as those selected for the platform study and the multiple-stop service study.

The en route portion of the same stops are summarized to indicate the total miles traveled and the total weight handled. From these totals, the pounds per vehicle hour en route for each weight group may be determined. This is different from multiple-stop service where an overall pounds per vehicle hour figure was used. In single-stop service, there is only one stop so the cost allocation among stops is not required.

The running cost per 100 pounds is obtained by dividing the running cost per mile by the pounds per vehicle mile. The pounds per vehicle mile may be obtained for each stop weight because only one stop is made in single-stop service. The pounds picked up or delivered at the stop is divided by the number of miles to obtain the pounds per vehicle mile.

The illustration also uses the same labor cost and vehicle cost per hour figures as those used in multiple-stop service examples. In preparing comparable studies, the analyst would determine the accurate labor and vehicle cost. It is likely, however, that a different mixture of employees and vehicles would perform single-stop service from those employed in multiple-stop service.

This brief explanation of single-stop service, and our discussion of multiple-stop service, gives the analyst enough information to complete a table similar to Table 12.35.

TABLE 12.35

DEVELOPMENT OF DIRECT COST PER 100 POUNDS
FOR LESS THAN TRUCKLOAD SINGLE-STOP PICKUP AND DELIVERY SERVICE

Line No.	Item	WEIGHT GROUP - Pounds					
		0-99	100-499	500-999	1000-1999	2000-4999	5000-9999
1.	Loading/Unloading:						
2.	Pounds Per Man Hour	315	905	1,575	2,250	3,390	5,140
3.	Labor Cost (Driver & Helper)	$ 20.037	$ 20.123	$20.504	$ 22.710	$ 24.326	$ 26.443
4.	Cost Per 100 Pounds (Labor)	$ 6.361	$ 2.224	$ 1.302	$ 1.009	$ .718	$. 514
5.	Pounds Per Vehicle Hour	315	905	1,675	2,415	3,700	5,825
6.	Vehicle Fixed Cost Per Hour	$ 3.579	$ 3.614	$ 3.743	$ 3.968	$ 4.581	$ 4.972
7.	Cost Per 100 Pounds (Vehicle)	$ 1.136	$ .399	$ .223	$ .164	$ .124	$ .085
8.	Total Cost Per 100 Pounds	$ 7.497	$ 2.623	$ 1.525	$ 1.173	$ .842	$ .599
9.	En route Operation:						
10.	Labor Cost (Driver & Helper)	$ 20.037	$20.123	$20.504	$ 22.710	$ 24.326	$ 26.443
11.	Vehicle Fixed Cost Per Hour	3.579	3.614	3.743	3.968	4.581	4.972
12.	Total Cost Per Hour	$ 23.616	$23.737	$24.247	$ 26.678	$ 28.907	$ 31.415
13.	Pounds Per Vehicle Hour (En route)	245	575	1,265	2,320	5,110	10,850
14.	Cost Per 100 Pounds	$ 9.639	$ 4.128	$ 1.917	$ 1.150	$ .566	$ .290
15.	Pounds Per Vehicle Mile	25	45	115	220	510	1,040
16.	Running Cost Per Mile	$ .360	$ .362	$ .369	$ .381	$ .413	$ .455
17.	Cost Per 100 Pounds	$ 1.440	$ .804	$ .321	$ .173	$ .081	$ .044
18.	Cost Per 100 Pounds - Single-stop Service (Lines 8, 14 and 17)	$ 18.576	$ 7.555	$ 3.763	$ 2.496	$ 1.489	$ .933

The cost to provide single-stop service for shippers is significantly higher per 100 pounds than multiple-stop service. This is due to the fact that more miles are traveled for less weight.

The illustrated study of pickup and delivery service is completed by combining multiple- and single-stop service into one cost. This is accomplished by using the number of stops in each weight group. The multiple-stop service cost is weighted by the relationship of the number of stops to the total number of stops. The single-stop service cost is weighted similarly. Data for these determinations has been produced in the tables developed from the field study.

TABLE 12.36

DETERMINATION OF WEIGHTED COST PER 100 POUNDS
FOR LESS THAN TRUCKLOAD PICKUP AND/OR DELIVERY SERVICE

Line No.	Item	WEIGHT GROUP - Pounds					
		0-99	100-499	500-999	1000-1999	2000-4999	5000-9999
1.	MULTIPLE-STOP SERVICE						
2.	Percent	94.6	92.9	92.4	87.8	79.5	65.0
3.	Cost	$ 5.309	$ 2.195	$ 1.336	$ 1.159	$ 1.033	$ .947
4.	SINGLE-STOP SERVICE						
5.	Percent	5.4	7.1	7.6	12.2	20.5	35.0
6.	Cost	$18.576	$ 7.555	$ 3.763	$ 2.496	$ 1.489	$ .933
7.	Weighted Cost Per 100 Pounds	$ 6.025	$ 2.576	$ 1.520	$ 1.322	$ 1.126	$ .942

The total on line 7 represents the total direct cost per 100 pounds to perform less-than-truckload pickup and delivery operations. The discussion to this point has been limited to less-than- truckload operations, but most LTL carriers also transport shipments in excess of 10,000 pounds. In some cases, such shipments are handled in pickup and delivery operations along with line-haul operations similar to those of the LTL shipments. To provide for this activity, Tables 12.37 and 12.38 construct truckload pickup and delivery productivity required to develop a cost per 100 pounds for this operating process. Table 12.37 illustrates productivity for the loading and/or unloading process; Table 12.38 illustrates factors for the en route portion.

TABLE 12.37

DEVELOPMENT OF PRODUCTIVITY PER HOUR
(Load/unload truckload operation)

Line No.	Weight Group	No. of Stops	Total Weight (Pounds)	Man Hours	Vehicle Hours	Pounds Per Man Hour	Pounds Per Vehicle Hour
1.	10,000 - 19,999	330	5,107,080	616.8	495.2	8,280	10,313
2.	20,000 - 29,999	84	1,416,258	138.5	108.5	10,226	13,053
3.	30,000 - 39,999	12	428,736	35.7	28.8	12,020	14,870
4.	40,000 and Over	4	195,417	14.4	11.7	13,560	16,700

TABLE 12.38

DEVELOPMENT OF PRODUCTIVITY PER MILE
(En route truckload operation)

Line No.	Weight Group	No. of Stops	Total Weight (Pounds)	Vehicle Hours	Vehicle Miles	Pounds Per Vehicle Mile	Pounds Per Vehicle Hour
1.	10,000 - 19,999	330	5,107,080	278.3	2,853.1	1,790	18,350
2.	20,000 - 29,999	84	1,416,258	51.7	540.6	2,620	27,400
3.	30,000 - 39,999	12	428,736	11.7	129.5	3,310	36,500
4.	40,000 and Over	4	195,417	4.7	56.3	3,470	41,400

TABLE 12.39

**DEVELOPMENT OF COST PER 100 POUNDS
FOR TRUCKLOAD PICKUP AND DELIVERY OPERATION**

Line No.	Item	WEIGHT GROUP - Pounds			
		10,000-19,999	20,000-29,999	30,000-39,999	40,000 And Over
1.	Loading and/or Unloading:				
2.	Labor Cost Per Hour (Driver & Helper - Table)	$ 26.591	$ 26.878	$ 27.247	$ 27.575
3.	Pounds Per Man Hour	8,280	10,226	12,020	13,560
4.	Labor Cost Per 100 Pounds	$ .321	$ .263	$ .227	$ .205
5.	Vehicle Fixed Cost Per Hour (Table 12.24)	$ 5.887	$ 6.143	$ 6.891	$ 7.211
6.	Pounds Per Vehicle Hour	10,313	13,053	14,870	16,700
7.	Vehicle Fixed Cost Per 100 Pounds	$ .057	$ .047	$ .046	$ .043
8.	Cost Per 100 Pounds (Line 4 + Line 7)	$ .378	$ .310	$ .273	$ .246
9.	En route Operation:				
10.	Labor Cost Per Hour (Driver & Helper - Table	$ 26.591	$ 26.878	$ 27.247	$ 27.575
11.	Vehicle Fixed Cost Per Hour (Table 12.24)	5.887	6.143	6.891	7.211
12.	Labor and Vehicle Cost Per Hour	$ 32.478	$ 33.021	$ 34.128	$ 34.786
13.	Pounds Per Vehicle Hour En route	18,350	27,400	36,500	41,400
14.	Cost Per 100 Pounds	$ .177	$ .121	$ .094	$ .084
15.	Vehicle Running Cost Per Mile (Table 12.24)	$ .486	$ .500	$ .529	$ .533
16.	Pounds Per Vehicle Mile	1,790	2,620	3,310	3,470
17.	Cost Per 100 Pounds	$ .027	$ .019	$ .016	$ .015
18.	Total Cost Per 100 Pounds (Lines 8, 14 and 17)	$ .582	$ .450	$ .383	$ .345

It should be apparent that a large data base is required for LTL carriers to properly develop similar costs for their pickup and delivery operating processes. Three general categories of data are required.

Shipment analysis requires the following data segregated according to single-stop service, multiple-stop service, and total service. Each must be summarized in preselected weight groups that include the following data:

1. Stop weight groups

    a) Number of stops

    b) Weight

    c) Average weight per stop

2. Shipment weight groups

    a) Number of shipments

    b) Weight

    c) Average weight per shipments

3. Number of shipments handled at stops, overall, per hour.

4. Number of shipments in each weight group picked up or delivered

    in each stop weight group.

5. Number of stops per hour, overall, while the vehicles are away

    from the terminal.

This data will provide the study framework in terms of the mix of activity in the pickup and delivery operation. It will determine the basis of cost distribution.

The second category is the determination of the types of vehicles and classifications of the employees.

1. Weighting of vehicle types used in each stop and shipment weight group.

2. Weighting of employee classifications used in each stop and shipment weight group.

The underlying productivity data includes:

1. Labor hours to load and/or unload shipments at stops in the same weight groups as the shipment and stop analysis just described. These hours include the time for both drivers and helpers, when helpers are used.

2. Vehicle hours at the stops by stop weight group. These hours differ from labor hours; they are elapsed hours at the stops.

3. Vehicle hours while the vehicle is moving, from the time it leaves the terminal until it returns.

4. Vehicle miles from the time the vehicle leaves the terminal until it returns.

5. Weight on vehicles while en route, from the time they leave the terminal until their return.

6. Items 3, 4, and 5 are not summarized in stop or shipment weight groups in the multiple-stop service because productivity is determined using overall weight.

After the field study is completed and the data summarized in accordance with these parameters, the analyst can begin to compile data into the schedules shown in this section.

Line-haul Analysis

The final operating process in the development of cost for pricing purposes in LTL general freight operations is line-haul. This process moves truckloads or near truckloads of LTL shipments between the carrier's terminals. Cost for the operation is a function of both time and distance. The driver labor cost and the vehicle fixed cost are determined on the basis of the number of hours per trip. The running cost is determined on the basis of the number of miles per trip. If drivers are paid on a mileage basis, their pay becomes a function of the number of miles traveled.

After the cost per trip is determined, the conversion to a cost per 100 pounds is accomplished by dividing the cost per trip by the average weight per trip. In most cases, LTL carriers do not maintain trip manifests that list the number and weight of shipments for each trip. For the field study period, such manifests must be prepared to make the conversion from a cost per trip to a cost per 100 pounds. Collection of this data can be accomplished using Form 3 in the Appendix.

The preparation of platform and pickup and delivery costs described earlier in this chapter illustrated a cost development for a carrier operating two terminals. In that case, a line-haul cost would be prepared only on a point-to-point basis between the two terminals. However, to fully illustrate the line-haul cost development, we will assume that the carrier operates several terminals.

The process begins much like the pickup and delivery cost development in that it is necessary to determine the weighting factors for both labor and vehicle costs. If carriers use different equipment and drivers in LTL operations between terminals, the analyst should perform an equipment and labor weighting to obtain one cost for each, per hour, by the length of the line haul.

The illustration in Table 12.40 assumes that only tractors and double trailers are used. The average of drivers operating tractors pulling double trailers in Tables 12.27 and 12.28 is used for the labor cost.

TABLE 12.40

DEVELOPMENT OF LINE-HAUL COST PER 100 POUNDS
FOR LESS THAN TRUCKLOAD TRAFFIC

Line No.	Item	LENGTH OF HAUL - Miles					
		25	50	100	200	400	700
1.	Equipment Fixed Cost Per Year (Table 12.14 and 12.15B)	$ 16,171	$ 16,171	$ 16,171	$ 16,171	$16,171	$ 12,251
2.	Use Factor - Hours	1,690	1,875	2,150	2,290	2,500	2,825
3.	Equipment Fixed Cost Per Hour	$ 9.569	$ 8.625	$ 7.521	$ 7.062	$ 6.468	$ 4.337
4.	Equipment Hours Per Trip	1.50	2.06	3.15	5.52	10.46	17.76
5.	Equipment Cost Per Trip	$ 14.354	$ 17.768	$ 23.691	$ 38.982	$67.655	$ 77.025
6.	Driver Cost Per Hour (Avg. Tables 12.27 and 12.28)	$ 20.326	$ 20.326	$ 20.326	$ 20.326	$20.326	$ 20.326
7.	Driver Cost Per Trip	$ 30.489	$ 41.872	$64.027	$112.200	$212.610	$360.990
8.	Running Cost Per Mile	$ .551	$ .551	$ .551	$ .551	$ .551	$ .551
9.	Running Cost Per Trip	$ 13.775	$ 27.550	$ 55.100	$110.200	$220.400	$385.700
10.	Driver Subsistence	-	-	-	-	-	$ 22.000
11.	Total Cost Per Trip (Lines 5, 8, 10, and 11)	$ 58.618	$ 87.190	$142.818	$261.392	$500.665	$823.715
12.	Average Load (Pounds)	17,750	18,000	19,250	21,700	25,800	28,600
13.	Cost Per 100 Pounds	$ .330	$ .484	$ .742	$ 1.205	$ 1.941	$ 2.880

The equipment use factor in line 2 is the number of hours per year the vehicles are used to operate between terminals 25 miles apart. As the length of the haul increases, so do the annual use hours. The figures representing annual use can be determined from a sample of trip times between terminals. If several terminals are operated, the trip times can be plotted on a line graph, and specific times at specific lengths of haul can be read from the graph. The number of trips per year times the hours per trip yields the annual vehicle hours.

The equipment fixed cost per hour times the number of hours per trip equals the equipment cost per trip. The same concept is applied to labor cost: the number of hours per trip is multiplied by the cost per hour to achieve the labor cost per trip.

The vehicle cost per trip is determined by multiplying the cost per mile by the number of miles for each length of haul.

Subsistence allowance for the driver is added at 700 miles because the trip cannot be made within the regular service hours.

The total of the vehicle fixed cost, the driver cost, the subsistence, and the vehicle running cost determines the direct cost per trip by the length of the haul.

The cost per 100 pounds is determined by dividing the cost per trip by the average load weight at each length of haul.

Cost Summary

The direct costs of all operating processes for LTL general freight transportation have now been demonstrated. These costs must be combined to achieve the total direct cost per 100 pounds. Combining these costs is done in two stages because the total terminal cost must be determined before the line-haul cost can be added. The total terminal cost includes one pickup, a platform handling at origin, another platform handling at destination, and one delivery.

TABLE 12.41

SUMMARY OF DIRECT TERMINAL COST
PER 100 POUNDS

Line No.	Item	WEIGHT GROUP - Pounds									
		0-99	100-499	500-999	1000-1999	2000-4999	5000-9999	10,000-19,999	20,000-29,999	30,000-39,999	40,000 & Over
1.	Pickup	$ 6.025	$ 2.576	$ 1.520	$ 1.322	$ 1.126	$ .942	$ .582	$ .450	$ .383	$ .345
2.	Terminal Platform	3.899	1.660	1.072	.777	.522	.273	.061	-	-	-
3.	Total Starting Cost	$ 9.924	$ 4.236	$ 2.592	$ 2.099	$ 1.648	$ 1.215	$ .643	$ .450	$ .383	$ .345
4.	Terminal Platform	3.899	1.660	1.072	.777	.522	.273	.061	-	-	-
5.	Delivery	6.025	2.576	1.520	1.322	1.126	.942	.582	.450	.383	.345
6.	Total 2 Terminal Cost	$19.848	$ 8.472	$ 5.184	$ 4.198	$ 3.296	$ 2.430	$ 1.286	$ .900	$ .766	$ .690
7.	Terminal Platform	3.899	1.660	1.072	.777	.522	.273	.061	-	-	-
8.	Total 3 Terminal Cost	$23.747	$10.132	$ 6.256	$ 4.975	$ 3.818	$ 2.703	$ 1.347	$ .900	$ .766	$ .690

Table 12.41 compiles all the costs developed for 2-terminal and 3-terminal handling. This cost is combined with the line-haul cost to achieve the total direct cost.

Generally, LTL shipments receive two platform handlings, one at the origin terminal and one at the destination terminal. Some LTL carriers operate terminals known as break-bulk stations where shipments are transferred across a third platform. In these instances, the analyst should add another platform handling to the 2-terminal portion of the table, which is constructed to determine the total terminal cost per 100 pounds. The analyst should also recognize that not all break-bulk stations are operated in the same manner. Whether a full additional platform handling cost should be added to all shipments depends upon the particular circumstances. In the illustration, we used three platform handlings for shipments moving 700 miles and over.

When the total terminal cost has been completed, including break-bulk costs, the total direct cost by the length of the haul can be established by adding the line-haul cost.

When the terminal direct cost and the line-haul cost are added, the result is the direct cost for handling LTL shipments. Indirect, or overhead, cost must be added to the direct cost to obtain the total cost at a 100 operating ratio, or the break-even point. Earlier discussion of indirect cost (Chapter 7) described the procedure to determine the ratio for most carriers.

The method used in this chapter to determine the ratio for LTL carriers is different from methods used for other types of carriers. The difference is primarily the handling of maintenance cost. When we prepared maintenance cost per mile, we included shop overhead, assuming that all LTL carriers operate their own shop. Another assumption is that the carrier loads each shop work order with overhead cost, so the summaries of cost per vehicle, or vehicle type, include all shop cost.

When the method in this chapter is used, the overall company overhead cost incurred in the repair shop becomes a direct cost because it is included in the maintenance cost per mile. If these costs were classified as direct cost in the overall ratio determination, they would be included in the study twice.

Table 12.42 is a chart of accounts that might be used to determine the indirect ratio for LTL carriers.

TABLE 12.42

SUMMARY OF OPERATING EXPENSES IN PERCENTAGES

Line No.	Item	Direct	Indirect	Total
1.	Officer and Supervisory Salaries	.43	5.24	5.67
2.	Clerical and Administrative Wages	-	3.45	3.45
3.	Drivers & Helpers Wages	34.08	-	34.08
4.	Cargo Handlers Wages	10.09	-	10.09
5.	Vehicle Repair & Service Wages	3.46	-	3.46
6.	Owner-Operator Driver Wages	3.23	-	3.23
7.	Other Labor Wages	-	.49	.49
8.	Federal Payroll Taxes	1.45	.40	1.85
9.	State Payroll Taxes	.16	.05	.21
10.	Workers Compensation	2.06	.17	2.23
11.	Group Insurance	1.46	.33	1.79
12.	Pension and Retirement Plans	.58	.46	1.04
13.	Other Fringes	-	-	-
14.	Fuel, Oil, and Lubricants for Motor Vehicles	3.46	.06	3.52
15.	Vehicle Parts	4.46	-	4.46
16.	Outside Maintenance	1.10	.15	1.25
17.	Tires and Tubes	1.68	.05	1.73
18.	Other Operating Supplies and Expenses	1.00	1.70	2.70
19.	Tariffs and Advertising	-	.14	.14
20.	Commission and Fees	-	.06	.06
21.	Officers, Employees, and Other General Expenses	-	.96	.96
22.	Gas, Diesel Fuel & Oil Taxes (Fed.)	1.26	.04	1.30
23.	Vehicle Licenses and Registration Fees (Fed.)	1.12	-	1.12
24.	Other Taxes (Federal)	-	-	-
25.	Real Estate and Personal Property Taxes	-	.27	.27
26.	Fuel and Oil Taxes (State and Other)	1.60	-	1.60
27.	Vehicle Licenses and Registration Fees (State)	.96	.12	1.08
28.	Other Taxes	-	.01	.01
29.	Liability and Property Damage	.28	1.99	2.27
30.	Cargo Loss and Damage Insurance	-	1.03	1.03
31.	All Other Insurance	-	.20	.20
32.	Communications	-	1.15	1.15
33.	Utilities	-	.96	.96
34.	Depreciation, Buildings, and Improvements	-	-	-
35.	Depreciation, Revenue Equipment	4.85	-	4.85
36.	Depreciation, All Other Equipment & Property	-	.49	.49
37.	Amortization	-	-	-
38.	Vehicle Rents With Driver	.02	-	.02
39.	Vehicle Rents With Driver - Vehicle Portion	1.02	-	1.02
40.	Vehicle Rents Without Driver	.16	-	.16
41.	Other Purchased Transportation	.12	-	.12
42.	Equipment Rents - Credit	(.06)	-	(.06)
43.	Total Operating Expenses	80.03	19.97	100.00

The chart of expense accounts in Table 12.42 produces an indirect ratio to total expenses of 20%. The figure shown as a direct cost in line 1 represents the cost of supervisors in the repair shop. Accounts split between direct and indirect cost include expense items for employees and vehicles included in the direct cost analysis, as well as indirect expenses for payroll taxes and fringe benefits for clerical staff and fuel and oil for company cars. Each expense account should be analyzed to determine the correct cost allocation.

The indirect ratio is calculated on total expenses rather than total revenue. The objective is to determine the total cost at the break-even point before profit is determined or included in the rate structure. If the ratio were determined on revenue, the cost would be understated by the difference in percentage between revenue and expense.

When the indirect ratio has been determined, the total cost in weight groups by the length of the haul is attained by adding the direct cost to the dollar amount of overhead, or indirect cost. Table 12.43 accomplishes that calculation.

TABLE 12.43

SUMMARY OF TOTAL COST PER 100 POUNDS BY LENGTH OF HAUL

Line No.	Item	0- 99	100- 499	500- 999	1000 1999	2000- 4999	5000- 9999	10,000- 19,999	20,000- 29,999	30,000- 39,999	40,000 & Over
						WEIGHT GROUP - Pounds					
1.	25 Miles										
2.	Total Terminal Cost	$19.848	$ 8.472	$ 5.184	$ 4.198	$ 3.296	$ 2.430	$ 1.286	$ .900	$ .766	$ .690
3.	Line Haul Cost	.330	.330	.330	.330	.330	.330	.330	.330	.330	.330
4.	Direct Cost	$20.178	$ 8.802	$ 5.514	$ 4.528	$ 3.626	$ 2.760	$ 1.616	$ 1.230	$ 1.096	$ 1.020
5.	Direct and Indirect Cost	$25.223	$11.003	$ 6.893	$ 5.660	$ 4.533	$ 3.450	$ 2.020	$ 1.538	$ 1.370	$ 1.275
6.	Cost at 93 O. R.	$26.989	$11.773	$ 7.376	$ 6.056	$ 4.850	$ 3.692	$ 2.161	$ 1.646	$ 1.466	$ 1.364
7.	50 Miles										
8.	Total Terminal Cost	$19.848	$ 8.472	$ 5.184	$ 4.198	$ 3.296	$ 2.430	$ 1.286	$ .900	$ .766	$ .690
9.	Line Haul Cost	.484	.484	.484	.484	.484	.484	.484	.484	.484	.484
10.	Direct Cost	$20.332	$ 8.956	$ 5.668	$ 4.682	$ 3.780	$ 2.914	$ 1.770	$ 1.384	$ 1.250	$ 1.174
11.	Direct and Indirect Cost	$25.415	$11.195	$ 7.085	$ 5.853	$ 4.725	$ 3.643	$ 2.213	$ 1.730	$ 1.563	$ 1.468
12.	Cost at 93 O. R.	$27.194	$11.979	$ 7.581	$ 6.263	$ 5.056	$ 3.898	$ 2.368	$1.851	$ 1.672	$ 1.571
13.	100 Miles										
14.	Total Terminal Cost	$19.848	$ 8.472	$ 5.184	$ 4.198	$ 3.296	$ 2.430	$ 1.286	$ .900	$ .766	$ .690
15.	Line Haul Cost	.742	.742	.742	.742	.742	.742	.742	.742	.742	.742
16.	Direct Cost	$20.590	$ 9.214	$ 5.926	$ 4.940	$ 4.038	$ 3.172	$ 2.028	$ 1.642	$ 1.508	$ 1.432
17.	Direct and Indirect Cost	$25.738	$11.518	$ 7.408	$ 6.175	$ 5.048	$ 3.965	$ 2.535	$ 2.053	$ 1.885	$ 1.790
18.	Cost at 93 O. R.	$27.540	$12.324	$ 7.927	$ 6.607	$ 5.401	$ 4.243	$ 2.712	$ 2.197	$ 2.017	$ 1.915
19.	200 Miles										
20.	Total Terminal Cost	$19.848	$ 8.472	$ 5.184	$ 4.198	$ 3.296	$ 2.430	$ 1.286	$ .900	$ .766	$ .690
21.	Line Haul Cost	1.205	1.205	1.205	1.205	1.205	1.205	1.205	1.205	1.205	1.205
22.	Direct Cost	$21.053	$ 9.677	$ 6.389	$ 5.403	$ 4.501	$ 3.635	$ 2.491	$ 2.105	$ 1.971	$ 1.895
23.	Direct and Indirect Cost	$26.316	$12.096	$ 7.986	$ 6.754	$ 5.626	$ 4.544	$ 3.114	$ 2.631	$ 2.464	$ 2.369
24.	Cost at 93 O. R.	$28.158	$12.943	$ 8.545	$ 7.227	$ 6.020	$ 4.862	$ 3.332	$ 2.815	$ 2.636	$ 2.535

TABLE 12.43 (continued)

SUMMARY OF TOTAL COST PER 100 POUNDS BY LENGTH OF HAUL

Line No.	Item	0-99	100-499	500-999	1000-1999	2000-4999	5000-9999	10,000-19,999	20,000-29,999	30,000-39,999	40,000 & Over
		WEIGHT GROUP - Pounds									
25.	400 Miles										
26.	Total Terminal Cost	$19.848	$8.472	$5.184	$4.198	$3.296	$2.430	$1.286	$.900	$.766	$.690
27.	Line Haul Cost	1.941	1.941	1.941	1.941	1.941	1.941	1.941	1.941	1.941	1.941
28.	Direct Cost	$21.789	$10.413	$7.125	$6.139	$5.237	$4.371	$3.227	$2.841	$2.707	$2.631
29.	Direct and Indirect Cost	$27.236	$13.016	$8.906	$7.674	$6.546	$5.464	$4.034	$3.551	$3.384	$3.289
30.	Cost at 93 O. R.	$29.143	$13.927	$9.529	$8.211	$7.004	$5.846	$4.316	$3.800	$3.621	$3.519
31.	700 Miles										
32.	Total Terminal Cost	$23.747	$10.132	$6.256	$4.975	$3.818	$2.703	$1.347	$.900	$.766	$.690
33.	Line Haul Cost	2.880	2.880	2.880	2.880	2.880	2.880	2.880	2.880	2.880	2.880
34.	Direct Cost	$26.627	$13.012	$9.136	$7.855	$6.698	$5.583	$4.227	$3.780	$3.646	$3.570
35.	Direct and Indirect Cost	$33.284	$16.265	$11.420	$9.819	$8.373	$6.979	$5.284	$4.725	$4.558	$4.463
36.	Cost at 93 O. R.	$35.614	$17.404	$12.219	$10.506	$8.959	$7.468	$5.654	$5.056	$4.877	$4.775

Direct and indirect costs shown for each length of haul are determined by dividing the direct cost in each category by the complement of the indirect ratio shown in Table 12.42. That table developed an indirect ratio of 20%, the complement of which is 80%. For example, the direct cost for shipments weighing 0 to 99 pounds on line 4 of Table 12.43 is $20.178. That figure divided by .80 is $25.223, which is the figure shown on line 5 of Table 12.43. This procedure was followed for each weight bracket and length of haul.

The result of these calculations is the break-even point or cost at a 100 operating ratio where cost and rate are the same. To develop a rate that will return a profit, cost must be developed at a higher operating ratio. Demonstrations of rate development throughout the book have been predicated upon an operating ratio of 93, which builds a 7% profit into the rate. The only reason 7% was selected was because we believe most carriers are familiar with that level.

Most regulatory agencies have used that figure as a benchmark in past rate-making proceedings. Today, carriers may use any margin of profit they choose, within the competitive environment.

We again emphasis that the methods and procedures used in this book develop the cost at a 100 operating ratio including only carrier operating income and expense. The cost of taxes based upon net operating income and the cost of borrowed funds are not included in the cost base.

Accordingly, taxes based upon net operating income, interest income, and interest expense resulting from carrier operations must be recovered from, or be added to, the difference between costs at a 100 operating ratio and the selected profit margin. Noncarrier income and expense are not included in these calculations.

The Rate Structure of LTL Carriers

Historically, LTL carriers have confronted two major issues in designing a compensatory rate structure. The cost study described in this chapter prepares a cost per 100 pounds for handling shipments of various sizes moving various distances, but it does not address the classification of commodities that requires different rates to reflect handling characteristics. Commodities transported by these carriers differ significantly and the differences must be accounted for in the rate structure.

The second issue is what carriers have described as "the small shipment problem." This problem is one of rate level. In many cases, the handling of small shipments on the basis of weight will not return sufficient revenue to cover the cost of their handling. To compensate for the inordinately higher cost, the industry has constructed charges per shipment in 25 and 50 pound increments, for shipments weighing up to 500 pounds. In effect, these rates become minimum charges that are designed to recover the higher handling cost.

The National Motor Freight Classification describes virtually every commodity that moves in the United States. Each of these commodities are assigned a rating that describes their relativity to other commodities. These ratings are established on the basis of density, packaging, and other transportation characteristics. Therefore, a cost study must be related to the classification of commodities. This relationship is determined by another analysis of the freight bills included in Table 12.19. The classification rating used on the freight bills should be determined and recorded in the data base.

The weighted average rating should be obtained for the entire sampling. From this analysis, the overall classification rating of all commodities handled during the study period can be obtained. The analysis should be further reduced to the classification of LTL shipments versus the rating for truckload shipments. This breakdown is necessary because the National Motor Freight Classification assigns different rating groups to truckload shipments and LTL shipments.

For purposes of the illustrated rate design that follows, the overall classification rating was class 70 for LTL shipments and class 35 for truckload shipments. This means that the cost developed represents cost for handling, on a weighted average, shipments rated as class 70 and class 35. Each of the other ratings in the rate structure are percentages of the rates at those points.

Many LTL class rates have historically been constructed in weight groups to reflect the decrease in rate per 100 pounds as weight increases. For purposes of the illustrations in this chapter, we have used Any Quantity, 2,000, 5,000, 10,000, 20,000, and truckload minimum weights. These weight groups conform with the weight groups selected in design of the cost study. The Any Quantity weight group includes shipments weighing between 1,000 and 2,000 pounds. Shipments weighing less than 1,000 pounds will be rated under a rule that will be described later in this chapter.

The classes selected for use in the following rate pages are believed to be reflective of classes predominately used in the National Motor Freight

Classification. Class 70 represents the rate necessary to recover the cost of handling all shipments, on a weighted average, in our example. Shipments with characteristics other than those at class 70 must be rated according to those found in construction of the classification. For example, if a commodity is rated as class 100, it cannot take the same rate as commodities rated at class 70. In our example, the class 70 rate is increased by 25% to reflect the class rating difference up to class 100.

TABLE 12.44A

DISTANCE CLASS RATES (Cents per 100 pounds)

MILES NOT OVER	MINIMUM WEIGHT IN POUNDS	100	92.5	85	77.5	CLASS 70	65	60	55	50
3	AQ					597				
5						598				
10						600				
15						602				
20						604				
25						*606				
30						609				
35						612				
40						616				
45						620				
50						*626				
60						632				
70						639				
80						646				
90						653				
100						*660				
110						666				
120						672				
130						678				
140						684				

continued

TABLE 12.44A *(continued)*

DISTANCE CLASS RATES (Cents per 100 pounds) (continued)

MILES NOT OVER	MINIMUM WEIGHT IN POUNDS	100	92.5	85	77.5	CLASS 70	65	60	55	50
150						691				
160						697				
170						703				
180						710				
190						717				
200						*723				
220						732				
240						741				
260						750				
280						760				
300						772				
325						784				
350						796				
375						808				
400						* 821				
425						836				
450						851				
475						867				
500						883				
525						901				
550						921				
575						942				
600						963				
625						984				
650						1006				
675						1028				
700						*1051				
725						1074				
750						1097				

Table 12.44A is an outline of the rates to be constructed for the Any Quantity class rates. Cost at a 93 operating ratio is entered in the rate table from the figures in Table 12.43 under the weight group 1,000-1,999 for each of the distances. The cost points are entered in the class 70 column since that is the overall commodity classification found in the freight bill analysis.

The rates between the cost points are then entered in increasing increments as distance increases. For example, the increase between the 25- and 30-mile distance brackets is only 3 cents, but the increase between 500 miles and 525 miles is 18 cents. These changes follow both the changes in cost and the changes in the width of the mileage brackets. As distance increases, the width of the mileage brackets also increases.

In feathering the rates between cost points on the mileage scale, the largest adjustments in the amounts of increase should occur at the change in mileage bracket width. Following these procedures will produce a smooth progression of rates through all distances. For example, an adjustment in amount of rate increase should occur at the 50-60 mile bracket because the bracket widens from 5 miles to 10 miles. The previous mileage bracket was 45-50 miles.

TABLE 12.44B

DISTANCE CLASS RATES (Cents Per 100 Pounds)

MILES NOT OVER	MINIMUM WEIGHT IN POUNDS	100	92.5	85	77.5	CLASS 70	65 RATE	60	55	50
3	AQ	746	709	671	638	597	574	552	530	507
5		747	710	673	639	598	575	553	531	508
10		750	712	675	641	600	577	555	532	509
15		753	714	677	643	602	579	557	534	511
20		755	717	679	645	604	580	559	536	513
25		758	720	682	648	*606	583	561	538	515
30		761	723	685	651	609	586	563	540	517
35		765	727	689	654	612	589	566	543	520
40		770	731	693	658	616	593	570	547	524
45		775	737	698	664	620	597	574	550	527

(continued)

TABLE 12.44B *(continued)*

DISTANCE CLASS RATES (Cents per 100 pounds)

MILES NOT OVER	MINIMUM WEIGHT IN POUNDS	100	92.5	85	77.5	CLASS 70	65 RATE	60	55	50
50		783	744	705	670	*626	603	579	555	532
60		791	751	712	676	632	609	585	561	538
70		799	759	719	683	639	615	591	567	543
80		808	768	727	690	646	622	598	573	549
90		816	775	734	697	653	628	604	579	555
100		824	783	742	704	*660	634	610	585	560
110		832	790	749	711	666	641	616	591	566
120		840	798	756	718	672	647	621	597	571
130		848	806	763	725	678	653	628	603	577
140		856	813	770	732	684	660	633	609	582
150		864	821	778	739	691	666	639	615	588
160		872	828	785	746	697	672	645	620	593
170		880	836	792	752	703	678	651	626	598
180		888	844	799	759	710	684	657	632	604
190		896	851	806	766	717	691	663	638	609
200		904	860	814	774	*723	698	669	644	615
220		917	871	825	784	732	706	677	650	622
240		927	881	834	793	741	714	686	657	630
260		938	891	844	802	750	722	694	666	638
280		950	903	855	813	760	732	703	674	646
300		965	917	869	825	772	743	714	685	656
325		980	931	882	838	784	755	725	696	666
350		995	945	896	851	796	766	736	706	676
375		1010	960	909	864	808	778	747	717	687
400		1026	975	923	878	* 821	790	759	728	698
425		1045	993	941	894	836	805	773	742	710
450		1064	1012	958	910	851	819	787	755	723
475		1084	1030	976	927	867	835	802	769	737
500		1104	1049	994	944	883	851	817	784	751
525		1126	1070	1013	963	901	867	833	799	766
550		1151	1093	1036	984	921	886	852	817	783
575		1178	1119	1060	1007	942	907	872	836	801
600		1204	1144	1084	1030	963	927	891	855	819
625		1230	1169	1107	1052	984	947	910	873	836
650		1258	1195	1132	1076	1006	969	931	893	855
675		1286	1222	1157	1100	1028	990	952	913	874
700		1314	1248	1183	1123	*1051	1012	972	933	893
725		1343	1276	1209	1148	1074	1034	994	954	913
750		1371	1302	1234	1172	1097	1056	1015	974	933

Table 12.44B is a completed rate page for the Any Quantity rates from 0 to 750 miles. The class 70 rates in Table 12.44A were enlarged to include the classification ratings from class 100 to class 50.

The class 100 rates were determined by multiplying the class 70 rates by 1.25 to increase them by 25%. This means that the class 70 rates are 80% of the class 100 rates. For example, the class 70 rate at a distance of 90 miles is $6.53. Increasing this rate by 25% produces a class 100 rate of $8.16. The $6.53 class 70 rate divided by the class 100 rate of $8.16 produces 80% ($6.53 ÷ $8.16 = 80%).

The remaining columns are percentages of the class 100 rates. The following chart indicates the percentage relationships to the class 100 rates:

Table 12.44B Column Headings	Percentage Of Class 100
92.5	95
85	90
77.5	85
70	80
65	77
60	74
55	71
50	68

These are the relationships indicated in the illustrations to demonstrate procedures to spread rates throughout the classification ratings. It is believed that these methods produce a rate structure that properly relates to the National Motor Freight Classification.

TABLE 12.45

DISTANCE CLASS RATES (Cents per 100 pounds)

MILES NOT OVER	MINIMUM WEIGHT IN POUNDS	100	92.5	85	77.5	CLASS 70	65	60	55	50
3	2,000	590	561	531	501	472	454	437	419	401
5		592	562	533	503	474	456	438	420	402
10		595	565	535	505	476	458	440	422	404
20		602	572	541	511	482	463	445	427	409
25		606	576	545	515	*485	467	448	430	412
30		611	580	550	519	489	470	452	434	415
35		616	585	555	524	493	474	456	438	419
40		621	590	559	528	497	478	460	442	423
45		626	595	564	533	501	482	464	445	427
50		633	601	570	538	*506	487	468	449	431
60		640	608	576	544	512	492	473	454	435
70		649	617	584	550	519	499	478	459	439
80		658	625	592	556	526	506	484	465	444
90		666	633	599	562	533	513	491	471	449
100		675	641	608	569	*540	520	498	477	454
110		684	650	616	576	547	527	505	483	459
120		691	656	622	583	553	533	512	490	465
130		699	664	629	590	559	539	518	496	471
140		706	671	635	597	565	545	524	501	477
150		714	678	643	605	571	551	530	507	483
160		721	685	649	613	577	556	536	512	489
170		729	693	656	621	583	562	542	518	495
180		736	699	662	627	589	568	548	524	501
190		744	707	670	634	595	574	554	530	507
200		753	715	678	641	*602	582	560	536	513
220		763	725	687	649	610	589	566	542	520
240		776	737	698	659	621	596	573	549	528
260		790	750	711	670	632	607	583	559	537
280		804	764	724	682	643	617	594	570	547
300		818	777	736	694	654	628	605	581	556
325		831	789	748	706	665	639	615	590	565
350		845	803	760	718	676	650	625	600	575
375		860	817	774	731	688	662	636	611	585
400		875	831	788	744	*700	674	648	621	595
425		891	846	802	757	713	686	660	632	606
450		909	864	818	773	727	700	673	644	618

(continued)

475		928	882	835	789	742	714	687	657	631
500		948	901	853	806	758	730	702	672	644
525		967	919	870	822	774	745	716	687	658
550		989	940	890	841	791	761	730	702	673
575		1010	960	909	859	808	778	746	717	687
600		1031	980	928	876	825	794	763	732	701
625		1053	1000	948	895	842	811	780	748	716
650		1075	1021	968	914	860	828	796	764	731
675		1098	1043	988	933	878	845	812	780	747
700		1120	1064	1008	952	*896	862	829	794	762
725		1143	1086	1028	971	914	880	846	810	777
750		1165	1107	1048	990	932	897	863	826	792

TABLE 12.46

DISTANCE CLASS RATES (Cents per 100 pounds)

MILES NOT OVER	MINIMUM WEIGHT IN POUNDS	100	92Ω	85	77.5	CLASS 70	65	60	55	50
3	5,000	449	427	404	382	359	346	332	319	305
5		450	428	405	383	360	347	333	320	306
10		452	430	407	384	362	348	334	321	307
15		454	432	409	386	364	350	336	322	309
20		457	434	411	388	366	352	338	324	311
25		461	437	414	391	*369	354	341	327	313
30		465	441	418	394	372	357	344	330	316
35		470	446	423	399	376	361	348	333	320
40		475	451	428	403	380	365	352	337	323
45		481	457	433	408	385	370	356	341	327
50		487	462	438	413	*390	375	360	346	331
60		494	468	444	420	396	380	365	351	336
70		501	476	450	426	402	386	371	356	341
80		509	483	457	432	409	392	377	361	346
90		517	491	464	439	416	398	383	367	352
100		521	495	469	446	*424	405	389	373	358
110		526	500	473	451	430	411	395	379	363
120		531	505	478	457	436	417	401	385	369
130		537	510	483	462	442	423	407	391	374
140		543	516	488	468	448	430	413	397	379

(continued)

TABLE 12.46 *continued*

DISTANCE CLASS RATES (Cents per 100 pounds)

MILES NOT OVER	MINIMUM WEIGHT IN POUNDS	100	92.5	85	77.5	CLASS 70	65	60	55	50
150		549	523	495	474	454	436	419	403	385
160		555	530	502	480	460	442	425	409	390
170		561	537	509	486	466	448	431	415	396
180		568	545	517	493	472	454	437	421	401
190		576	553	525	499	478	460	443	426	407
200		583	560	533	505	*486	467	449	432	413
220		590	567	540	513	493	474	456	438	419
240		597	574	548	521	502	483	464	445	426
260		604	582	557	528	512	492	474	454	435
280		613	590	565	536	523	503	483	464	444
300		623	599	574	546	534	514	494	473	454
325		633	608	583	556	546	526	505	485	464
350		643	618	592	568	559	538	517	496	475
375		653	628	601	580	572	551	529	508	486
400		666	638	611	592	*585	563	541	519	497
425		681	652	624	605	599	575	553	530	508
450		694	667	638	618	613	588	565	542	520
475		708	682	651	631	627	601	578	554	531
500		722	698	664	644	641	614	591	566	543
525		736	714	681	658	654	628	603	578	555
550		751	730	697	671	667	641	616	591	566
575		768	746	713	684	680	654	628	603	577
600		785	762	730	698	693	667	641	615	589
625		802	779	747	713	706	680	653	627	600
650		820	795	764	728	719	693	666	639	612
675		838	811	781	750	733	706	679	651	624
700		856	827	797	763	*747	719	691	663	635
725		874	844	814	777	751	732	704	675	647
750		892	871	830	800	765	745	716	687	658

TABLE 12.47

DISTANCE CLASS RATES (Cents per 100 pounds)

MILES NOT OVER	MINIMUM WEIGHT IN POUNDS	100	92.5	85	77.5	CLASS 70	65	60	55	50
3	10,000	261	248	235	222	209	201	193	185	177
5		262	249	236	223	210	202	194	186	178
10		264	250	238	224	211	203	195	187	179
15		266	252	239	226	212	205	197	189	181
20		268	255	241	228	214	207	199	191	182
25		270	257	243	230	*216	209	201	192	184
30		273	259	246	232	219	211	203	194	186
35		278	263	250	236	223	214	205	197	189
40		283	268	255	240	227	218	208	200	192
45		289	275	260	245	232	223	213	204	196
50		296	281	266	251	*237	228	219	209	201
60		304	289	274	257	243	234	225	215	206
70		312	296	281	265	250	240	231	221	212
80		320	304	289	273	257	246	238	228	218
90		328	313	297	280	264	252	244	234	224
100		336	322	305	288	*271	259	251	241	231
110		342	330	312	295	278	267	257	247	237
120		349	338	320	303	285	274	263	253	242
130		356	346	327	310	291	281	269	258	248
140		363	352	334	316	298	287	275	264	253
150		370	358	341	322	303	293	281	270	258
160		377	364	347	328	309	299	286	275	263
170		384	370	355	335	315	305	292	281	268
180		391	377	362	342	321	310	298	286	273
190		398	384	370	349	327	315	304	291	278
200		405	391	377	355	*333	320	310	296	283
220		412	398	385	361	339	326	315	301	288
240		419	406	393	368	347	333	321	307	294
260		427	414	401	378	357	343	329	315	304
280		435	422	409	391	368	354	340	325	313
300		443	430	417	403	379	365	351	336	323
325		452	441	426	414	390	376	361	347	332
350		462	452	437	425	402	387	371	357	341

(continued)

TABLE 12.47 *(continued)*

DISTANCE CLASS RATES (Cents Per 100 Pounds)

MILES NOT OVER	MINIMUM WEIGHT IN POUNDS	100	92.5	85	77.5	CLASS 70	65	60	55	50
375		473	463	449	436	417	399	382	368	352
400		484	473	462	447	*432	413	395	380	364
425		495	483	473	460	445	426	408	393	376
450		507	494	585	473	458	440	422	406	388
475		520	506	597	486	470	453	435	418	399
500		534	518	510	499	482	465	447	429	411
525		545	531	521	511	494	477	458	439	420
550		555	544	533	522	505	488	468	449	430
575		566	558	546	533	516	498	478	459	439
600		577	571	559	544	526	507	488	467	447
625		588	582	571	555	536	517	498	476	456
650		600	593	582	566	546	527	508	485	465
675		612	604	593	577	556	536	516	494	473
700		624	615	603	587	*565	545	524	503	481
725		635	625	613	597	576	554	533	512	489
750		646	636	623	607	586	564	542	521	498

TABLE 12.48

DISTANCE CLASS RATES (Cents Per 100 Pounds)

MILES NOT OVER	MINIMUM WEIGHT IN POUNDS	100	92.5	85	77.5	CLASS 70	65	60	55	50
3	20,000	196	186	176	167	157	151	145	139	133
5		197	187	177	168	158	152	146	140	134
10		198	188	178	169	159	153	147	141	135
15		200	190	180	170	160	154	148	142	136
20		202	192	182	172	162	156	149	144	137
25		205	195	185	174	*165	158	152	146	139
30		209	198	188	179	168	161	155	148	142
35		214	203	193	181	172	165	158	152	145

(continued)

40	220	209	198	186	176	169	162	156	149
45	225	214	203	191	180	173	167	160	153
50	231	220	208	196	*185	178	171	164	157
60	238	226	214	202	190	183	176	169	162
70	245	233	220	208	196	189	181	174	167
80	252	239	227	214	202	194	186	179	171
90	259	246	233	220	207	199	191	184	176
100	266	252	239	226	213	205	197	189	181
110	273	259	246	232	218	210	202	194	186
120	280	266	252	238	224	215	207	199	191
130	288	274	259	245	230	221	213	204	196
140	296	281	266	251	237	227	219	210	201
150	303	288	273	258	242	233	224	215	206
160	311	295	280	264	249	239	230	220	211
170	318	302	287	270	254	245	236	225	216
180	325	309	293	276	260	250	241	231	221
190	332	316	299	282	266	256	247	236	226
200	340	323	305	289	272	262	253	241	231
220	347	330	312	295	278	267	258	246	236
240	353	337	318	301	282	272	262	252	241
260	361	344	325	307	289	278	267	257	246
280	369	351	332	314	295	284	273	262	251
300	377	358	339	320	302	290	279	268	256
325	386	367	347	328	309	297	285	275	262
350	395	376	355	336	316	304	292	282	268
375	404	384	363	343	323	311	299	288	274
400	415	394	373	353	332	318	307	295	281
425	426	404	383	362	341	327	315	302	288
450	437	415	393	372	350	336	323	310	296
475	448	426	403	381	359	345	331	318	304
500	459	437	413	390	367	353	339	326	312
525	470	448	423	399	376	362	347	334	320
550	481	458	433	409	384	371	356	341	327
575	492	468	443	419	392	379	364	349	335
600	503	478	453	428	400	387	372	357	343
625	514	488	463	437	409	396	380	365	351
650	525	498	473	446	420	405	388	373	359
675	536	508	483	455	430	414	396	381	366
700	547	519	494	464	440	423	405	388	374
725	558	530	504	474	450	432	413	396	381
750	569	541	514	484	460	441	421	404	398

TABLE 12.49

DISTANCE CLASS RATES (Cents Per 100 Pounds)

MILES NOT OVER	MINIMUM WEIGHT IN POUNDS	45	40	37.5	CLASS 35	35.1	35.2	35.3	35.5
3	AS PROVIDED	162	155	147	130	125	120	115	110
5	IN THE	163	156	148	131	126	121	116	111
10	CLASSIFICATION	164	157	149	132	127	122	117	112
15		165	158	150	133	128	123	118	113
20		167	159	151	134	129	124	119	114
25		169	161	153	136	131	126	121	116
30		171	164	155	137	133	128	123	118
35		174	168	158	139	135	131	125	120
40		179	172	162	143	138	134	128	123
45		185	176	167	148	142	138	131	126
50		191	181	172	153	147	141	135	130
60		197	186	176	158	151	144	139	134
70		203	191	182	162	155	148	143	138
80		209	196	188	167	160	152	147	142
90		214	201	194	171	165	156	151	146
100		219	207	200	175	170	161	156	150
110		225	213	206	180	175	166	161	154
120		232	220	212	186	180	171	166	158
130		239	227	218	191	185	177	171	162
140		246	234	223	197	190	182	175	166
150		253	241	228	202	195	188	180	170
160		259	247	233	207	200	192	184	174
170		265	253	238	212	205	196	188	178
180		271	259	243	217	210	200	192	182
190		278	266	248	222	215	205	196	186
200		285	273	253	228	220	210	200	190
220		292	279	258	234	225	215	205	194
240		298	286	263	239	230	220	210	198
260		305	292	269	245	235	225	215	202
280		313	298	275	251	240	231	220	207
300		320	304	281	257	246	236	225	212
325		327	312	287	262	252	242	230	217

(continued)

350		335	318	293	268	259	248	235	224
375		344	324	299	275	266	234	240	231
400		353	330	307	284	272	261	245	237
425		362	336	315	291	279	268	251	243
450		372	343	322	298	286	275	258	249
475		383	350	330	307	294	283	265	256
500		394	358	338	315	302	290	272	263
525		405	366	346	323	311	298	280	270
550		414	375	354	331	319	306	287	277
575		423	384	362	339	328	313	294	284
600		432	393	370	346	335	320	301	291
625		441	402	378	354	342	327	308	291
650		450	412	386	362	349	334	316	298
675		460	422	394	370	357	341	323	305
700		471	432	402	378	365	348	331	312
725		482	442	410	386	373	353	338	320
750		493	453	419	395	380	361	346	328

Tables 12.45 through 12.49 are rate tables that result from entering costs for each of the weight groups included in the study. After the rate is entered in each table from the cost study, the same procedure is followed as described in connection with the Any Quantity rates. Rates are feathered into the class 70 mileage scale, and expanded to reflect the classification ratings using the percentages listed above.

After the rate tables are completed, another table is necessary to provide assistance in properly relating the rates. The purpose of the table is to determine whether the range of application of rates are consistent through the mileage and weight brackets. The range of application is another way to describe the degree of breakback throughout the rate structure. Breakback weight is the point at which the rate at the actual shipment and the rate at the next higher minimum weight produce the same charge. The range of application is the spread of weight at which a single rate applies.

TABLE 12.50

STATEMENT SHOWING THE DEGREE OF BREAKBACK IN RATE STRUCTURE
Classes 70 and 35

Any Quantity Truckload	Minimum		Minimum 2000 Lbs.		Minimum 5000 Lbs.		Minimum 10000 Lbs.		Minimum 20000 Lbs.		Minimum	
	Range of Miles		Range of Miles		Range of Miles		Range of Miles		Range of Miles		Range of Miles	
	Rate	Application	Rate	Application	Rate	Application	Rate	Application	Rate	Application	Rate	Application
25	606	0-1601	485	1602-3804	369	3805-5854	216	5855-15278	165	15279-32970	136	32971-40000
50	626	0-1617	506	1618-3854	390	3855-6077	237	6078-15662	185	15663-33081	153	33082-40000
100	660	0-1636	540	1637-3926	424	3927-6392	271	6393-15720	213	15721-32864	175	32865-40000
200	723	0-1665	602	1666-4036	486	4037-6852	333	6852-16336	272	16337-33529	228	33529-40000
400	821	0-1705	700	1706-4179	585	4180-7385	432	7386-15370	332	15371-36216	284	36217-40000
700	1051	0-1705	896	1706-4168	747	4169-7564	565	7565-15575	440	15576-34363	378	34364-40000

If the range of application is not consistent throughout the mileage scale, the rates should be adjusted until they are. This will mean that not all rates are equally distant from class 70 for LTL rates or class 35 for truckload rates. The primary target is to remain as close to the cost points as possible. The secondary target is to maintain a relationship to the classification ratings. The third target is to achieve a smooth progression of rates through the distances.

To capture these objectives, the design of a full rate structure becomes more of an art because several trials are necessary to find the best fit. Once the analyst has found the best fit for the structure, it is helpful to plot one scale of rates from each of the charts in a line graph to get a better view of the flow of rates through the distances. A typical graph would use the horizontal plane for distance and the vertical plane for rate. The lines should flow evenly between the points, and should be nearly parallel to each other.

An example of the flowing of rate relationships is our illustration in the 20,000 pound minimum weight chart where rates are shown to a breakback point of approximately 34,000 pounds, a wide range of rates. This means that the cost points for 30,000-39,999 shipment weights are not used, and the next higher rates are for truckload quantities. The range of application of rates for truckload quantities goes up to 40,000 pounds.

This does not mean that only shipments up to 40,000 pounds can be rated under the Truckload classifications. Those rates may be used for any truckload weight, though they may be too high to be competitive at the higher weights. If this is true, a study similar to that described in Chapter 9 may be necessary to establish cost-based rates for shipments weighing over about 50,000 pounds. These heavier shipments are normally handled directly in a fashion similar to specialized carriers. Such studies, and resulting rates, are expected to be lower than those used in developing the rates illustrated in this chapter.

At the lower end of the rate structure, small shipments require special rates in order for the carrier to recover its incurred cost. This can be accomplished through rules such as minimum charges or small shipment charges.

TABLE 12.51

MINIMUM CHARGE

The minimum charge per shipment shall be as follows:

(a) For shipments transported distances not exceeding 100 miles:

WEIGHT OF SHIPMENT (In Pounds)		Minimum Charge in Dollars
Over	But Not Over	
0	25	10.50
25	50	13.00
50	75	15.50
75	100	18.50
100	150	21.00
150	200	24.00
200	250	27.75
250	300	31.00
300	400	35.00
400	500	39.00
500	-	45.00

(b) For shipments transported distances exceeding 100 miles:

WEIGHT OF SHIPMENT (In Pounds)		Minimum Charge in Dollars
Over	But Not Over	
0	25	10.50
0	100	17.50
100	150	22.00
150	200	27.50
200	250	33.00
250	300	39.00
300	400	45.00
400	500	51.00
500	-	58.00

Table 12.43 contains the source data from which Table 12.51 is constructed. The cost per 100 pounds at a 93 operating ratio is averaged for shipments weighing 0 to 100 and moving through 100-mile lengths of haul. The average is $27.241 for shipments weighing an average of 54.1 pounds. Multiplying the cost per 100 pounds by .541 produces the cost per shipment of $14.737, which is entered in subparagraph (a) in Table 12.51 in the 50-75 pound weight group. The amount is increased slightly because 54.1 pounds is at the lower end of the weight group.

The same procedure is followed for the next weight group in Table 12.43 to obtain the figure for the higher weights in Table 12.51 for shipments with an average weight of 222 pounds (as shown in Table 12.19). The cost per shipment of $32.763 at that average shipment weight is entered in the 200-250 weight group. The rates between the 50-75 weight group and the 200-250 weight group are then filled in to complete the table.

Subparagraph (b) is completed using the same procedure, except that the source for the cost information is the lengths of haul over 100 miles.

Another rule carriers may consider to address the small shipment situation might be "Small Shipment Service." The intent of this rule is to offer the shipper a reduced rate from the Minimum Charge rule in return for certain considerations. Such a rule may be written as shown in Table 12.52

TABLE 12.52

SMALL SHIPMENT SERVICE

Rates provided in this item shall apply only when the shipping document is annotated by shipper, certifying that the shipment meets the requirements of this item, and requesting Small Shipment Service. Rates in this item will apply only to prepaid shipments, released to a value not to exceed 50 cents per pound or less, weighing under 500 pounds, and moving for distances not to exceed 500 miles. Rates in this item do not apply to:

1.   Shipments containing any commodity rated above class 100.

2.   Shipments weighing less than 100 pounds which contain more than 5 pieces, or any shipment which contains more than 5 pieces per 100 pounds.

3.   Shipments which require Temperature Control or COD services.

4.   Shipments picked up or delivered to private residences of retail customers.

5.   Shipments containing personal effects, baggage or used household goods.

6.   Shipments moving on Government Bill of Lading.

Rates provided in this item do not alternate with other rates and charges in this tariff, and rates provided in this item may not be used in combination with any other rates.

The charge for Small Shipment Service shall be:

WEIGHT OF SHIPMENT (In Pounds)		Charge in Dollars
Over	But Not Over	
0	25	13.50
25	50	13.50
50	75	13.50
75	100	13.50
100	150	18.00
150	200	23.00
200	250	27.50
250	300	31.50
300	400	36.00
400	500	40.50

To find the rates in Table 12.52, find the average of the Minimum Charge rates in each of the weight brackets and reduce that figure by 10%. For example, the average of subparagraphs (a) and (b) for the weight groups between 0 and 100 pounds in Table 12.51 is $15.00. Reducing the average by 10% produces the figure used of $13.50. When the shipper qualifies, a 10% reduction from the Minimum Charge is realized.

Other rules, such as split pickup and delivery, are discussed in Chapters 9 and 11. The procedures for establishing these rates for LTL carriers is the same as for other carriers, except that the application of many of the rules is different. Other rules in the old common carrier tariffs remain as they were.

Appendix A
Forms for Collection of Data

FORM 1
PICKUP AND DELIVERY OPERATION PERFORMANCE SURVEY

Company _____

Terminal Address (city) _____

Driver _____

Date _____

Power Unit Fuel:

☐ Gas ☐ Diesel ☐ LPG

Truck: ☐ 2-Axle ☐ 3-Axle

Tractor: ☐ 2-Axle ☐ 3-Axle

Equipment (Check appropriate box):

a. ☐ Full ☐ Semi

b. Number of Trailers ☐ 1 ☐ 2

c. Length of Trailer(s)

1st Trailer Length _____ ft. 2nd Trailer Length _____ ft.

Jeep Used:

☐ Yes ☐ No

Converter Gear Used:

☐ Yes ☐ No

Commodity _____

How Packaged _____
(Cartons, Bundles, Barrels, Sacks, etc.)

Time Out for Meals:

From _____ m to _____ m

Was shipment on pallets or skids?

(Check one) ☐ Yes ☐ No

SHIPMENT INFORMATION	Location (1)	Time (2)	Speedometer Reading (3)	Shipment Weights in Pounds		No. Pcs. (5)	Number of Helpers		Type of Power Equipment Used (Fork Lift, etc.)	Number Used	
				Load (4A)	Unload (4B)		Yours (6A)	Theirs (6B)	Type (7A)	Yours (7B)	Theirs (7C)
Left Terminal											
Arrived											
Started Load or Unload											
Finished Load or Unload											
Left											
Arrived											
Started Load or Unload											
Finished Load or Unload											
Left											
Arrived Terminal											

Remarks: Explain unusual delays, etc. _____

FORM 2

SUMMARY OF PLATFORM HOURS AND WAGES

Carrier _____ Terminal _____ Date _____

| 1 | 2 | 3 | 4 Hours Worked (From Timecard) | | | 5 | 6 | 7 |
Name	Wage Rate for Day	Description of Help (PU Driver, Dock Hand, etc.)	ST	OT	Total	Hours Spent Other Than Platform	Platform Hours	Office Use Only

NOTE: Individual platform hours sheets must be attached to this sheet.

FORM 2.A
INDIVIDUAL PLATFORM HOURS

Carrier _____   Terminal _____

Name _____   Date _____

Straight Time Rate _____   Overtime Rate _____

Time Start _____   Time Quit _____

Lunch from _____ to _____

Time Start Platform	Time Leave Platform	Leave Blank	

FORM 2.B
TERMINAL PLATFORM SHIPMENT ANALYSIS

Carrier_____   Terminal_____   Date_____

F/B or I.D. No.	Weight	No. of Pieces	Check One	
			Across Platform	Not Across Platform

F/B or I.D. No.	Weight	No. of Pieces	Check One	
			Across Platform	Not Across Platform

FORM 3
LINE HAUL LOAD ANALYSIS

Carrier _____   Reporting Terminal _____

Date	Trailer Number	Trailer Length (Feet)	Origin	Destination	Heaviest Mark (Check One)		Total Weight	Comments
					Under 10,000#	10,000# or Over		

NOTE: Every trailer moving in line haul service must be listed — both EMPTIES and LOADED. Note in comments any unusual circumstances such as movements of single boxes, overloads, etc.

FORM 4
REVENUE EQUIPMENT INVENTORY

Carrier _____   Date _____

1 Equipment	2 Year	3 Make	4 Check One		5 Type of Equipment	6 Type of Body	7 Special Equipment	8 Length of Bed (Feet)	9 Type Serv. (Check One)			10 Fuel (Check One)			11 No. of Axles	12 Tires		13 Tare Weight of Vehicle w/o Load	14 Vehicle Book Cost Less Tires	15 Special Equip. Cost (See instr.)	16 Service Life
			New	Used					Local	Line	Comb.	Gas	Dsl	LPG		No.	Size				

FORM 5
SPECIALIZED CARRIER TRIP PERFORMANCE REPORT

Carrier _____

Equipment Nos. _____

Driver Name _____

Load Tag Number _____

Date _____

Receiving Destination _____

Net Weight Loaded _____

Commodity _____

Leave Yard (Gate) _____

Odometer Reading (Tenths) _____

Time of Day (Hr/Min): _____ AM/PM

Time Out for Meals: From _____ to _____

Odometer Reading (Tenths) _____

Arrive Yard (Gate) _____

Odometer Reading (Tenths) _____

Time of Day (Hr/Min): _____ AM/PM

| Arrive Shipper Gate | | Leave Rack Time | Arrive Load Rack | | Leave Shipper Gate | | Arrive Unload Gate | | Arrive Unload Rack | | Leave Rack Time | Leave Unload Gate | | Comments |
Odometer	Time		Odometer	Time	Odometer	Time	Odometer	Time	Odometer	Time		Odometer	Time	

INTERMEDIATE CHECKPOINTS

Location	Odometer	Time	Location	Odometer	Time	Location	Odometer	Time	Comments

FORM 6
USED HOUSEHOLD GOODS EQUIPMENT LIST

Carrier _____

Date _____

1 Equipment Model	2 Model Year	3 Make	4 Type of Equipment	5 Type of Body	6 Fuel	7 Length of Bed (ft)	8 No. of Axles	9 Tare Weight	Purchase			13 Cost of On Board Equipment
									10 Year	11 New/Used	12 Price	

FORM 7
HOUSEHOLD GOODS TRIP PERFORMANCE

Company _____

Terminal Address (city) _____

Date _____

Driver _____ Helper _____ Helper _____

EQUIPMENT

Equipment Number _____ Truck _____ Tractor _____ Trailer _____

Gas or Diesel _____

Body (Van, flat, hi-cube) _____

Body Length _____

Number of Axles _____

USE SEPARATE
FORM IF EQUIPMENT
IS CHANGED

LEAVE TERMINAL

Speedometer reading _____

Time of day _____ AM/PM

RETURN TO TERMINAL

Speedometer reading _____

Time of day _____ AM/PM

TIME OUT FOR MEALS

From _____ AM/PM to _____ AM/PM

ACTIVITY

1 Equipment Number	2 Waybill Number	3 Inter	4 Intra	5 Location	LOADING										UNLOADING						DRIVING		
					Place		Time		10 No. of Helpers	11 Pounds (Actual)	Place		Time		16 No. of Helpers	17 Pounds (Actual)	18 Miles	19 Time	20 No. of Helpers
					6 Dock	7 Res.	8 Start	9 Finish			12 Dock	13 Res.	14 Start	15 Finish					

Return to Terminal

Explain any unusual delays, give time and reason:

_____

FORM 8
PLATFORM LOADING – UNLOADING

Company _____

Terminal Address _____

Date _____

1	Type of Shipment		4	Time		LOADED			UNLOADED		
Waybill Number	2 Inter	3 Intra	Number of Men	5		6	Total Man-Hours 7		8	Total Man-Hours 9	
				Hours	Minutes	Wt. of Shpment	Hours	Minutes	Wt. of Shpment	Hours	Minutes

Index

Index - Tables